WARWICK SCHOOL
A History

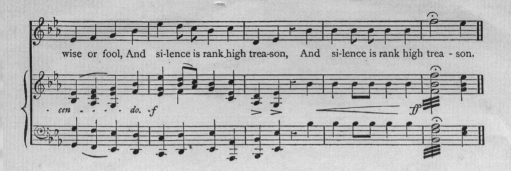

wise or fool, And si-lence is rank high trea-son, And si-lence is rank high trea - son.

Lent Term.

2 Now bounds the ball on the Fives-court wall,
   Or the Mile or the Quarter we run ;
   If we bruise our shins where the football spins,
   I' faith ! it is part of the fun.
   Chorus, &c.

Summer Term.

3 In the cricket field the willow we wield,
   Well equipped for the struggle and fit ;
   We've skill and we've pluck, and with moderate
   luck
   We'll cheer for the conquering hit.
   Chorus, &c.

4 And we plunge in the cool of the shady pool,
   And Stoneleigh's lawns are green ;
   And the flickering steel of the bicycle wheel
   On Edgehill's height is seen.
   Chorus, &c.

Winter Term.

5 There's plenty of fun though the summer's
   done,
   And skies are leaden and gray ;
   If frost and snow are keen, we'll show
   That we can be keen as they.
   Chorus, &c.

6 So sing with a will, tho' the winds blow chill,
   While we toughen our sinews and muscles,
   Close on the ball we'll follow all
   In our hard-fought football tussles.
   Chorus, &c.

Concluding Verses.

7 Though Latin and Greek are hard to speak,
   And Euclid's a sore vexation,
   Be plucky and work, for fellows who shirk
   Will be plucked in Examination.
   Chorus, &c.

8 Stick hard ! for your lives ! to Grammar and
   Fives,
   Greek, Algebra, Football, and Science ;
   If they're well gripped, then fully equipped,
   We'll face the world with defiance.
   Chorus, &c.

9 Though all things must return to dust,
   Old friends let nothing sever ;
   But as you grow older stand shoulder to
   shoulder !
   Hurrah ! boys ! Warwick for ever !
   Chorus, &c.

*The two following extra verses were composed by the reviser, and sent with the request that they
should be sung at the inauguration of the Song :—*

To come after Verse 8.

Serene and great may our Ship of State
   Ride safely the dangers round her ;
With men like *Peel*[1] at the good ship's wheel,
   She never, God grant, shall founder.
   Chorus, &c.

May our Warwick boat long proudly float
   In fair or in stormy weather,
Through work or play with a stroke like *Way*,
   To teach us to pull together.
   Chorus, &c.

---

[1] The Speaker of the House of Commons, a Governor of the School, to whose speech on Prize Day the
School owes this Song.

WARWICK SCHOOL
A History

G N FRYKMAN AND E J HADLEY

GRESHAM BOOKS LTD
in partnership with
WARWICK SCHOOL
2004

© Warwick School 2004

Published by
Gresham Books Limited
46 Victoria Road
Summertown
Oxford
OX2 7QD

In partnership with
Warwick School
Myton Road
Warwick
CV34 6PP

ISBN 0 946095 46 9

Design and typesetting by John Saunders Design & Production
Printed and bound in the United Kingdom at the University Press, Cambridge

Foreword

PROFESSOR ERIC W IVES, OBE

Oliver Cromwell famously said that he wanted to be painted "warts and all". That should be the standard whenever we record anything, and not least when telling the story of a school. Few of the school histories on library shelves achieve this. They read instead like a sequence of obituaries for long-dead headmasters, interspersed with the recycling of honours boards.

Readers look for three things. Certainly, the story of heads and staff – and with all their idiosyncrasies. We remember them not by what they taught – or failed to teach us – but by their character, personalities and quirks. Second, there is the development of the school – size, recruitment, buildings, curriculum, external relations. There is much more than 200 years between what Warwick offers today and what it offered at the start of the nineteenth century, or even 75 years ago. Finally, there are the boys; as visiting speakers almost always say at Speech Days, it is they who matter. The story of Warwick School is the story of the experience of the boys, that life outside the classroom which is what makes a school such as Warwick distinct.

By these modern criteria, the existing *History of Warwick School* by the great Victorian educational historian AF Leach is somewhat wanting. In this 21st century history, Gervald Frykman and Eric Hadley have taken on the wider challenge of telling how it was. Or, one should say, how it was and is, for the life of a school is ongoing, and Frykman and Hadley will be out of date the moment this book comes off the press.

Research is ongoing, and for the story of Warwick to be continued in a future edition, it is vital that readers respond with their knowledge, memories and memorabilia. The appointment of Gervald Frykman as school archivist has been a great success. In the past, few educational institutions paid proper attention to past material, and to recover it takes determination, protective clothing and a nose for secrets. So let us not repeat the unconcern of the past. We must preserve the material of today so that when, in the future, our successors ask, "What were they like?" and "What was Warwick like?" they can do so with some hope of discovering.

Eric Ives
Chairman of Governors 1985-2003

Contents

❦

Part Two: The Post-War Era

List of colour plates

❧

Acknowledgements

The writing of this book would not have been possible without the co-operation of many people and organisations, together with the encouragement of all those who have wondered for years why nothing has been written about the school since 1906. There is no doubt that an apparent shortage of archives held many people back from trying to update AF Leach's *History of Warwick School,* and it is to the eternal credit of Dr PJ Cheshire, who created the post of School Archivist in January 2002, and Mr EB Halse, who found so much historic material secreted around the headmaster's house later that year, that this omission has at last been rectified.

In thanking all those whose memories of the school have been enshrined in print, pride of place must go to Mr Ralph Thornton, former Second Master, whose legendary knowledge is a source of amazement. Several Old Warwickians, too, have been kind enough to write commissioned articles, which not only join a growing collection of such items deposited in the school archives, but from which extensive quotations have also been made in the text of this book. This is exactly the technique used by AF Leach, who, unlike the authors, was a professional historian. However, also unlike the authors, Leach had no connection with the school and, therefore, had no background knowledge of it.

The authors have been fortunate in being able to track down several living descendants of major players in the school's history, and their contributions, in terms of supplying photographs and diaries, and in correcting factual inaccuracies, have been invaluable. Particular thanks must therefore go to Mr Christopher Riding, Mrs Ros Partridge and Mrs Caroline Sterratt.

Tracing the subsequent career paths of the several headmasters who were sacked from the school has been made a great deal easier by the informed enthusiasm of John Blatchly, former Headmaster of Ipswich School, the staff of Ilfracombe Museum and the Anglican Church archivists in Vancouver, Canada.

The long residence of the school in the town has ensured that quite a lot of relevant material has ended up in the Warwickshire County Record Office, and the staff there could not have been more helpful in their guidance and in readily granting permission for a large number of their copyright images to be published in this book. Specifically, these are: PV WAR Eas 4, CR 1709/337, PH 352/187/167, PH(N)

600/11, PV WAR Col 2, CR 2851/33 and 34, PH 143/819 and 820, HR 83/40, CR 1886/M328, CR 1618 sheet 12, CR 919/2/4, CR 919/214, 25" OS map 33.14 1925 and MA 1966.

The pictures in this book were collected by Gervald Frykman from a wide variety of sources. Copyright images, apart from those from WCRO, are reproduced with permission and come from Aerofilms Ltd, from the Francis Frith Collection and from the library of Corpus Christi College, Oxford. Many of the photographs reproduced from some older editions of Warwick School's magazine, *The Portcullis*, were taken by Mr Keith Brocklehurst. It would not be right to omit the enormous contribution made to this book, in terms of both traditional and digital photography, by Mr Peter O'Grady, and, indeed, by all our colleagues, both past and present, who have given so generously of their anecdotes, their memories and their proof-reading skills. Finally, Mrs Kathryn Frykman's exhaustive efforts, as well as those of her friends Angela Robinson and Norma Jones, in harmonising the styles of two very different authors, editing and proof-reading the entire work deserve very public thanks.

Gervald Frykman – Warwick School Archivist
Eric Hadley – Editor, *The Portcullis*

May 2004

Introduction

꤯

There has been a school in Warwick in continuous existence at least from the days of King Edward the Confessor (who reigned 1042-1066), when the fledgling town possessed a school under the tutelage of All Saints' Church. The earliest appearance of the town of Warwick in history is an entry in the Anglo-Saxon Chronicle under the year 914, and for a long time this has been taken as the date of the foundation of Warwick School.

Very little documentary evidence exists before 1545, when King Henry VIII "established [ie, presumably re-founded] the King's New School of Warwick". The premises were soon to be in the Guild Hall, which then became part of the Lord Leycester Hospital, and later St Peter's Chapel over the East Gate. The location of the school for most of the 17th century is still not known for sure. Between 1697 or so and 1879, the school was run in the old College of the Vicars Choral in St Mary's churchyard and was primarily a day school, but it also took boarders from time to time – when the health of the sometimes geriatric headmasters allowed. The education, typically for the time, emphasised the Classics above all.

The move to the open fields site, south of the River Avon, in 1879 eventually brought about a steady rise in numbers: in 1878, there had been 44 boys in the school, whereas the total in 1906 was 110. In that year of crisis, a merger with the King's Middle School in Warwick encouraged the name Warwick School, which had come into use during the 1880s, to be universally adopted, rather than The King's School or The King's Grammar School, and also resulted in an immediate doubling of numbers.

The size of the school in the 1930s reached 350, with 18 staff and a sixth form of about 40. By the 1960s, there were over 750 pupils and 45 staff. This expansion in numbers, together with a broadening of the curriculum, produced a continuous demand for new buildings. The original Science Block of 1905 survives in its third guise as the modern Music Department, and the Engineering Shop of 1910 is still used for its original purpose. More modern buildings include the Memorial Gymnasium and new Science Block of 1957, the Guy Nelson Hall and Languages Block of the early 1970s, the new Sports Hall and Arts Block of 1994 and the Bridge House Theatre of 2000, as well as the new Junior School buildings of 2002.

In 1894, the headmaster of the time, JP Way, was puzzled as to why King Henry VIII founded a new school in Warwick, and wondered what had existed before. He commissioned the eminent historian AF Leach to investigate the history of Warwick School, with a mission to prove that it was one of the country's oldest foundations. Leach's book was eventually published to subscribers at a cost of 5s (and to non-subscribers for 10s) in 1906 and was for almost the whole of the next 100 years the most up-to-date history of the school!

The publication of Leach's book unfortunately coincided with the total economic collapse of the school, whereas this new history not only examines the reasons for the crash, but also celebrates the school's subsequent huge expansion and success throughout the twentieth century and beyond. In Part 1, Gervald Frykman explores the history of the school up to the watershed year of 1946, and in Part 2 Eric Hadley examines in detail the modern, post-war life of the school.

WARWICK SCHOOL
A History

PART ONE

*The History of Warwick School
up to 1946*

CHAPTER 1

Pre-Conquest Beginnings

✦

It is perhaps ironic that just as the institution which was to become Warwick School was moving to its present site in 1879, and, after a few set-backs, was getting ready for its huge expansion throughout the 20th century, a disastrous fire in Birmingham Public Library destroyed a great deal of the recorded history of Warwickshire, including, we must suppose, that of its oldest school.

Early documentary evidence for the existence of a school in Warwick rests entirely on a couple of documents written in 1123 and now in the Public Record Office. It would seem that there was a collegiate church of All Saints in the grounds of the castle, which claimed that it was the mother church of Warwick, and a newer collegiate church in the town, called St Mary's. Both of these churches were claiming the right to run a school, and King Henry I (who reigned 1100-1135) decreed, in Latin, that All Saints "have all its customs and the ordeals of iron and water, as well and lawfully as they used to have them in the time of King Edward, and of my father and

The portion of the charter of 1123, now in the Public Record Office, dealing with the school.
The whole claim for its antiquity is based on the three words in the penultimate line –
tempore Edwardi regis or "in the time of King Edward".

brother, and have the school in like manner." This is evidence that the Church of All Saints was entitled to govern and keep a school in 1123, as it had done under William II (who reigned 1087-1100), William the Conqueror (who reigned 1066-1087) and Edward the Confessor (who reigned 1042-1066).

The rival claims of the two collegiate churches to run the school in 1123 were settled in a rather elegant manner: the two churches were united into one, and the small town grammar school passed the next 400 poorly-documented years under the auspices of St Mary and All Saints until the cataclysmic period of the Reformation.

If the school existed in the time of Edward the Confessor, then it most probably began in the early 11th century, or possibly from the time of the earliest mention of the name of the town of Warwick in the Anglo-Saxon Chronicle in the year 914. It is fair to mention, however, that no record of the school, nor indeed the church of All Saints in Warwick Castle, can be found in the Domesday Book of 1086, when Warwick was a royal borough, and there is only a passing reference to St Mary's. So, although within the past 100 years the tradition has grown that Warwick School was founded in the year 914, there is nothing to prove it, nor to disprove it. Perhaps the best compromise is to say that the modern Warwick School is the legitimate successor to the old town grammar school, for which documentary evidence goes back at least some 1,000 years.

CHAPTER 2

The Mediaeval Period

Our knowledge of events in Warwick, and its grammar school, would no doubt be much greater had it not been for another disastrous fire – the Great Fire of Warwick in 1694 – which destroyed some 250 houses in the town, and the nave and tower of St Mary's Church. The old south porch of St Mary's had contained an incomparable library of manuscripts and early printed books, started by the Warwick-born John Rows (or Rous), the father of English antiquarianism. Rows very possibly attended his local grammar school early in the 15th century, but his chief claims to fame are his two works, *The History of the Kings of England* and *The History of the Earls of Warwick*, also known as the Rouse Roll, begun in 1477. Rows was a chantry priest for 42 years at Guys Cliffe, near Warwick, and very helpfully tells us that the school was held in the old church of St John the Baptist, "whyche stondythe yet in the Market Styd, and is nowe the comon Scolehouse for gramarians." It is clear that the school was still there at the time of the dissolution of the monasteries – in 1539, "reparacions upon the Scolehouse in the market" cost 9s 10d (worth about £190 in 2003 values), as well as 3d (about £5) "for a key for the Scolehouse dore". The calculations of the purchasing power of the pound given above, and those found throughout this book, are by courtesy of Economic History Services and are intended to make financial comparisons more effective.

There is some evidence that there was an associated elementary school, a "song-school" or "petites school", for teaching the six boys in the choir of St Mary's the rudiments of grammar and of music before they passed on to the grammar school proper.

CHAPTER 3

The Reformation and Early Elizabethan Period

Along with all other monasteries, hospitals, colleges and chantries in Warwickshire, the "College of Warwick" was surrendered to King Henry VIII at some stage before 1545, and the various properties started to be sold off. The townspeople of Warwick saw to it that they salvaged what they considered to be the most beneficial of these institutions, namely, St Mary's, St Nicholas and Budbrooke parish churches and the grammar school, and obtained a grant from the king for their preservation. In the Chantries Act of 1545, the Guild of Holy Trinity and St George "received therefore £39 13s 4d whyche was expended and bestowed for the optayning and establysshement of the Kings maiesties foundacion of the parrishe churche of Warwick and the Kings new scole within the same town". Although the Guild was itself a victim of the Reformation, it had done enough. A Latin charter, dated 15th May, 1545, effected the incorporation of the town of Warwick and the re-foundation of the school. The new Burgesses would pay the vicar of St Mary's "£20 per year and 40s more" and the "Master or Pedagogue of our school" £10 per year, and provide a convenient house "for the dwelling and living of the same Vicar and Schoolmaster". Furthermore, the king would "fully create, erect, found, ordain, make and establish to endure for all future times a Free School in the said town of Warwick, of a Master or Pedagogue; and that the said school so by us founded, created, erected and established shall for ever be called and named in the vulgar tongue *The King's New Scole of Warwyke*." The schoolmaster was to be appointed by the crown, and there was a clear intention that he and the vicar of St Mary's should live in the same house. Henry VIII's charter also makes it clear that the King's School should continue to be a grammar school, training pupils in "more polite literature", that is, Classics.

AF Leach's researches found that the earliest date for which a definite name could be given to any schoolmaster of the King's School was 1580. The indefatigable Elizabethan historian John Fisher records that in that year "Mr Humfrey Waryng" was paid £13 8s 8d as vicar of St Nicholas Church and £10 "for teaching the free gramer skole the said yere". Thomas Kemp, an old pupil of the school and an eminent local historian, if ever there was one, subsequently reported (in 1910) that the line of schoolmasters could be taken right back to the Reformation using the Corporation

The charter of 1545, re-founding "The King's New School of Warwick",
preserved in the Public Record Office.

Accounts Book of 1546-1569, which is preserved in the County Record Office, having
been given back to the Mayor of Warwick by Thomas Kemp's son-in-law in 1957. This
document is extremely difficult to read, but the list as given by Thomas Kemp is:

    1546 Leonard Cokks (with Humphrey Wering as usher)
    1547 John Skirrow (also organist of St Mary's Church)
    1564 Brownswood
    1565 Raffe Gryffen
    1568 Master Bolton
    1580 Humphrey Wering

A John Brownsword was appointed schoolmaster of the grammar school at
Stratford-upon-Avon in 1565, having had teaching experience in Macclesfield and
Warwick, so it would seem that "Brownswood" and John Brownsword are one and
the same person. Raffe Gryffen (or Griffin), known locally as "Mr Griffin the
Preacher", became the first Master of the Lord Leycester Hospital in 1571.

Also in the Corporation Accounts Book is a reference to "The Queen's Majesty's
Players", who performed in the schoolhouse "before Mr Bailiff, and other his
company" and were paid 20s for doing so. However, any hope that a young William
Shakespeare, who belonged to a group of that name, might therefore have acted in
this performance is dashed by working out that he would have been no more than
four years of age when the performance took place at some time in 1568.

By the time Queen Elizabeth I visited Warwick in 1572, the Recorder of the town
was able to tell her that her father had endowed the town, "injoyning them withall to
keepe a vykar to serve in the church and divers other ministers, with a skolemaister
for the bringing up of youth in learning and vertu." The school, having outgrown its
cramped home in St John's Church in the Market Place, moved to the old Guild Hall,
then called the Burgers' Hall, in what is now known as the Lord Leycester Hospital.

The previous premises passed to the crown and were subsequently let to a tanner called Thompson. For this knowledge, we have to thank John Fisher and his Black Book of the Corporation, kept between 1561 and 1588.

The next important episode in the life of the school is its appearance in the foundation deed of Thomas Oken's charity in 1571. Warwick's greatest benefactor left "45s to a learned schoolmaster towards the augmenting of his wages to and for the teaching of a grammar school in the said town of Warwick, and if he should not be learned or should not use himself diligently, then to some other good use or uses as should be thought most meet by the bailiff and principal burgesses and the said three most substantial commoners of the eight wards." He also provided for elementary education by giving "40s to the use of the schoolmaster to be found and kept in the town of Warwick for ever to teach petties and poor men's children within the same town". In later years, this payment was made to the master of Bablake School (then pronounced Boblic), which took over the school-room at the East Gate at some time after it was vacated by the grammar school. The site is now occupied by King's High School for Girls. Thomas Oken died in 1573 and is commemorated by a brass memorial in St Mary's Church.

At the same time that Oken's bequest was being formulated, Robert Dudley, Earl of Leicester, who was the younger brother of the Earl of Warwick, visited the town. The Earl of Leicester had persuaded Queen Elizabeth I to allow him to found a hospital in either Warwick or Kenilworth, and he visited both towns in 1571 to decide on a site. The bailiff and burgesses of Warwick nearly wrecked their chances, apparently, by being offhand and rude to the earl, but the situation was rescued when one of the burgesses showed him the Burgers' Hall by the West Gate, "and the Earl alighted and went into the same and so into the chappell, and liked well thereof." He was given the whole property, including the "skolehouse", which the burgesses did not want to hand over, but this was only after he threatened to go to Kenilworth if he did not get the lot. The new Master of the Hospital was awarded a salary of £50 per year, which was more than double that of the vicar, and five times that of the schoolmaster. The burgesses tried to get an alternative meeting-hall and school-house built, and were eventually awarded St Peter's Chapel over the East Gate, but AF Leach doubted whether the school ever moved out of the Guild Hall – that is, until the Great Fire of Warwick more than 100 years later. This was hotly disputed by EG Tibbits in his unpublished 1960s book, *Warwick Charities*, still in type-script and preserved in the Warwickshire County Record Office. Tibbits showed that in the Account Book of Thomas Oken's Feoffees, payments were made as follows:

1586-7: "for reparacions doone on the Skolehous called Estchappell".
1588-9: "to the said Accomptants 1s by them paid this yere for some reparacions on the Estchapell wherin the free gramer Scole is kept as in the mending of the leades thereof".

It is likely, therefore, that the school stayed in what is now the Lord Leycester Hospital for about 30 years, from the 1540s to the 1570s, and then moved to St Peter's Chapel over the East Gate, where it may have stayed until the very end of the 17th century.

It has to be said, though, that if the school stayed at the East Gate, then the following entry from 1615 in the Corporation Minute-Book, as reported by AF Leach, is difficult to explain, there being no record of schoolmasters named Carter or Goodwick:

> Agreed that Wm Carter be put out of his possession of St Peter's Chappell, and that the same be let to Richard Goodwick att will from yeare to yeare at 20s a yere and keeping repayre.

In short, therefore, the small matter of the location of the school for almost the whole of the 17th century is still extremely uncertain.

CHAPTER 4

Later Elizabethan Times and the Seventeenth Century

Humphrey Wering almost rivals George Innes (who ran the school from 1792 to 1842) in the length of time that he served the school. He died in 1593, and was thought by AF Leach to have been succeeded by one Thomas Hall. More recently-discovered evidence, however, suggests that Thomas Hall was the schoolmaster from 1589 to 1594. At any rate, once in the job, he immediately petitioned the bailiff and the rest of the burgesses that he should not have to read the Common Prayer in church, and that the number of rival schoolmasters "might bee within this borough abated". Thomas Hall was an extremely outspoken man and in 1618, when he was vicar of St Mary's, "preached invective sermons and reproachfull and scandalous speeches against the Bayliffe and Burgesses." As late as 1631, Mr Hall, although "now aged", was still in conflict with the authorities, complaining about his salary at St Mary's. He died in 1639 but had long since handed over the schoolmastership to a man whose fame spread throughout Europe – John Owen, the Latin epigrammatist.

The most likely date of Welshman John Owen's move to Warwick is 1595, when Thomas Hall became vicar of St Mary's. John Owen was born around 1564 at Bettws Garmon, near Snowdon, and was educated at Winchester and New College, Oxford, from where he graduated as a Bachelor of Civil Law in 1590. John Owen had started writing epigrams, or witty Latin verses, while at Winchester – indeed, education there was largely devoted to the production of them – and his were good enough by the time he reached 16 years of age to be used in a ceremony held when Queen Elizabeth I paid a state visit to Sir Francis Drake on his ship at Deptford, on his return from sailing around the world. John Owen began publishing his epigrams in 1606, whereupon they met with almost instant success throughout Europe. With the aid of contemporary translations into English, French, German and Spanish, he earned himself the pseudonym of "The English Martial". We know precious little, however, about his time at Warwick. It may be that the school was at St Peter's Chapel over the East Gate at this time, but we only know the names of two of his pupils.

The effect of a Chancery decree in 1614, referring to "the schoolmaster of the Free Grammar School and his successors, being sufficient painful and diligent in

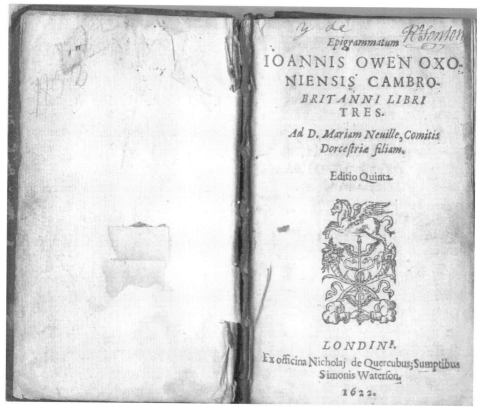

The copy of John Owen's Epigrams, published in 1622 and owned by the school.
(Warwick School Archives)

their places", was to double John Owen's salary to £20 per year – but the local parsons had theirs tripled, which must have caused some resentment.

John Owen died in 1622 and was buried in the old St Paul's Cathedral. In 1906, all that AF Leach was able to relate of his successors was that in 1636 King Charles I came to Warwick and was presented with a valuable silver cup, being "recevid by the Bailive, Principale Burgesses and Assistants, and oracion made by Mr Dugard Scolemaster of the King's Gramer Schole in Warwick". It is Mr Thomas Dugard, in fact, whom we have to thank for filling in a huge gap in the known history of the school. In the early 1670s, a questionnaire was sent out to all Free Schools in the Midlands by one Christopher Wase, and the scores of letters he received back, including two concerning Warwick, are now preserved as the Wase School Collection in Corpus Christi College Library, Oxford. The school archivist had found references to Wase in the County Record Office in 2003, but it later came to light that AF Leach had, in fact, discovered this collection in time for his essay on Warwick School – essentially a summary of his 1906 book – in *The Victoria History of the County of Warwick, Vol. II (1908)*, but nobody at the school ever seems to have been informed of it. Evidence for this is that the list of headmasters on the Honours Boards in Big School, painted during the First World War, never contained the extra names from the Wase Collection, although they did include Thomas Kemp's list, given on p 7.

The schoolmaster of 1673, William Martin, obviously felt that he was not up to the task of assembling all that was known about the school and decided that one of his predecessors, Thomas Dugard, who had left the job 25 years previously, was a much better candidate. Other evidence, in fact, suggests that William Martin was hardly up to the task of teaching at all! In his letter to Christopher Wase, dated November 1673, William Martin writes hurriedly, on the grounds that a messenger is waiting to take his reply to Oxford:

> Honoured Sir
> There have been two returns I think of our Carrier since he brought me yr letter, which delay should not have been but that I was very willing to have spoken with one Mr Duguard my worthy friend whom I succeed in this place, before I tenderd any thing in answer to yrs but now meeting with yr opportunity by a friend of sending to you, I thought myself obliged to send yr at draft with this satisfaction, that yrs came safe to me, and another before from Mr Wright from Worcester to your same purpose, yr concerns of which I have not neglected, as you will assuredly find e'er long by an Account from Mr Duguard, not only of this but of some other neighbouring schools. Pardon I beseech you my rude writing occasioned by my friend's hast.
>
> I am, Honoured Sir, Your very humble servt Wm Martin
> Warwick November ye 19th–73

In contrast, Thomas Dugard's reply to the Wase questionnaire is a model of precision. Thanks to it, the sequence of schoolmasters is now clear. Dugard wrote:

> The King's School of Warwick was founded by King Henry the Eighth in the 37th year of his reign, and in the year of our Lord 1545. The king gave only ten pounds yearly for the master, to which afterward were added by the corporation four pounds for an house for the Master, and forty shillings by Mr Thomas Oken, a Burgess of the Corporation.

MASTERS OF THE SCHOOL

Mr Thomas Hall	Afterward Minister of St Mary's in Warwick the space of 46 years. He had been schoolmaster 5 years. Entered upon the school about the year 1589.
Mr John Owen	The Epigrammalist
Mr Whitaker	
Mr John Biker	20 years afterward Vicar of Dunchurch and Rector of Frankton in Warwickshire.

Rev Thomas Dugard's grave monument of 1683 in Barford church.
(GN Frykman)

Mr Carr	
Mr Ward	Afterward Rector of Shistock in Warwickshire.
Mr Daniel Clark	Afterward Rector of Fenny Compton in Warwickshire
Mr Thomas Du-Gard	Now Rector of Barford in Warwickshire. He entered upon the school in the year 1633, was Master of it 15 years. In his time the Masters 16 pounds per annum was raised to 36 pounds per annum. And 10 pounds yearly allowed for an usher. Of the 36 pounds four and of the ten pounds two were given by Mr William Viner, then living in Warwick and father of Sir Robert Viner, now Alderman of London.
Mr Thomas Glover	Who entered ann. 1649.
Mr William Martin	Now Master, who entered ann. 1660.

Tho DuGard

Although the increase in stipend from £10 in 1545 to £12 in 1571, then £16 and finally £36 may seem significant, the period was one of massive inflation: Dugard's £36 bought hardly more than the £12 in 1571. However, the arrival of an usher meant that there was now a staff of two. At this time, an important distinction was made between boys born in Warwick and those from outside the borough – and only the former were to be taught free of charge. It was also stated that the school was only for boys who already knew the elements of grammar, once again indicating the importance of the petty school in getting them ready for entrance to the main grammar school.

Thomas Dugard does not seem to have provoked the wrath of the Parliamentarians, for he stayed in office at the school throughout the Civil War period. This was typical of Warwick folk at the time, given the protection afforded by the Greville family of Warwick Castle. Indeed, Dugard seems to have been on comfortable terms with the noted Puritan, Robert Greville, the second Lord Brooke. In 1648, Thomas Dugard started his second career, that of Rector of Barford, where he stayed for the next 35 years, until his death in 1683, and there is a fine slate memorial to him in the chancel of Barford Church. His successor as schoolmaster, Thomas Glover, became Rector of St Nicholas Church in Warwick in 1662 and died early in 1672.

In the early 1660s, the Town Council ordered that the £10 salary of the usher should not be paid to "Mr Martin, Head Schoolemaster, he having noe Usher, nor the 40s, formerly given to the Usher by Mr Oken, untill further order". This has been taken to mean that since there was no assistant teacher, the school was in one of its periodic declines. William Martin died in 1687, and the appointment of his successor by King James II was a blatantly political piece of interference, in exactly the same way that the king tried to install a Catholic President of Magdalen College, Oxford. The Oxford college had an almighty struggle to remove the interloper, and, indeed, still celebrates the restoration of the previous President and Fellows in 1688 with a magnificent dinner. St Mary's Church and The King's School, Warwick, had to suffer Mr William Eades in a similar way, but for a longer period, and the battle commenced in grand style almost immediately. On the one side was Warwick Corporation, and on the other were Eades, the King and his Chancellor, the infamous "Hanging Judge Jeffreys". Eades was a belligerent man, and his relatives were even worse. He started by demanding his full salary, with all the extras, as vicar, "for I have had no curate by my appointment, neither shall any preach in my pulpitt that you shall appoint. Pick what sense your malice will permit you out of this, and I doe expect to be paid it forthwith."

The mayor claimed that he had been physically threatened by Eades' brother, "a wild debauched young man... He broke out into a violent passion against me as mayor, repeating the God-damming himself many times over, if he did not kill me whenever he saw me." Eades was in London when told of the mayor's complaints, which included the accusation that he could not read Latin. Eades whined back that the Lord Chancellor "is better satisfy'd concerning me, and it is probable your designs may prove to my advantage." The next report was that his father, "who hath no more breeding than he hath given his son, did report in publick that his son had gotten the better of the corporation, and that in a few days they would have a messenger to fetch them up to London". The Corporation retaliated by ordering that "the lease of the house wherein Mr John Edes, the vicar's father, now liveth" would be transferred to someone else. The counter-blow was the dissolution of the Corporation itself in 1688, followed in rapid succession by the landing of William of Orange, the jailing of Judge Jeffreys and the flight of James II to France. William Eades, however, was for the moment untouchable – but he still wanted to be paid. The revived corporation, however, resolved on June 1st, 1689, "to signify how unreasonable they think Mr Eed's proposals and presente what they shall think fitt for the speedy removall of the said Mr Eeds from the church of St Mary and from the Freescoole".

By August 1689, the Corporation was plotting to side-line William Eades by setting up a rival Grammar School. This was on the grounds that "by the neglect or ignorance of our present schoolemaster the free schoole here is gone much to decay." In the following year, Eades finally got his money but was forced to have nothing more to do with the school, except retain the nominal title of Master. All the teaching was to be done by an Usher, or Ushers, appointed by the Corporation, and the Corporation became entitled to ask for Eades' resignation, as and when it thought fit. William Eades continued to be a thorn in the Corporation's side for the rest of his life – the collective sigh of relief must have been extremely audible when his death was finally announced in 1707.

After the dramas of the Restoration years, we find that few records exist, but one shows a definite name for the schoolmaster in 1697 – Thomas Gilpin – and he had resigned by 1698, to become rector of Fringford in Oxfordshire. In the Corporation accounts of 1693-4 is the rather large sum of £3 0s 8d (worth about £270 in 2003)

King Henry 8th College. Warwick 18 Ap. 1835

old Mulberry Tree

A previously unpublished, unsigned pencil drawing of "King Henry 8th College", 1835.
The steps by the mulberry tree and the boundary wall are all that survive.
(WCRO)

"for mending the windows at the free school", and this is supposed to have been the result of the traditional "barring-out" of the schoolmaster over Christmas – what we would now call a very destructive pupil riot.

The Great Fire of Warwick in 1694, although it did not destroy the room used by the school (wherever that was!), nevertheless caused a great deal of re-allocation of buildings and resources, and around 1697 the King's School moved to the old College of the Vicars Choral in St Mary's churchyard, situated between the east end of the church and The Butts. The mediaeval buildings may have been picturesque, but they were totally unsuitable, and a great deal of money had to be spent, not only at the start, to buy them (at a discount price of £260 – worth about £20,000 in 2003), but also over the next 200 years, to stop them falling down. This unequal battle was finally lost in 1880, with not a little help from some unsympathetic governors.

Between 1698 and 1701, the schoolmaster was one John Curdworth, who was also assistant at St Mary's, but about whom very little else seems to be known.

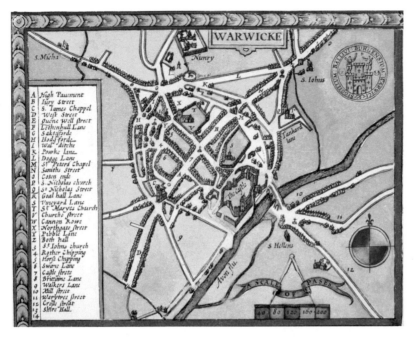

1. John Speede's map of Warwick, published in 1610. The various locations of the school are clearly visible:
a) St John's Church
b) The Guild Hall (by St James' Chapel)
c) St Peter's Chapel over the East Gate
d) The College in St Mary's Churchyard.
The modern location of the school is just off the right hand side of the map.
[WCRO]

2. The letter written by Thomas Dugard to Christopher Wase in 1673, outlining the history of the school as he knew it.
(By kind permission of the President and Fellows of Corpus Christi College, Oxford)

3. (*Left, top*) The modern external
appearance of the Lord Leycester Hospital. The
schoolroom was on the first floor,
parallel with the street.
(PJ O'Grady)

4. (*Left, bottom*) The stairs leading up to
the Guild Hall, or former schoolroom, of the
Lord Leycester Hospital.
(PJ O'Grady)

5. St Peter's Chapel over the East Gate, where
the school was situated for some part of the late
16th and early 17th centuries, pictured in 1811.
[WCRO]

6. The parchment of appointment given to
Rev Herbert Hill in 1842, together with the
Great Seal of Queen Victoria.
(WCRO, photo by PJ O'Grady)

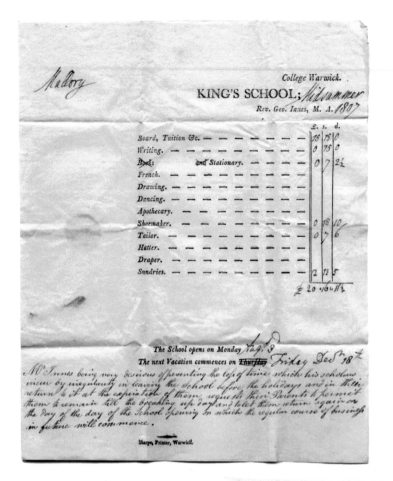

8. (*Right*) A ground plan of the College, drawn on the 1851 Board of Health map. The green area at the top of the map is the garden of Landor House. (WCRO, photo by PJ O'Grady)

9. (*Bottom right*) Schoolboy graffiti in St Mary's churchyard, pictured in 2003. (GN Frykman)

7. School bills, written in George Innes' own hand, dating from 1807. [WCRO]

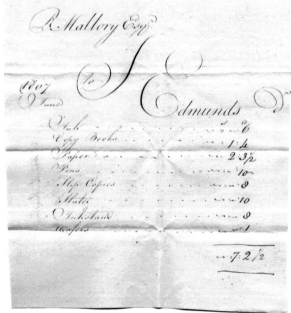

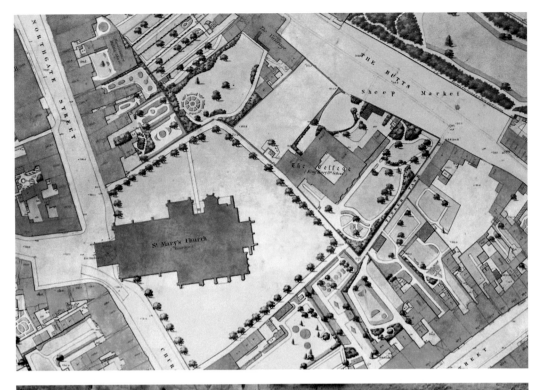

10. The site of the former College in St Mary's churchyard, pictured in 2003. (GN Frykman)

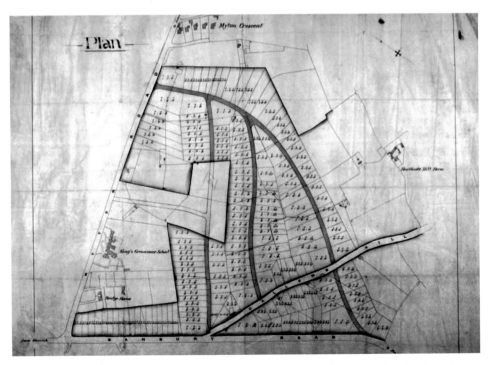

11. A plan dating from the mid-1880s from the Warwick Castle archive, showing how the present school fields could have become a Victorian suburb. (WCRO, photo by PJ O'Grady)

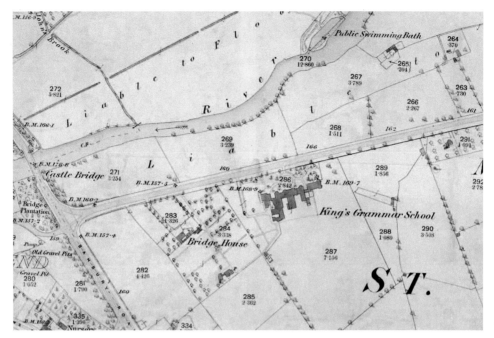

12. Part of the 1886 Ordnance Survey map of Warwick, showing the brand new Grammar School before the Limes were planted and the Junior House was built. The swimming bath used by the boys is at the top of the map. (WCRO, photo by PJ O'Grady)

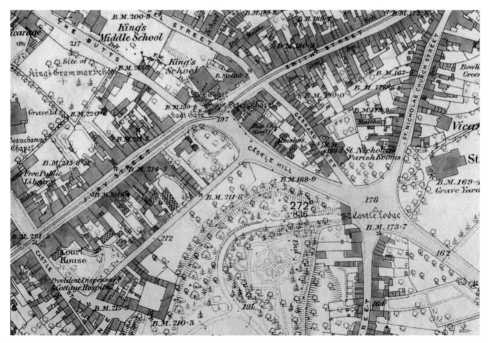

13. The centre of Warwick on the 1886 Ordnance Survey map, showing the site of the newly-demolished College and two new schools – the King's Middle School and the King's School, now known as King's High School for Girls. (WCRO, photo by PJ O'Grady)

14. The medal awarded by the governors to Robert Johnson as the most outstanding pupil at the school in 1885. (PJ O'Grady)

15. Possibly the earliest surviving photograph of the present school buildings, taken from near the River Avon around 1890. (Warwick School Archives)

CHAPTER 5

The Eighteenth Century

For virtually the whole of the 18th century, there were only three schoolmasters of The King's School in its new home in the College of the Vicars Choral in The Butts.

In November 1701, Rev Richard Lydiate, aged 28, was appointed to be "Master of the Free School and lecturer of St Mary's Church". He had gone to Winchester College as a pupil in 1685, and then automatically to New College, Oxford, in 1689. Initially, he was paid to do three jobs – master, usher and lecturer – but dropped his work as lecturer (assistant) at the church in 1706, on the grounds that the school was flourishing. The fact that seats for 60 boarders were reserved in the west gallery of St Mary's supports the idea that numbers were buoyant at this time. As regards day-boys, free education was still provided for boys born in Warwick itself, or whose parents had lived there for at least seven years.

The major event of Richard Lydiate's time was the Exhibition Foundation of Fulke Weale, a prosperous woollen-draper, whose will of 1729 provided "towards the mainte-nance and education of two young men at a time, natives of Warwick". Fulke Weale Exhibitions, given to boys leaving the school and intended to fund them entirely through university, were fiercely contested for the next 200 years; excellent investments in property meant that the scholarships increased handsomely in value. It is interesting to note that, in 1910, a boy claimed – and received – a free education at Warwick School, on the grounds that he was a great-great-great-great-great-great-great nephew of Fulke Weale, who had done so much to help the school in previous years. This boy, providently named Sidney Fulke Weale Matthews, "was not an intellectual boy, and had no chance of winning his forebear's prize, but by sheer worth managed to get a commission in the Indian Army" (according to HS Pyne, his headmaster) – he was mentioned in despatches in the Afghan War. More extraordinarily, his younger brother, Edward Weale Matthews, who joined the school in 1921, did get the coveted Fulke Weale Exhibition, to go to Sandhurst, in 1931. Despite never even entering the sixth form, he left the school, aged 19, from form Vb. That the Matthews family continued to regard the Fulke Weale Exhibition as their personal prerogative is clear from the fact that the now Major EW Matthews applied for the Exhibition for his three sons in 1952, despite the fact that they were ineligible because they were not yet at the school. The school did, in fact, award a moderate remission of fees for two of them, but it was not a happy arrangement, and the whole saga must have convinced the school authorities that the usefulness of this Exhibition had come to an end.

Richard Lydiate died late in 1730 and was buried in St Mary's churchyard. He was immediately succeeded by his son Francis, who had been born in Warwick in 1709 and had followed in his father's footsteps to Winchester and New College, Oxford. Rev Francis Lydiate was also vicar of Budbrooke. We know virtually nothing of his 32-year schoolmastership, except that he was paid £31 18s per year as vicar of Budbrooke, £40 per year as schoolmaster and £12 per year as usher, and that in 1762 he was buried, like his father, in St Mary's churchyard. However, in the June and July 1928 editions of *The Portcullis*, there are extracts from an 1811 autobiography of Richard Lovell Edgeworth (1744-1817), "inventor, educationalist and Enlightenment polymath", and father of the Irish author Maria Edgeworth (1768–1849), which make it clear that he studied under Francis Lydiate at Warwick:

> After a few months of preparatory discipline, I was taken to school at Warwick and placed under the care of Dr Lydiat, on the 26th of August, 1752, a day memorable to me. A new world now opened to my view. I was about eight years old; I had been bred up with much tenderness and had never before lived with any companions but my sisters. The noise and bustle and roughness of my school-fellows at first confounded me; I had been sufficiently tainted with Irish accent, and Irish idiom, to be the object of open ridicule, and much secret contempt. I beat one boy, who was taller than myself, for mocking me; and in a short time I acquired the English provincial accent of my companions so effectually, as to give no fair pretence for tormenting me on this subject.

Most of the extracts concern fights that he had and the constant bullying by older boys, but he does make it clear that a fellow pupil and great friend of his was Christopher Wren, the great-grandson of the architect of St Paul's Cathedral, London. Edgeworth spent his first Christmas holiday away from home in Wellesbourne, but he became ill:

> After my return to school, my progress in Latin was prevented by hooping cough; cut off from all occupation and amusement, my time pressed heavily, and I should have been in a miserable situation, had I not been treated with the utmost kindness and tenderness by Dr Lydiat and by his sister, who managed the house. My father soon came from Bath and took me away with him.

Despite our lack of knowledge of standards of education, or, indeed, virtually anything about the school at this time, Rev James Roberts, who succeeded Francis Lydiate in 1769 and was schoolmaster until 1791, seems to have afflicted Warwick with the malaise of the 18th century in general, for he was, in short, something of a disaster. The son of a country parson in Gloucestershire, he took his MA at Magdalen Hall, now Hertford College, Oxford, in 1762. In 1776, the receiver of Henry VIII's charity was ordered not to pay the usher's salary until there should be an usher. This may well have been an attempt to force Rev Roberts to employ someone to do the teaching that he was obviously not doing, and, indeed, a succession of ushers came and went, earning up to £30 per year, including, at one point, Roberts' own son. Despite his incompetence, Roberts had his salary increased to £75 per year and even managed to get a petition from the inhabitants of Warwick dismissed; it had demanded "the removal of the said James Roberts from his office of Master of the Free Grammar School for neglect of his duty". Long after James Roberts' death in 1791, Lord Brougham's Commission stated: "The School seems to have fallen into great decay under Mr Roberts, who had been School-master from the year 1763. Towards the latter part of his mastership there were no boarders and few, if any, free scholars."

CHAPTER 6

Rev George Innes

In Felix Farley's Bristol Journal of July 21st, 1792, the following advertisement appeared:

> The King's School, at the College, Warwick, will open at Michaelmas next (not on the 14th of August as before advertised), under the Rev. Geo. Innes MA, Fellow of Magdalen College, Oxford, and Second Master of Rugby School. Boys under the age of twelve years only will be admitted, and on the following terms: Board and tuition, Twenty five guineas per ann. (washing not included) – Entrance Two Guineas. Masters will attend to teach Writing, French, Dancing, Drawing and Musick.

George Innes was the son of the Rector of Devizes. Born in 1759, he was expelled from Winchester in 1777 for his part in a riot but was, nevertheless, admitted to Merton College, Oxford, and in 1788 he became a fellow of Magdalen College, Oxford. From 1783, he had been a teacher at Rugby School, where, after dealing with a pupil riot, he became Second Master in 1787. A notice outside Rugby School nowadays proudly proclaims that it was there that the Riot Act was read for the last time, and that it was this that brought the Great Rebellion of 1797 to an end. Innes might well have become Head Master of Rugby if he had stayed on, but he came to Warwick in 1793, with a wife who, it is alleged, was the main cause of the move. The portrait of Rev George Innes now in the Pyne Room was presented to the school by St Mary's Church in 1923.

Despite his length of service, records from Innes' time are very scarce. However, his great-nephew, Charles Innes of Harrow, Middlesex, wrote to the school in 1911:

> Gentlemen. As a descendant of the late Rev George Innes who in 1837 was Head Master of the King's School, The College, Warwick, I am destroying many letters of no value. Amongst them, however, I came upon an "Exoneration of the Land Tax" for the School dated 16th November 1814. Before destroying this, I write to ask you if you would care to have it. The school (in the Exoneration) is styled "The Free Grammar School alias the King's School at Warwick". It is duly sealed and signed. The tax exonerated appears to have been for a sum of nineteen shillings per annum.
>
> I know not what changes may have taken place, but if of any service to you I shall be happy to send it. The Rev George Innes was my Great Uncle.
>
> I am, Gentlemen, Yours faithfully, Chas E Innes.

A photograph of the portrait of Rev George Innes
now owned by the school.

The certificate referred to is the oldest archive in the possession of Warwick School and is on permanent display in the Foundation Office, near St Mary's Church. The writing on the back is in the hand of George Innes. Another fascinating Innes autograph surfaced in the Warwickshire County Record Office, just as this book was going to press, in the form of a school bill of 1807. Innes' hand-written complaint at the bottom of the bill, warning parents about unauthorised holidays, is just as valid today as it was 200 years ago!

Despite the job advertisement, when Innes started there were only one or two day-boys and no boarders. He increased the numbers to nine or ten day-boys, had a school-room built for him by the Corporation and maintained a flourishing boarding house for 15 to 20 years, before he became a victim of gout. He had an assistant master in the early years, and again when he was very, very much older. In 1816, the school-master's salary was increased from £75 to £135. From this time onwards, Innes seems to have taught only those day-boys who really insisted on coming to school. Their fees were 1½ guineas on entering (a modern £93) and 10s a year for "warming and cleaning the school" (£30). As was typical of the time, Innes had acquired the living of Hilferton in Wiltshire in 1798 in order to augment his salary.

In 1832, there were 13 pupils at the King's School, but they did their lessons at home, only coming in to school to have what we would now call a tutorial. Innes only taught Classics; for other subjects, such as English and arithmetic, the boys had to seek out other tutors – for example, at Bablake School, which was at the Eastgate. The boys made full recreational use of St Mary's Churchyard and organised many races around it, even using the gravestones for steeplechases. For this information, and much else besides for the period 1832–38, we have to thank Archdeacon James Baly, who in June 1902, seven years before he died, wrote a long article, published in full in the July 1902 edition of *The Portcullis*, which was extensively quoted by AF Leach. Baly had entered Mr Innes' school at the age of eight in 1832 and learnt nothing there except Latin and Greek for the next six years:

> When free from gout, the old gentleman would take his seat in a very old and roomy desk, raised on a platform about a foot from the floor, with room enough for half a dozen boys to stand on at one time; quite enough, though, for when I went to the school in 1832, there were only thirteen boys; and during my six years' stay I do not remember there being more than sixteen or eighteen boys at one time.
>
> The school building consisted of two large rooms; the outer one was quite bare of furniture except a row of low cupboards, the top of which served as a bench for sitting. They were all empty and never used while I was at the school. The inner room was the class room; a row of eight desks, much cut and carved with designs of the human figure, or the names of successive owners, was fixed at one end of the room on the same level as the floor; these were occupied by the younger scholars. On the side wall, facing Mr Innes' desk, were four or five desks raised above the floor, which were the seats of the elder scholars. The two rows were in chronic hostility, and even during the time of lessons, missiles and winged words of wrath passed from one to the other.
>
> There was no assistant-master until the last two or three years of Mr Innes' mastership, when the Rev. Henry Gem was appointed; and from that time the greater part of the schoolwork was conducted by him, and more was done.

In October 1833, at an enquiry into the state of Warwick Corporation, Innes, described as "Master of the Free School", had to defend himself against an accusation by a half-blind ex-soldier, John Morris, that he had promised, and then withdrawn, the offer of the valuable Fulke Weale Exhibition, or scholarship, to his son. When he entered the school, the boy was the only pupil and therefore seemed bound to get it. The fact that he left the school at the age of 14, however, automatically precluded him from getting the Exhibition. Extracts from the report of the dialogue between Innes and the Commissioner, R Whitcombe, contain some astonishing revelations:

Whitcombe: When you applied for the School, did you make any inquiry as to the nature of what was taught there?

Innes: I did not conceive it necessary. I thought I was to teach Latin.

W: How long did you take boarders?

I: Perhaps, from fifteen to twenty years. I parted with them merely at last because my health would not endure it, and I was obliged to give it up.

W: Was your health sufficiently good to allow you to attend to the School?

I: Yes, I always attended to my school, even though I had but one or two boys; I scarce ever omitted a day.

W: Has there ever been any period during your Mastership in which there has been no boy at the School?

I: I do not think that there has ever been such a period. I cannot state, but from memory I am sure that there has never been a period in which I have not had one or two.

W: When you first took to the School, you taught nothing but Latin and Greek, and you have adhered to that course ever since?

I: Yes.

W: As far as your Free Scholars are concerned, you have only, generally speaking, taught Latin and Greek, unless paid for?

I: No. I made a compendious form of Arithmetic, of my own, and taught it to those Boarders only who were remarkably quick and attentive.

W: Since you have been Master, have the Corporation been in the habit, from time to time, of visiting your School?

I: Never.

W: Have you ever been called upon by the Mayor, or any of the Members of the Corporation, to give an account of the way in which the School is going on?

I: Never.

W: Have they ever interfered with the management of the School?

I: Never, I always conceived I was perfectly independent of them.

W: As you have stated, you frequently at various times have had but two or three boys at your school?

I: Yes.

W: At this time, your attention to the School has not been during the whole of the school hours?

I: Not so long; they learn their lessons at home, and when they come I hear them, and then they go back.

W: In case of boys not coming regularly to the School, do you make any enquiries?

I: No, mine is a very small establishment. I seldom received any information from parents. I never choose to send a boy to inquire against another boy, because I think it might make him false for life.

W: When any one absented himself from School, what measures did you take?

I: I take their word for the cause of their absence, unless, which is very rare, I have any other opportunity of inquiring.

W: About how long, in the course of the day, have you been in the habit of being in the School?

I: Every other day there is a half holiday; on Monday, Wednesday and Friday. I enter at about a quarter or half past ten, until 12 or one; and in the evening, from a quarter to half past two until four.

W: Do they learn any lessons in the School?

I: No; I have often wished them to come to construe their lessons over one with another, but I cannot accomplish it.

W: How long together have you been absent from the School?

I: Once I was absent five months. I was at Torquay, attending to one of my family, who was exceedingly ill; but my School was amply provided for, at my own expense, during the time; and I have twice or three times been absent for a week.

W: When you have actually been residing in Warwick, have you ever been absent from the School any series of days?

I: I do not remember having been absent from my School two days, or scarcely to have given a holiday in the year. I beg to say that in forty-one years it may have escaped my memory. I do not remember to have been absent for any number of days in my life. I do not think I can recollect having been absent for one or two days.

Prior to this, Mr George Greenway, the Receiver of Henry VIII's Charity, had been asked some questions about the school, and about a Decree of Charles I's time, by Mr Whitcombe and the other Commissioner, Mr AE Cockburn:

Q: Can you tell us any thing about the present state of the Free School?

A: No, I believe there are about twenty. I was once of that School, when there were only about ten boys.

Q: Does the Decree say any thing as to the reception of Boarders?

A: I am not aware; I believe there were ten Day-boys when the School was in the most flourishing state, and about sixty Boarders.

Q: Are there any Boarders now?

A: None. The School was established at the Reformation, when Popery was no longer in power, in order to teach and encourage Protestantism, the Classics, before that period, having been taught by the priests.

Q: Might not the School be made subservient to the different situations of the town, and more consistent with the character of Warwick?

A: It is entirely a matter of opinion.

Q: Do you not think, if it were a School of General Education, and there was no charge of a guinea and a half entrance, there would be more Day-boys?

A: Probably there would.

Q: Has not the School been nearly deserted?

A: Yes. It was so before Mr Innes's time; I believe it was so in 1790, or 1791, when Mr Roberts was the Master. Under Mr Lydiat it was a flourishing School. It has commonly been the case, when they have a new Master it flourishes, but when they get old it dwindles away.

Q: Have the Boys educated there been the sons of gentlemen?

A: Yes. There was a Smith, whose father kept the School at the Chapel, who had the Exhibition to Oxford, but he did not conduct himself well and was expelled, and became a journeyman butcher. It is said he is now dead.

Q: When I say gentlemen, I mean the sons of the higher order of tradesmen?

A: Yes.

Q: Would the lower orders probably have sent their boys, had it not been for the entrance-money?

A: They might, but it is not probable they would.

Q: What class of Boys go to the Bablake School?

A: The poorer class.

Q: How many boys are educated there?

A: About 100.

Q: Is there a National School?

A: Yes. There are about 80 on the list, and about 70 attend.

Innes died in office in 1842, at the age of 82. His grave tablet is in the north transept of St Mary's Church. Why he stayed on well past his prime, as it were, is easy to determine. His successor had exactly the same problem – there was no pension. In 1842, a petition quoted an earlier Chancery report which stated that:

The Free Grammar School is in an inefficient state in consequence of the limited system of instruction, caused by the advanced age of the master and other causes, and that it would be of the utmost benefit to the borough were the system of education to be extended beyond the teaching of the Classics to the useful branches of literature and science, for at present scholars have to go to other teachers for writing and arithmetic, the teacher attends two and a half hours in the morning, and about an hour and a half in the evening and there are half holidays on three days a week. The pupils learn their lessons at home and only come to school to repeat them.

The charity trustees felt that the death of Innes was "an opportunity to alter the scheme of education", and this was endorsed by the Town Council and a town public meeting:

NEAR THIS PLACE

REPOSE THE MORTAL REMAINS OF THE

REV. GEORGE INNES. M.A. 50 YEARS MASTER OF

KING HENRY THE EIGHT'S SCHOOL AT THE COLLEGE IN THIS TOWN;

WHO DIED 17TH. JULY 1842, IN HIS 83RD. YEAR.

AN ACCOMPLISHED SCHOLAR AND GENTLEMAN.

TO STRICT INTEGRITY, AND INDEPENDENCE OF CHARACTER,

HE UNITED CHRISTIAN SIMPLICITY, HUMILITY, AND LOVE.

SHE, WHO ALONE SURVIVES OF THOSE WHO BEST KNEW HIS

WORTH, HAS ERECTED THIS TABLET TO HIS MEMORY.

Rev George Innes' grave tablet in St Mary's Church, Warwick.
(GN Frykman)

All this will entail repairs to the school buildings, an increase in salaries due to the master and usher, and a plan for instruction in commercial and general education, and in grammar, and other learning fit to be taught in a Grammar School

The death of George Innes was recalled, nearly sixty years later, in two anonymous articles in *The Portcullis* of November and December 1900. An interesting reference is made to the initials carved into the wall of St Mary's churchyard, still clearly visible to this day:

I will describe the state of things as they existed in 1840, when I was first introduced to the shrine of learning at King Henry the Eighth's school, generally spoken of as "The College." It was arranged that I should commence school upon the following morning, and I accordingly made my way to the only entrance, viz. a door leading from the church-yard, where now some initials are to be seen, but by far the greater number have been erased by "the hand of time," the soft sandstone of the walls not being of sufficiently durable material to hand them down to posterity, as fondly hoped by those who carved them.

The lids of the desks were decorated in various ways, as suggested by the genius of the boys, coupled with the efficiency of the pocket-knives they possessed; but the one chief feature and by far the grandest design was a canal which had been cut along their entire length, indicating a general engineering skill, which had obviously overcome many difficulties in its construction. Only one slight defect need be mentioned; there was no "fall," but this was treated as a trifle. Reservoirs were introduced at intervals to contain the ink which was propelled along the canal by the aid of pens, &c, as opportunity occurred; the "working" of the undertaking usually resulted in very dirty hands and distinct and original designs in ink upon the face.

As the health of the headmaster became more enfeebled, the small boys saw less and less of him during the later portions of his life. He would occasionally hear us our declensions, or conjugate a verb, and at such times would secure a small lock of the hair between his thumb and forefinger, so that he could at once, upon hearing a false quantity, or a wrong pronunciation, apply the "thumb screw" very effectually, as he said in a kindly voice, but too slowly, "You foolish boy! you stupid boy!" screwing up the hair all the while with a special cunning peculiar to himself.

There was nothing approaching a fixed time for lessons, but we were expected to be in attendance in case we were called up. The "big fellows" also were by no means overworked, their lessons were soon over and then the games began, being organised and presided over by them, with a view to their own pleasures, which consisted chiefly in making the small boys do what they wanted.

Thus things passed on, but it was not to last much longer, for on our way to school one morning in July, 1842, we were told our old Master was dead, and shortly after, a handsome (to our eyes) brass plate was exposed in the engraver's window, recording the event. After his death, the house and school were thoroughly repaired and altered, the work taking up a considerable time, during which it was still a favourite resort for play.

It must be remembered, that except for the richer classes, who could afford to send their boys to the more expensive Public Schools, this was the best education to be obtained at that time.

Innes' last surviving pupil, Samuel William Cooke, died in 1911. Colonel Cooke, a local soldier, deserves to be remembered as the founder of the school's Cadet Corps in 1884. Quite what Colonel Cooke would have thought of the introduction of four King's High School girls to Warwick School's CCF in September 2003 is best left to the imagination!

CHAPTER 7

Rev Herbert Hill

In August 1842, a committee of trustees of the Charity of King Henry VIII and Warwick Town Council, as already mentioned, saw the death of George Innes as an opportunity to draw up a new scheme for the regulation of the school, of which the main points were as follows:

1. That the Headmaster should be a graduate of an English University and in Holy Orders. That his salary should not be less than £200 per annum, and that he should be at liberty to take boarders.

2. The Usher or undermaster should be appointed by the Headmaster who should be competent to teach as well the Classics as mathematics and the higher branches of arithmetic and should be well versed in Literature, Geography and Science and should be a fit person in his habits and temper to have charge of education and that his salary should be £80 per annum.

3. That a Writing Master should be appointed by the Headmaster at a salary of £40 per annum.

4. That the management of the school should be confided to the Headmaster entirely.

5. That besides the Classical languages there should be taught in the school mathematics, the higher branches of arithmetic, general English Literature, geography, English composition, sacred and profane history, the lower branches of arithmetic, reading and writing, and that in addition to the above branches of education it was desirable that there should be taught in the school, French, German and other modern languages, and that instruction should be given in the Arts and Sciences to such scholars as might be willing to contribute to the expense thereof, and that the Headmaster might provide proper Masters and Lecturers to teach the same as he might think fit and proper and circumstances might from time to time require.

6. That the Headmaster should make a yearly report to the Governors as to the number of scholars, in addition to half yearly reports on their progress and on the general state of the school.

7. That the Governors should consist of the Earl of Warwick, the Recorder of

Rev Herbert Hill, photographed probably on his retirement in 1876.
(Warwick School Archives)

Warwick, the Mayor of Warwick, two representatives of the Town Council and two representatives of the Trustees, who should be visitors of the school.

The creation of a board of governors was a clear attempt to supervise what went on in the school. No minutes of their early meetings have survived, but the governors may well have restricted their activities to reading the headmaster's reports. This revolutionary scheme was confirmed, with only small amendments, by the Court of Chancery in January 1845.

The Court had, in the meantime (late in 1842), appointed Rev Herbert Hill to be the new Headmaster. Born in Streatham (which is near London but was then in Surrey) in 1810, the son of the Chancellor of Hereford Cathedral and Rector of Streatham, Herbert Hill went to Winchester, like his predecessor, and then New College, Oxford, where he became a Fellow, as was usual, two years after his admission. In 1833, he was appointed tutor to Dr Arnold's son at Rugby School, joining the staff around 1836.

Within two years of his arrival at Warwick in 1843, the boys had a playground, boarding was re-introduced (and, for the first time, a bed was provided for each boy!), and a proper teaching staff was employed. In 1844, the school had 52 pupils, a more or less constant figure for many years to come.

The early years of Herbert Hill's tenure of office are recalled in an article by TF Inman, dated October 1900 and published in the March 1901 edition of *The Portcullis*:

> I went to the school as a boarder just as our dear old master, Herbert Hill, had been appointed. The school had been shut up for a year. My journey from Bath was chiefly by coach. There was then railway only from Gloucester to Birmingham.
>
> On arriving I was taken into the dining room, a large but low room covered with books on one side. Mr Hill had just come back from Coventry with toys for his children, and was kneeling on the floor showing them to them. He was tall, with a slight well-made figure. You were at once struck by his eyes, very bright bluish grey. Hair long and curling, of a very dark auburn beginning to show a little grey. Fair complexion and remarkably beautiful hands, the last very artistic-looking.
>
> I have sometimes wondered how it was that Mr Hill had so great control over the boys. He was little given to punishment. He would at times call a boy aside and speak to him kindly and earnestly and with considerable effect. He was devoted to books, and was for a time sub-librarian at the Bodleian, but he was by no means a mere book-worm, and constantly was with us at cricket. He knew what to see and what not to see. Those who have read "Tom Brown's School Days" will know how common fighting was amongst the boys at that time. I think that, like Dr Arnold, he was not too ready to see and stop a fight.
>
> One of the Rugby ways he brought with him was to have the boarders or some of them into his drawing room on, I think, Sunday evenings. Mr and Mrs Hill were delightful hosts.

Hill "used to keep a list of the boys admitted" but later confessed to having lost it. Near the end of his career, he purchased a splendid book, the King's Grammar School Roll Book, and this book has survived. It records, in each headmaster's own hand, which boys were admitted from 1871 onwards, and quite often a few extra details are added, such as Oxbridge scholarships, canings and expulsions, and the occasional unfortunate death: infectious diseases were a recurring nightmare for all boarding school headmasters at this time. This unique archive from the old school was discovered in the summer of 2002, in a very poor state, and it was immediately re-bound. There are three companion hand-written volumes, and, together, they record all pupils admitted from 1871 to 1994.

Hill made a great point of learning huge chunks of the Classics by heart. In 1848, the poet Wordsworth came to stay with the headmaster – Hill had married the poet Southey's daughter, Bertha. Her aunt was Coleridge's wife, and even Matthew Arnold visited the school more than once. "Small games" were played at the school;

football and cricket, on Saltisford Common. There were six forms, I, II and III being the Lower School, and IV, V and VI the Upper School. It would seem that the term "Head Master" was first used for Herbert Hill. Innes was usually referred to as the "Master" of the King's School.

Sabine Baring-Gould, the writer of the hymns *Onward, Christian Soldiers, Now the Day is Over* and *Through the Night of Doubt and Sorrow*, was a pupil for some months in 1846, before he got whooping-cough and was ordered abroad. However, he has his portrait proudly hanging in the vestry of Warwick School chapel. His obituary in *The Portcullis* of March 1924 rather sanctimoniously announces that not only had he inherited "the family estates of Lew Trenchard, which comprised 3,000 acres, and presented himself to the rectory of that place in 1880", but also that he had "married a Yorkshire mill girl whom he had well educated, and who made an excellent wife". When he was 34, Baring-Gould, a Yorkshire curate at the time, met Grace Taylor, an illiterate mill girl of 16, and "had her educated" for two years. The marriage lasted for 48 years, and the couple had 15 children. This extraordinary liaison between a prolific author, expert on folk music, self-proclaimed squire and rector, and a mill girl is said to be the basis of George Bernard Shaw's *Pygmalion*, and, subsequently, the musical *My Fair Lady*. One touching story is that at a children's party one evening he apparently called to a young child: "And whose little girl are you?" The child burst into tears and, with quivering lip, said: "I'm yours, Daddy."

The 1851 Census records that Herbert Hill, aged 40, and his wife Bertha, aged 42 (who was born in Keswick, Cumbria), lived in the College with their seven children, aged between one and eleven. The elder three were born in Grasmere, and the younger four in Warwick. The household also included seven servants. In this crowded home, he somehow found the space and time to write at least one published book: Crockford's Clerical Directory of 1860 quotes him as having written *Short Sermons on some Leading Principles of Christian Life* (published by Masters at 6s in 1854). The same directory lists Hill as being the Domestic Chaplain of the Earl of Warwick.

Life at the King's School in the 1860s was illustrated in an anonymous article published in *The Portcullis* in July 1900. It starts by describing the headmaster:

> Tall, thin, erect, an excellent scholar, and a good man, he was much respected by his old pupils. The school hours were 9 o'clock until 12, and from 2 o'clock until 5, except in the winter, when as there were no lights, we were dismissed at dusk. In those days we all wore mortar boards, and carried our books in blue bags, which together with hockeys (if that game happened to be on then), and caps, were popped under the desks during school hours. At 9 o'clock and 2 the boys were summoned to school, not by a bell, but by the headmaster vigorously caning a door which opened against the outer wall of the schoolroom, and as the Master waited until all in the playground were in, a laggard stood a good chance of receiving any small balance of caning which might have belonged to the door.

In the 1860s, Hill's large family suffered much ill-health, and, to quote Leach, "the same lassitude for a thankless task which had overtaken his predecessor" overtook Hill. The 1860s saw many educational reforms and three important Acts of Parliament. The inspector who visited Warwick in 1865-6 found 44 boys at the King's School, of whom four were boarders. In 1867, the Town Council was becoming obsessed with "commercial education" and recommended the forming of two schools: a classical school, with boarding, and an entirely distinct commercial school. The Charity Commission found a great deal of money locked up in local charities, and a public meeting in 1868 suggested that this money be applied to the modernising of the school. It is somewhat ironic to learn that Thomas Oken's Charity, which had been subsidising the salary of the headmaster since the sixteenth century, was virtually crippled by this reorganisation. This modernisation also required Hill's retirement, which he was not willing to allow – on the grounds that, like his predecessor, he did not have a pension.

All these public discussions, not to mention Hill's advancing age, had the effect of reducing pupil numbers to 28, including one boarder (who was Hill's nephew). Hill reported in 1868 that the three boys from parishes outside Warwick paid an annual fee of 10 guineas, and the twenty-four from Warwick paid 4 guineas per annum. He further reported that nine boys learned Greek; twenty-six learned Latin; and two, being quite young, were taught a common English education. With the exception of three or four of the youngest boys, they all learned French. Some were taught Euclid; and others, algebra. None of them learned the Church Catechism, but nearly all were taught Scripture History. Their ages varied from 8 to 16, the majority being between 11 and 14. The 1868 report suggests that there were two other teaching staff besides Herbert Hill: Mr Montague and Mr Palmer.

By 1872, numbers were back up to 54 – but all were day-boys. Public confidence had been somewhat restored by lack of change. The scheme published in 1873 provided for three schools: a Grammar School for 250 boys, including 70 boarders; a Middle School for 100 boys; and a Girls' School for 80 girls. The Schools Inquiry Commission had classified schools into three grades:

First Grade: For boys intended for the Universities, leaving school at 18 or 19.
Second Grade: For boys intended for the professions, the Army and the Civil Service, leaving school at 16 or 17 years of age.
Third Grade: For boys, the sons of small traders, farmers and skilled artisans, leaving school at 14 years of age.

The Grammar School was to be Second Grade, that is, for boys from 8 to 17 years of age, at fees of £6 to £12 per year (worth £250 to £500 in 2003). The boarding fee was to be fixed at £35 per year (£1,500).

The increasing numbers caused additional premises to be sought, and, for a while, Landor House (at that time called Eastgate House) in Smith Street was used for accommodation for extra classes, described by EG Tibbits as "a Modern department of the Grammar School, which had been set up as a result of popular clamour". When the boys moved out (the new Middle School was ready in 1878, and the Grammar School in 1879), King's High School for Girls was at last able to move into Landor House and get under way with 22 girls, aged between 5 and 15.

Life at the King's Grammar School in the 1870s was illustrated in an anonymous article in *The Portcullis* of June 1900, and it described, in particular, the intense rivalry which existed between the King's School and the Bablake (or Boblic) boys in the period immediately before both schools were found new homes. This included snowball fights "with stones placed inside the snowballs thrown by the enemy – a Boer-like expedient never adopted by our fellows."

Hill prophesied that the Middle School would under-sell the Grammar School among the townspeople and that the boarding fee was far too low. Local worthies argued vehemently that the proposed Grammar School should be First Grade, with no charge for extra Greek and with a discount for local boys, and the leaving age raised to 18. This huge row, with the Earl of Warwick at its centre, was largely based on the fear of Liberals and Non-Conformists getting a foothold in the management of the school, and was only resolved in 1875, when the scheme for the three separate schools was finally set up. It may have taken 30 more years, but Herbert Hill was proved right when unfair competition caused the complete economic collapse of Warwick School.

Ironically, one of the consequences of the educational reforms of the 1860s and 1870s was that The King's School was now to have a new board of governors – and the Earl of Warwick became the first chairman of that board in 1875. The new school site, called the Myton site, was chosen by the new governors in 1876, after they had considered, and then abandoned, the idea of a move to land in St John's; the Charity of King Henry VIII had been instructed to allocate 12 acres at Myton for new Grammar School buildings and to provide a yearly sum to support them. The Earl of Warwick expressed his "fierce opposition" to the Myton site – he owned the land in St John's and, unlike the Charity, would not have been expected to give the land away. The other governors presumably saw through this, and the administration of both the Myton site and the annual grant was transferred to a new trust, The King's School Foundation. Shortly afterwards, Herbert Hill retired, with a testimonial of "a Silver Salver, of the value of £20, with an appropriate inscription, and a Purse of £1,180", donated by friends and former pupils. This would be worth about £45,000 in 2003. In 1880, he was appointed to the Mastership of the Lord Leycester Hospital and died in 1892, aged 81. In his obituary in *The Portcullis*, JP Way wrote:

> He was the last of the old line of Head-masters of the King's School who received their appointments directly from the Lord Chancellor, sealed with the Great Seal.

It was with great excitement that members of the upper-fifth Archives Group discovered the original 1842 parchment and Great Seal for Herbert Hill's appointment, apparently unseen for decades, in the Warwickshire County Record Office in September 2003.

CHAPTER 8
Rev William Fisher MacMichael

William Fisher MacMichael was the son of John Fisher MacMichael, Canon of Ripon Cathedral and Head Master of Ripon Cathedral School. He studied mathematics at Downing College, Cambridge, and also rowed for his university in 1868 and 1869. He was ordained in 1871 and, after a short period as Chaplain of Downing, joined the staff of Cheltenham College in 1872, before coming to Warwick in 1876.

He deserves to be remembered as the headmaster who brought the school down from the town to its present site, but is peremptorily dismissed by Leach as "not a success", on the grounds that "he appears to have been somewhat too robust in his treatment of the boys." He was, at the time, a bachelor, and he imported his mother and sister to help him run the boarding side, but he lost popularity by being extremely "high church". Indeed, one of the many complaints against him was that he had given 12 boys at Cheltenham in 1875 a book entitled *The Altar Manual*. In 1878, there were 44 boys in the school, and seven letters of complaint were sent to the governors. There were charges of "wilful cruelty, unfairness and incapacity", but the governors declared the charges unfounded. It is interesting that there are several clues still existing to the "high church" nature of the school – one of the most obvious being the holy water stoup, or piscina, set in the wall to the south side of the altar in the chancel of the chapel. The chancel was not, of course, built by MacMichael, but by JP Way in the 1890s.

MacMichael was the first Headmaster of the new school buildings, which were opened on 1st August, 1879. They had been designed by John Cundall (1836-1889), who was also responsible for a number of buildings in Leamington, including the Town Hall. At one point, Cundall was asked to "place the building at an angle with the road instead of parallel to it in order to avoid a North aspect for the Class Rooms and Dormitories", but this idea was not followed, and the result is the frontage we know today. The governors' minutes of August 1879 state: "The governors then proceeded to the new Grammar School buildings to attend the opening ceremony. After a short service in the chapel the distribution of prizes took place in the large School Room. The Chair was taken by Lord Leigh and the prizes were distributed by Lord Brooke." Comforts were few: the governors' minutes suggest, for example, "that the providing of seats for the Masters in Chapel be postponed". These new

Rev WF MacMichael and his wife, seated at the further end of the second row of seats of a
charabanc in Devon, taken around 1910.
(Ilfracombe Museum)

buildings cost £12,300, plus £1,500 for the chapel, and the only items brought down
from the old site in St Mary's Churchyard were enough oak beams to make the headmaster's pig-sty. The bell from the Eastgate Chapel, dating from 1730, was installed
in the tower, where it survives to this day in fine condition. The redundant College
buildings were at one stage considered for the newly-established King's High School
for Girls, but that idea was rejected by the governors. The old buildings were sold
for £1,800 (worth about £100,000 in 2003) and were demolished in 1880. The site is
now a peaceful garden, although in 1904 it was being suggested that it should be
used as a playground for the boys of the cramped Middle School on the other side of
The Butts – and connected to it by a subway! The haste with which the demolition
was done suggests that the governors were pleased to be rid of the crumbling old
buildings. All that remains is the gateway, steps and outer wall of the school-yard, on
which are inscribed several sets of initials, carved, Leach presumed, by generations
of idle boys. He spotted them at the end of the 19th century, and they are still there.
One or two of the graffiti, very helpfully, carry a date – one is dated 1878. Even only
20 years after the demolition, alarm was being raised that there was no pictorial
record at all of the old school, but etchings and at least one photograph surfaced in
Edwardian times.

MacMichael was keen to modernise the teaching, even if he knew nothing of the subject; before the move to Myton Road, "it was resolved that Dr Tibbits and Mr James Baly be a committee to confer with the Head Master as to the best method of teaching chemistry in the school" and that "one of the class rooms on the ground floor to be fitted up as a laboratory." However, the governors also minuted "that the Head Master be authorised to charge the pupils in the Chemistry classes the cost of materials used in class experiments". As regards boarding, "the dormitory on the 1st floor containing 21 cubicles to be furnished." The location of the original chemistry laboratory was almost certainly the ground-floor teaching room nearest the chapel (fitted out as the reprographics room in 2002), and in the corridor outside it was the "school museum" – cases with a more or less random collection of objects of interest. It is difficult to establish who else, apart from MacMichael, was on the teaching staff at this time. One other member of staff is recorded as having made the move from St Mary's to Myton Road along with the headmaster, and that is Mr E Iremonger. His carved plaque in the dining room records his years of service as 1876–80.

As soon as he had settled the new school in, MacMichael was in conflict with the governors again. A tetchy exchange obviously took place: "A letter from Mr MacMichael having been read requesting to be informed whether the governors wished him to undertake services in the chapel, it was resolved that Mr MacMichael be requested to inform the governors what kind of services he proposed to establish." The answer, of course, was the normal rites of the Church of England. In June 1880, Mr MacMichael wrote to the governors, expressing his intention to resign at Christmas. The governors minuted: "The Governors, in accepting the resignation at Christmas of Mr MacMichael, desire to express their sense of the assiduity, integrity and zeal with which he has always discharged his arduous duty." He appears not to have taught again but, having been a curate at St Paul's, Leamington, while he was the headmaster at Warwick, he went on to hold three further curacies in Cambridge, Luton and Torquay, before being appointed vicar in 1886 at Lee in north Devon, three miles from Ilfracombe, at a salary of £186 per year. MacMichael made national news in 1904 when, acting as a guide to two couples who wanted to walk along the beach from Lee to Ilfracombe, he caused the entire party to be cut off by the tide, and he, one of the men and both ladies had to be hauled up the cliffs by rope. He died in 1924, aged 80, and has a splendid memorial at Lee Church.

CHAPTER 9

Rev William Grundy

Rev William Grundy was born in 1850 and was educated at Rossall School and Worcester College, Oxford, where he became a Fellow in 1875. He lectured at Oxford before becoming the Headmaster's Assistant at Rossall School in 1878, and he came to Warwick at the age of 31 in January 1881. He was a red-head and very energetic, being a fives player of national standard. He also excelled at chess and took a great interest in philosophy. He was a merciless flogger of boys and took great exception to "idleness". His technique with idle boys was to put the bottom two boys in each class on a "satisfecit", and if they had not improved in a fortnight, they were flogged. These lists, or Form Orders, were read out in Big School on Saturdays, and the floggings (over the shoulders) took place shortly afterwards in his study. The term "Form Order" is still used at Warwick School. Those at the bottom of the list are no longer flogged, but there is still a type of "satisfecit" – a report card. The earliest surviving school list is a Form Order from August 1881, on which the boys are not arranged alphabetically, but in descending academic order. One consequence of this, and of promotion on merit rather than by age, is that, of the top three boys in the school, two were fifteen years old, and the third, the ultimately tragic Wilfrid Gibson – the most brilliant boy the school had yet seen – was fourteen. One puzzling aspect is that several older sixth-formers are stated to be on "Special Work". It is explained in an article in *The Portcullis* of July 1924 that the work of boys who were not expecting to be entered for national examinations (which at the time were Oxford Local Junior and Senior) was not marked. Such boys presumably stayed at the school largely to benefit from the sporting facilities and fixtures.

Grundy married in 1881, and his unmarried sister acted as matron. In his own energetic way, he instituted the annual school sports, concerts, paper chases, swimming races, debating, essay societies, a Tuck Shop (in the small room by the main doors of the school), the first school magazine, the Rifle Corps, the Master's Book (discussed below), science teaching, a carpenter's shop, school lists and school rules, and he also appointed a "School Clerk". It is clear from the surviving cricket score books from the early 1880s that Grundy regularly played in the school team and was both a very successful batsman and bowler.

Found in the headmaster's house in 2002 were two archives of exceptional value and interest: two bound volumes, called the Master's Books, in which each head-

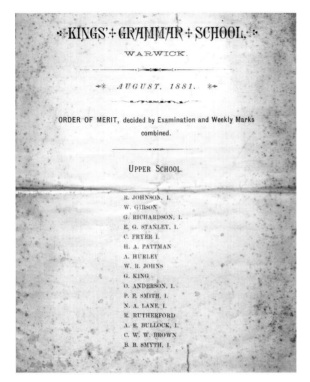

The earliest surviving school list,
dating from 1881.
(Warwick School Archives)

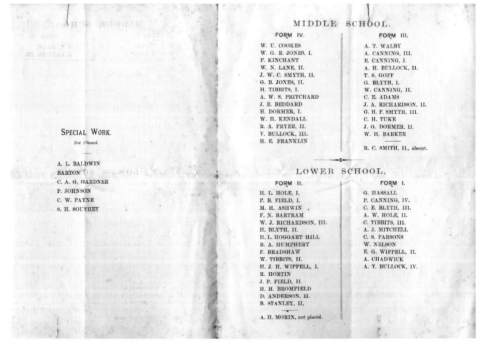

master from 1881 to 1906 recorded virtually everything of importance which happened at the school. Volume I was started by Grundy and finished by his successor, Rev JP Way. Grundy was the first headmaster to leave any appreciable written records, for in this book he started to write down notices which he gave out, and kept a record of the achievements of the school. The book must have been available to the teaching staff to read, because sometimes notices are addressed to them directly, but it must also have been brought daily into assembly in Big School, to have whole-school notices read out. Volume II, begun in 1894, has a handsome red binding, but on it are some extraordinary black marks. These correspond exactly to where the headmaster would have held the book, round the spine, while striding into assembly, but give the impression of somewhat excessive perspiration!

An 1881 Prospectus in the County Record Office shows that there was a teaching staff of three (plus the headmaster, who taught all the Classics in the school), and two "Drawing Masters", together with a local organist to teach "Vocal Music". Relations between the head and his staff do not seem to have been very cordial. Early in Volume I of the Master's Book, Grundy berates his staff in no uncertain terms:

> There is one other point to which I wish to direct the especial attention of Masters. It will be seen by reference to entry under date June 1, 1882, that I have already had cause to complain of disorder at meals. During the vacation very strong representations have been made to me upon the same point, and it is only after much anxiety to me, and a conjunction of favourable circumstances – simple good fortune, in fact – that the school has avoided a serious injury. As I have no definite information as to the date of the disorder complained of, it would be ill-natured on my part to assume that Masters have disregarded previous instructions, but I take this opportunity of emphasising all I have said upon the subject. Unless there is considerable improvement, it will be necessary to make regulations with regard to supervision at meals which, although they exist at most schools, I should prefer in the interest of assistant masters to avoid until my staff is larger. What I have said refers to resident masters only.
>
>   [undated, Sept 1882]   W Grundy

It must be borne in mind that the implied riots in the dining room involved no more than 30 or 40 boys, and that Grundy's complaint about staff supervision only applied to a couple of men. There was a dramatic rise in the number of boarders: from 8 in 1880, to 26 in 1881, and 70 in 1884. By 1885, the total number of boys reached 135, with six assistant masters, and Grundy applied to the governors to build a new boarding house, attached to the sanatorium, but this was refused, so he resigned at Easter 1885 and took the headmastership of Malvern, where he had exactly the same effect on numbers. An extremely dynamic man, he died of a seizure in 1891 at Malvern, and the whole school was made to file past his body.

Forty years later, it was being claimed that the sixth form of 1882-1884 was extraordinarily good, with three pupils in particular gaining national recognition for

Rev William Grundy, photographed around 1885.
(Warwick School Archives)

their examination results – Wilfrid Gibson, Robert Johnson and Gerald Richardson, all of whom are at the top of the 1881 school list. Their subsequent scholarships at Oxford University are proudly recorded in the Master's Book, and each was used as an excuse to award the whole school a half day's holiday. To quote from an article in *The Portcullis* of July 1924, lamenting the early death of Robert Johnson: "To pass from an elementary school to a good Oxford degree, now not unusual, was then a very rare achievement, and in Warwick quite a novelty." Johnson, who had been on the staff of King Edward VII School, Sheffield, was the first boy to win an Oxford Scholarship after the new 1875 scheme had creamed off many local boys to the King's Middle School, and, in fact, he had won a scholarship from the newly formed Middle School to its more august and senior partner in 1878. It is extraordinarily fortunate that, somehow, the magnificent medal given to Robert Johnson by the governors in 1885, in celebration of his outstanding achievement, is now back in the possession of the school. Wilfrid Gibson, as will be seen later, suffered an even earlier death than Robert Johnson.

Pasted into Volume I of the Master's Book, in an extremely fragile state, is the oldest existing set of school rules, initialled by Grundy himself in 1884, and they give a vivid description, not only of the behaviour of boys which he felt had to be curtailed, but also of the rule-bound lives which they were forced to lead.

KING'S GRAMMAR SCHOOL, WARWICK
Rules

1. Either College caps or hats with the School ribbon are to be worn outside the School. Hats with the School ribbon are preferable on week-days, but College caps should be worn on Sunday. Blue caps may be worn inside the School gates except on Sunday.
2. No boy may either use or possess a Catapult. Pistols, Cannons, and fire-arms of every sort are prohibited.
3. Stone throwing and dirt throwing of every description is prohibited.
4. During School hours there must be no shouting, whistling, noise or disorder, in any portion of the School buildings.
5. Neither desks nor doors are to be slammed.
6. Day boys may go upstairs for any purpose connected with their work; otherwise, the whole building above the ground floor, including the staircase, is out of bounds for them. Boarders in their own interest should see that this rule is observed.
7. Boys are cautioned against trespassing over the boundaries of the playground at the back of the School.
8. All writing upon walls, doors, or school furniture; cutting names or devices on desks; or in any way defacing school property is forbidden.
9. Boys are to come into Big School for prayers immediately the bell rings at 4.30, without waiting to get their hats or books.
10. Prefects are to take Roll-call at 4.30pm, in accordance with instructions.
11. A Prefect must be present at all out-matches.
12. Prefects are to wear tassels upon their College caps, and Prefects only.
13. The beds and grass in front of the School are out of bounds. Boys are particularly cautioned against treading upon the grass borders.
14. No flowers in the front are to be touched, nor is any damage to be done to the hedges or shrubs.
15. Nothing is to be thrown out of the windows.
16. Boys must not enter or leave any portion of the School buildings by means of the windows.
17. Playing or loafing about in front of the School is forbidden. Masters will interpret this rule as occasion requires.
18. Taking any article from another boy's desk, peg or shelves is strictly forbidden.
19. It is forbidden to climb about any portion of the School buildings.

20. Damage done should be immediately reported to the Head Master by the boy himself.

Boarders had their own extra set of rules:

1. On Week-day mornings the Dormitories are closed at 8, on Sundays at 8.30. They are opened in the evening at 9. On half-holidays they are open for half an-hour after dinner; also on half-holidays during the Cricket season from 6 to 6.30pm, and during the Football season from 4.30 to 5pm. The wardrobe keeper will attend after dinner on half-holidays to give out clothing, and will open the Dormitories in succession in other days for the same purpose and at the same time. On all other occasions, except those specified above, admission to the Dormitories must be obtained by application to the matron.

2. Clean linen will be given out to all boys twice a week, but collars and cuffs can be obtained from the wardrobe keeper any day after dinner, unless she sees reason to refuse. No collar or handkerchief will be given out on such occasions unless the one in use is returned. Boys who have got their feet wet are to make immediate application to the matron or wardrobe keeper for a change, without waiting till the usual time.

3. After games, and in the evening, boys must change their boots for house shoes before entering the Dormitories. No boots are to be taken into the Dormitories.

4. Only Prefects may have ink in the dormitories.

5. Boys are forbidden to take eatables or drinkables to the Dormitories.

6. Boarders in Dormitory A must go to bed directly after evening prayers unless they have leave to sit up. Boarders in Dormitory B must continue their evening preparation from the time prayers are ended till 9.45pm, unless they have special leave to go to bed, and must go to bed at 9.45 unless they have special leave to sit up. Boarders in Dormitory C must also continue their evening preparation till 9.45, unless [the document is damaged at this point, so the rest of Rule 6 is slightly speculative] they have special leave to go to bed. Prefects may work till 10.30 if they have special leave. Preparation after prayers will continue in the Class rooms. No boy may be in a Class room after 9pm without special leave. All lights are to be out at 10.45pm.

7. The Prefect in Dormitory A must see that there is silence in the Dormitory for three minutes when boys first go to bed, that prayers may be said without inter-ruption.

8. No boy may be out of his own cubicle, except in cases of necessity. This does not refer to Prefects in discharge of their duty.

9. There may be no loud talking in dormitories, and no talking whatever after 10 o'clock in Dormitory A, and after 10.45 in Dormitories B and C.

10. A set of shelves is provided in the Reading-room for each boy, marked with the

number of his cubicle. Hooks and rails are similarly numbered on the first floor. Boys have a right to the set of shelves and to the hook and rail bearing the number of their cubicle, and must keep their books, caps, hats and coats in the proper place.

11. No Boarder (with the exception of the house Prefects) may possess or use matches, set alight any material, or in any way interfere with the gas. The slightest infringement of this rule will be severely punished. This rule does not apply to the laboratory, when a master is present.

12. No Boarder, (unless a Prefect) may enter any town or house or go into any shop without leave. The River will be considered the boundary between the School and the town of Warwick; and the Canal-bridge between the School and Leamington; no boarder, therefore, may cross either bridge without leave. Prefects may be excepted from this rule, at the discretion of the Head Master, by formal application at the beginning of each term.

13. No Boarder may be absent from any meal without special permission.

14. Leave will not be given to visit friends or relatives in the neighbourhood without written invitation.

15. Card-playing, raffles, and every description of gambling and betting are prohibited.

16. All Boarders, without exception, must wear College caps on Sundays, whether within or without the gates.

The following rules were added in 1885:

1. Bathing immediately after dinner is forbidden: half an hour must elapse.
2. No boy is allowed to bathe more than twice in the same day.
3. The Kitchen and Pantry are all out of bounds except by leave of a master.
4. All lights must be out at 11.30.

The bathing-place used by the school until 1911 is clearly marked on old maps: a segment of the River Avon was diverted through a pool on the far side of the river, almost opposite the school. Boys presumably swam across, or used a boat, rather than walk all the way up to the road bridge and back down the other side.

Individual staff must have kept records of marks, because the weekly totals of marks were so important in arranging the boys in descending academic order. Grundy also started a whole-school Mark Book, in which the form position of every boy was to be written each week. It is in these three surviving books, covering the years 1882-1906, that we find the very young John Masefield, future Poet Laureate, not doing very well at all in his form orders. His short career at the school is discussed later.

CHAPTER 10

Rev Philip Edwin Raynor

For the summer term of 1885, a 28-year-old locum from Marlborough, one Rev Philip Edwin Raynor, became acting headmaster. He had applied, along with JP Way, to succeed Grundy, but lost out to his more senior Marlborough colleague (who was unable to take up the post immediately). Numbers fell back to 93 during this time. After his 'baptism of fire' at Warwick – Grundy must have been a very hard act to follow – Raynor got married and took up headmasterships in Tasmania and Adelaide. In 1894, he returned to England to be Headmaster of Ipswich School, from where he was sacked in 1906 for being a bankrupt, as a result of personally subsidising his staff's poor salaries. Although at Ipswich he was referred to as a "learned and courteous man", the Warwick School chief examiner's comments about Raynor a decade earlier are not complimentary. In the Master's Book, after he had left, was written:

> I regret very much that there seems to be such a falling off this year in the general results. I trust that the new Head Master will soon be able to stimulate Forms V and IV to more industry. I trust also that he will be able to improve the relaxed discipline so that the work of the viva-voce may be more easy and more pleasant.

In 1907, WVP Hexter – indefatigable Old Warwickian (OW) secretary, former pupil (1885–91) and member of staff (1909–14) – recalled:

> There had been an interregnum of one term; interregnums are of necessity unsatisfactory, and this was no exception. The discipline and organisation of the school had, in fact, fallen to pieces considerably.

Raynor actually date-stamped his entries in the Master's Book. He was a very keen cyclist, and he represented Oxford against Cambridge in a five-mile race on his penny-farthing. Some time later, he and his wife cycled around Tasmania on a tandem, which must have been quite an achievement in the 1890s. After his bankruptcy in Ipswich, he ended his career as a vicar in Tingewick, Buckinghamshire, and died in 1930. It is perhaps significant that his period at Warwick has been 'airbrushed', as it were, from his biographical entry in *Who Was Who, Volume III*, and it is also surprising that there is no mention whatsoever of the entire episode in the governors' minutes. Indeed, it is tempting to speculate that Way may have employed Raynor himself – the governors certainly did not!

CHAPTER 11

Rev John Pearce Way DD

Not only do we have thousands of words of Rev John Pearce Way's writings preserved in the Master's Books, but he seems to have been the first headmaster to have deliberately saved anything for posterity. Carefully stored in their original envelope are the first drafts of the 1892 Warwick School Song. The words "Warwick School" may now at last be used correctly, because it would seem that JP Way coined the name. The earliest surviving written record of the use of the name Warwick School is a concert programme from 1887, which beats the first edition of *The Portcullis* by a few months. That first edition of *The Portcullis*, in March 1888, clearly announces that it is "The Chronicle of Warwick School", yet Grundy's set of School Rules of 1884 emphatically uses the old name of King's Grammar School. So we can credit JP Way, very early in his headmastership, with introducing the use of the name Warwick School, even though he had absolutely no legal authority to do so. It took another twenty years or so before the old name faded from common usage, especially amongst the townsfolk. This process was undoubtedly helped by the legal changes involved in the "fresh start" of 1906, but it is interesting to note that the army was remarkably reluctant to acknowledge the change of name and was still referring to "The King's School Contingent" in its inspection reports of the Corps in the 1930s.

Born in 1850 in Bath, the son of Rev John Hyne Way, the incumbent of Christ Church, Bath, JP Way was 35 years old when he came to Warwick in September 1885. He had been educated at Somerset College (now Bath College) and Brasenose College, Oxford, where, being a keen rower, he was stroke of the Oxford Eight from 1874 to 1875. He tutored in Oxford before joining the staff of Marlborough College, becoming a housemaster there in 1877. AF Leach says: "In his classes there was no room for an idle boy. His special hatred was cribbing." At Christmas 1890, he married Gertrude Leach, who was 18 years his junior, and the prominence this announcement is given in the first published history of the school, together with the obvious closeness of the historian and the headmaster, leads one to suspect that Gertrude Leach might have been a relative – not a daughter, given that AF Leach married in 1881, but perhaps a niece.

Arthur Francis Leach (1851-1915), educated at Winchester and New College, Oxford, was a historian of prodigious energy, and he rapidly became the acknowledged expert on the historic schools of England. After he resigned his Fellowship of

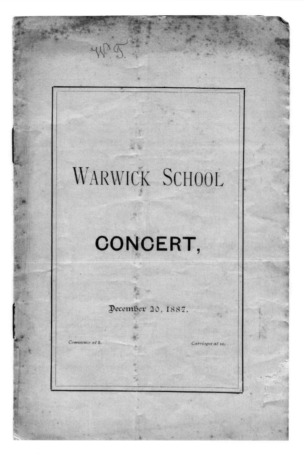

The earliest surviving use of the name Warwick School,
on a concert programme from December 1887.
(Warwick School Archives)

All Souls, Oxford, on his marriage, he worked for the Endowed Schools Department of the Charity Commission and, later on, the Board of Education. His work on Warwick School was only a small part of his output, some of which is as follows:

Visitations and Memorials of Southwell Minster (1891)
English Schools at the Reformation (1896)
The Building of Beverley Bar (1896)
History of Winchester College (1899)
Beverley Town Documents (1900)
History of Bradfield College (1900)
Early Yorkshire Schools (1903)
History of Warwick School (1906)

Milton as Schoolboy and Schoolmaster (1908)
Education Charters and Documents 598 to 1909 AD (1911)
Victoria County History (1911) – numerous articles on schools
Early Education in Worcester (1913)
The Schools of Mediaeval England (1915)

It must have been frustrating for Leach, described as "a Charity Commissioner steeped in muniments", to have had so little documentary evidence to go on as regards the early history of Warwick School. It must also have been somewhat galling to have "lost" JP Way to Rossall School so early in the writing of the book, and to sense, too, that things were going horribly wrong with the school at the start of the 20th century. It is perhaps for these reasons that not only is so much of his book taken up with the history of the town of Warwick, rather than its school, but also that it took twelve years to be published. It is noteworthy that not everyone thought highly of Leach: his writings on the tortured political and educational 'see-sawing' in Warwick in the 19th century were described as "typical of the smug complacence of the mid-Victorian education fanatics" by EG Tibbits in his monograph on Henry VIII's Charity, preserved in the County Record Office.

There were still just six forms in the school at the start of Way's time: VI, V, IV, UIII, LIII and Lower School. UIII became 3a, and LIII became 3b; and the Lower School was subsequently divided into Remove and Shell. Marks were awarded purely to generate a weekly form order, and much of the marking must have been done by verbal answers. The school's preserved Mark Books start in 1882, but it is only in Way's time that they develop merely from school lists into collections of marks. These so-called marks were, in fact, rank orders within the form, and it was upon them that periodic promotions to the next form were made – or, indeed, they were made the basis of the queue outside the headmaster's study for a flogging! The fact that a boy was only promoted when he seemed academically ready for it meant that you could get very young, bright boys in the sixth form and, conversely, very old, slower boys languishing in the 'sink' form, LIII or 3b. They merely repeated each year of work until they coped – or left!

JP Way introduced setting for mathematics teaching and also introduced classes for army entrance. Greek, being an optional extra, never attracted more than about 30 boys in the whole school at any one time. This naturally limited entrance to Oxford and Cambridge universities, which insisted on candidates offering Greek. JP Way, being a realist, however, developed what he called the "modern" side, in which German took the place of Greek. Although it does not seem to have survived, JP Way made reference to the "punishment book ... a dismal and melancholy book in which the headmaster entered the names of boys who had been guilty of gross misconduct or gross idleness".

It is quite difficult to work out exactly who was on the staff of the school at any one time, but it is clear that Barry Meade, who taught from 1882 to 1893, held the position

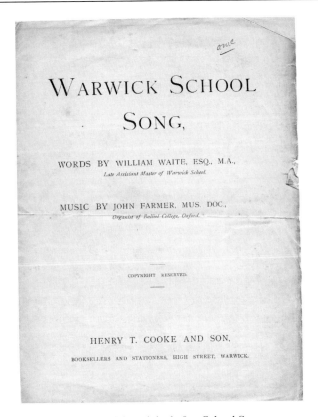

The cover of the original 1892 School Song.
(Warwick School Archives)

of "Senior Assistant Master". His successor as Senior Master was a man who joined the staff early in Way's time, Robert Davies. Davies' role in the economic crash of 1906 is discussed later.

William Waite taught English and history at Warwick from 1888 to 1891 (coincidentally, exactly the years that John Masefield was a pupil at the school) but died, tragically young, in Australia in 1893. His memorial was the first school song, published as *Cantate Varvicenses* in *The Portcullis* of June 1889. The Latin title means "Sing, Warwickians!" This magazine, the successor to Grundy's *The Varvicensian* of 1884–5, first appeared in March 1888, and eight editions were published in that year alone. In 1891, the Speaker of the House of Commons, later Lord Peel, offered £5 for the best school song, and a revised version of Waite's poem, with rather more blood-curdling words, and punning references to Peel himself, was chosen as Warwick School's first official school song in 1892, with music by Dr Farmer, composer of the Harrow School songs. Way carefully stored away Waite's original version, and it is rather a pity that this gem of its period is not performed more often.

There is no doubt that JP Way's lasting memorial, as he would have wished, is the chapel in the form in which we now know it. Before 1886, there was no chancel, the communion vessels were pewter, the side walls were merely painted, there was no lighting, and a harmonium accompanied the singers. There was, indeed, a custom for the bigger boys to kick the little boys if they presumed to sing! The organ, costing £500 (worth about £25,000 in 2003), was installed in 1886, and a choirmaster and organist, AG Warren, was appointed. In 1893, JP Way organised the building of the chancel and commissioned the oak stalls around the whole building to a design by WF Unsworth of Dean's Yard, Westminster Abbey. The whole work was paid for by subscriptions (the subscribers' names are carved in the oak) and two bazaars at Warwick Castle, which raised over £800 (worth more than £35,000 in 2003). Lady Warwick herself donated the pulpit; JP Way, the silver gilt communion service, hall-marked London 1893, which has survived in beautiful condition and is still in regular use. The chalice is set with semi-precious stones and has a very attractive base. The altar rails of the new chancel, which have since been taken down, were given in memory of Henry Daunt, who died at the school in 1893, aged 17. A brass plaque commemorating his death is now on the wall of the chapel gallery. JP Way took great pride in the chapel and strongly objected to some of the boys' behaviour on one St David's Day:

> The supporters of gallant little Wales may be *patriotic*, but they should first of all show due reverence to the place where they and their comrades worship God. They should also shew due respect to their Masters.
>
> To wear a *9-inch leek* in the button hole at Chapel or in form is scarcely consonant with either.
>
> If boys in future wear abnormal or outrageous button-holes they must expect to pay some penalty for the privilege.
>
> March 1, 1893   JP Way

Outside the chapel, JP Way organised an army of pupil conscripts to level the cricket pitch, which, until 1887, seems to have had mediaeval-type ridges and furrows:

> I must appeal to the good sense of boys to avoid damaging or doing anything that may be likely to damage the New Rails of the Pavilion. They are very light, as it was not thought necessary to put up heavy ones. Now that we have one of the best School Pavilions in the County, we ought all of us to do our best to keep it in good order. Prefects & Captains are especially requested to check those who may not shew good sense in this matter.
>
> Even jumping over the rails with poles damages the turf, or the place where we hope to see some turf grow.
>
> [undated, 1887]   JP Way

In the same year, the Limes were planted to mark Queen Victoria's Golden Jubilee year:

It has been thought that some members of the school may like to leave behind them some inexpensive memorial of the fact that they were members of the school in the Jubilee Year of Queen Victoria.

I have enquired the price of trees, which are much wanted in the field where there are scarcely any except in the hedgerows. I find that good Lime Trees about 10ft high can be procured for 2/- also trees of other sorts.

I shall be glad to receive at once the names of those who may be willing to give a tree. I shall be happy to have them planted & to put up any protection necessary against the sheep of the field, unless donors prefer to do it themselves. Names may be given in to the Captain of Games or the Captain of the Ground or to me.

March 5, 1887   JP Way

It was originally intended to plant 36 trees, according to an early *Portcullis* of 1888:

Although we shall not receive much benefit from them, still, future generations of Warwick boys, when lying beneath their shade, will gratefully think of us and the event which the trees commemorate. We have also been enabled, owing to the generosity of the Governors, to build a spacious Pavilion. Panels with the names of the XI and XV of each year painted in white, are to be placed in the Pavilion.

The pupils of 1887 celebrated the Golden Jubilee on June 28th in great style, according to an anonymous report in a 1907 *Portcullis*:

Breakfast over, a select party of us went to the Boat Club by invitation of NW Brown, known to many generations of OWs as Norman; we rowed up to the baths and had a swim, after which we went up to the Town, which made a brave appearance with its gay display of bunting, flags etc.

At eleven o'clock brakes were to start for Stoneleigh, where Dr Way was giving us a picnic, as well as we knew how to enjoy one!

Our first procedure on arriving at the end of our journey was to find a suitable place for a dip; we were great bathers in those days! A perfect looking spot was chosen, and the first valiant man took a header and was unfortunate in finding the bottom very near the surface, a fact which the want of clearness of the River Avon had not disclosed! After bathing we dispersed till lunch time; some played cricket, some hunted the wily bird's nest, and a small section of us captured a donkey and had turns in equestrian, or should I say, asinine exercise. When he was let go, he rejoined the herd of deer of which he was apparently the self-constituted leader. Presently the lunch signal was given; and how my mouth waters as I recall the lamb and mint sauce, meat pies, fruit tarts and so on.

After further rambles we returned to Warwick, the brakes this time taking the road past the Abbey and coming into Warwick by the Guy's Cliff Road. On our arrival we gave three hearty cheers for Dr and Miss Way, who had arrived home before the brakes, and were in front of the headmaster's house.

After tea we went to the Common to see the fireworks, which Mr Stanton, the then Mayor, had presented to the Town. A huge bonfire was blazing on the highest point, and a fine display of fireworks was shown. The illuminations in the Town were charming, those on the East and Westgates especially so.

On going back to school we were in time to see the end of the school illuminations from the Castle Hill. The whole building was studded with flaming petroleum cans, and the effect was magnificent, in fact so good was it, that the illuminations were repeated the following night.

Now that he had a flat cricket field, JP Way encouraged the pupils to practise:

A Court for "Imitation-Cricket" has been laid down in the field for the use & pleasure of boys. But as the material is not quite firm enough, I must ask boys not to walk upon it, still less to play upon it until leave is given. The same will apply to the fives court – which in the absence of frost it has, at last, been possible to mend.

April 28, 1888   JP Way

(1) It seems to be necessary both for the sake of the safety of boys, as well as in the interests of the preservation of the fabric, that I should put all roofs & the tops of walls out of bounds as far as the school premises extend. I hope this will be thoroughly understood; no excuse will be taken. Prefects are requested to enforce this.

(2) The Games Committee have published a most salutary rule concerning bowling at nets, which I feel bound to approve and enforce, both as Headmaster & as Housemaster, as it will be calculated to diminish the chance of serious accidents to boys under my care.

(3) I must remind those who are addicted to the practice of stone throwing that it is most strictly forbidden in or near the School premises, both on account of damage to the person, & damage to the fabric. I should suggest more practice with the cricket ball instead.

June 19, 1888   JP Way

Next, in 1890, a gymnasium was added, and compulsory physical education first established. The building, now part of the Sixth Form Centre, was built as a memorial to Wilfrid Gibson, who, as mentioned previously, was the school's brightest-ever pupil up to this time, but who had, sadly, drowned in the Avon shortly after going up to Oxford.

It has long been thought that the playing of hockey was a relatively late innovation at Warwick School. However, the following entry from Volume I of the Master's Book shows that, like Rev Herbert Hill in the 1860s, JP Way encouraged the game:

As the hockey season has commenced, I feel bound, both as a Housemaster & as Head Master, to warn boys against the danger that is incurred, if boys will violate the published rule of the game, which *forbids the raising of the hockey stick above the shoulder* either at the commencement or end of the swing of the stick. I have seen bad accidents result from the violation of this rule, & I must ask the Captains of sides to enforce it. At first the enforcing it may cause interruptions to the game, but the custom of observing the rule will soon be established.

Feb 1, 1889   JP Way

JP Way's promotion of hockey had obviously not lasted long, for in the March 1895 edition of *The Portcullis* is a letter to the editor, asking:

Could not a Hockey Club be established at this Ancient School?

However, in 1901, hockey was "reintroduced after a lapse of 10 years", during which time soccer was enthusiastically played.

Way's success in attracting pupils put a great strain on the existing space for boarders. The governors 'dragged their feet', as they had done with Grundy, but Way's response was to go ahead and build, "on his own responsibility", a new Lower School and Boarding House. It was opened in 1889, with 40 boys, and the first housemaster was Rev FJG Page. JP Way, naturally enough, had to make up some more rules:

The brand new Junior House, photographed around 1890.
(Warwick School Archives)

All offences committed by Boys residing in the Lower School House, that may be of such a nature as are generally dealt with by the *Housemaster* rather than the Form-master should be reported to Mr Page, & will be dealt with by him. The offences would include such as continued idleness (after the usual Form-master's methods have failed), "cribbing", lying, bad language or gross misconduct of any kind. These are the usual offences that are reported to me as Housemaster in the case of boys in the School House.

May 10, 1889   JP Way

In January 1895, the total number of boys in the school had reached 168, but Way resigned in 1896, the same year in which he was awarded his Doctor of Divinity degree, in order to become Headmaster of Rossall School. At this point, of course, he was able to sell back to the governors "his" Junior House – for the extremely large sum of £3,500. A clue as to why he went to the Lancashire coast lies in his love of sailing. He owned a 15-ton yacht, the "Blue Dragon", and sailed extensively around the Hebrides. A history of Rossall School says that, as a headmaster, "he never displayed emotion. He appeared detached, aloof, almost a spectator of what was going on around him. He was entirely unaffected and free from the more terrifying aspects of schoolmasters." He retired from Rossall in 1908, made his home in Tiverton, Devon, and died in 1937.

Something else from Way's time which is still very much in use is the school motto *Altiora Peto* – "I Seek Higher Things." He announced this in characteristic fashion:

As I can find no trace of an existent school motto, I have selected one which embodies, in one phrase, as many of the aims of school life as is possible. I hope that it will meet with the hearty approval of all the members of the school and that they will live up to it. It is one I thought of first for the School House; but the School House and School should, I believe, have the same motto: Altiora Peto.

July 23, 1893   JP Way

The school badge at the time depicted a Portcullis, and it was still being used as a cap badge until the 1970s. The justification for this emblem was that it was used by Henry VIII as a badge. King's High School has, of course, retained it to the present day. School uniform, as such, was not worn compulsorily until the 1930s. Blazers and badges were earned – for example, by playing in the Rugby XV. In *The Portcullis* of July 1903, we have descriptions of two blazers available:

First eleven blazer: special pocket Grand Azure, charges a Crown Tudor, a rose Lancaster, a Portcullis Argent en surtout; partition engrailed.
New general blazer: dark blue flannel coat, with white silk portcullis worked on pocket.

In July 1904, it is stated in *The Portcullis* that blue and white stripes "have been long in use in the school, both as a School ribbon, a 1st XI and 1st XV ribbon, and a School jersey".

JP Way made an attempt at creating a new school badge by combining the shields of Edward the Confessor and Henry VIII. This strange combination of two shields can still be seen on the covers of old books in the school library. By 1904, another version had crept into use, and this one, a blue and white striped shield with a bear in the top left-hand corner, can be seen very prominently in the centre panel of the west window of the chapel to this day. That this window was given to the school by HS Pyne in 1925 implies that he, too, regarded this emblem as the official school badge, although he chose JP Way's Victorian version to be printed on the front cover of the oldest surviving printed Prospectus in the school archives in 1919. One puzzling aspect of the stained-glass window is that the shield is surmounted by a Dean's Hat – black, with cords and hanging tassels. This shield is that of the pre-reformation College of Warwick, and its unauthorised use by the school (according to powerful voices on the governing body, complaining that they had not been consulted) meant that it was left to GA Riding, in 1931, to design the school badge which has been in use ever since. This combined certain elements of Edward the Confessor's shield (the cross and the martlets, ie, sparrows without feet) and Henry VIII's (the fleur de lys). The blue and white stripes so prominent in the "unauthorised" school badge are those of Roger de Newburgh, Earl of Warwick in 1123, and still feature as strongly in many items of the modern school uniform as they did in Victorian times.

JP Way enlarged the Cadet Corps that had been founded by his predecessor in 1884, and it became attached to the Second Battalion of the Royal Warwickshire Regiment. By the late 1880s, practically every boy in the school joined when he reached the correct age. In 1887, the Corps adopted a full dress standard uniform of scarlet, with blue facings and helmets. The earliest photo we have of the Cadet Corps dates from 1903, and this shows that there are 60 boys in uniform, when the total number of boys in the school was 100 or less. The Corps had been awarded new hats "like Colonial Police" late in 1902, and in 1908 the uniform was changed to khaki, "exchanging the old leggings for putties". Incidentally, it is rather alarming to read that in 1899 "the much battered carbines no longer adorned the walls of Big School." Carbines (shortened rifles, originally used by mounted soldiers) were presumably found to be useful for schoolboys because they were lighter than normal rifles. The carbines are very clearly visible in the 1903 photograph. A clue as to why they were taken down from the walls of Big School, and, it is to be hoped, stored somewhat more securely, is that there was a fatal accident involving one in 1897, more details of which are given later.

One of JP Way's most famous pupils was the future Poet Laureate, John Masefield. His rather pathetic marks in tests are recorded in the Master's Book, and his distinct lack of progress in the Form Orders can be found in the school Mark Books. It is only fair to record, however, that he won the Lower School Prize for Divinity and English in 1888, soon after he arrived at the school, and that the governors' minutes for 1890 report that he was awarded a scholarship of "half remission of fees". There is preserved a delightful Sports Day programme from 1890, in which J Masefield, with

𝔚𝔞𝔯𝔴𝔦𝔠𝔨 𝔖𝔠𝔥𝔬𝔬𝔩.

HEADMASTER'S REVIEW,

JULY 1891.

FOR LATIN PROSE.

1.—Having heard this, the ambassadors asked where the soldiers stood.

2.—Cæsar set out (*proficiscor*) to the camp at Gergovia and sent the cavalry to reconnoitre (*exploro*).

3.—So cruel (*crudelis*) was he that he wished none to be spared, for he himself pitied (*miseret*) none.

4.—The General told the scouts (*exploratores*) not to return till they had ascertained (*cognosco*) what was being done.

5.—You must not lose (*tero*) time; the sword (*gladius*) must decide (*discepto*) the matter (*res*).

6.—Do you think that the city that that man founded (*condo*) will be taken by such men as these are?

7.—If you had set out for Rome you would have been wise.

8.—Translate into Oratio Obliqua:—Go away home; I shall not advise you what to do.

Write distinctly, and leave a margin on the right; the Upper III. may leave out (7) and (8).

The Latin test set to all boys below the sixth form in July 1891.
(Warwick School Archives)

his own individual dark-blue-coloured vest, ran two under-12 races. It may not be mere coincidence that he left the school (later claiming that he had run away to join the training ship *Conway* in Liverpool) after a particularly gruelling Latin test in the summer of 1891, on the eve of his 13th birthday – a Latin test which, according to the custom of the time, was set to all boys below the sixth form and was written personally by the headmaster. In the Master's Book is pasted a copy of this Latin test – and John Masefield's mark in it (10%), which is not, perhaps, surprising considering that it would now be considered difficult for 'A'-level pupils!

The marks obtained by some of the boys in the 1891 Latin test,
including John Masefield's 9 out of 85.
(Warwick School Archives)

JP Way was quite content, it seems, to allow senior pupils to write and edit *The Portcullis*, although he became incandescent with rage about the implied criticism in the following letter, which was written by a pupil and published in the February 1896 edition:

> Dear Sirs – In that well-known and much-prized literary effort the School Prospectus these words occur: "Prizes are given for good work in the Choir." Yours truly has been in the said Choir for nearly five years, and has never heard of any prize being given. We venture to hope that this may be altered, as at present it is rather misleading.
>   Yours most sincerely, "Magna est Veritas et Praevalebit." (At least we hope so).

The Latin must have especially upset JP Way, for it means "Great is Truth and it will Prevail." In the Master's Book, he fumes:

> I have to express my great regret that such should have been written, should have been admitted, and should remain for ever as a blot upon the pages of what is in other respects the most interesting issue of the Portcullis that has ever appeared.
>   March 2, 1896   JP Way

It is to the school's great regret that no Prospectus from JP Way's time seems to have survived.

The behaviour of the boys during JP Way's time brought forth a continuous stream of notices in the Master's Book, be they about smoking, snowballing, golfing or even the maltreatment of sheep. The latter was almost his last notice of all before he left, and includes an unusual hint of violence:

497

Notice

I again remind boys that even the possession of Smoking paraphernalia of any kind will be treated as evidence of actual smoking.

I am resolved to keep it down; and any boys who disobey in this matter will be punished with the utmost severity & if necessary removed.

Nov 6. 94

J.P. Way.

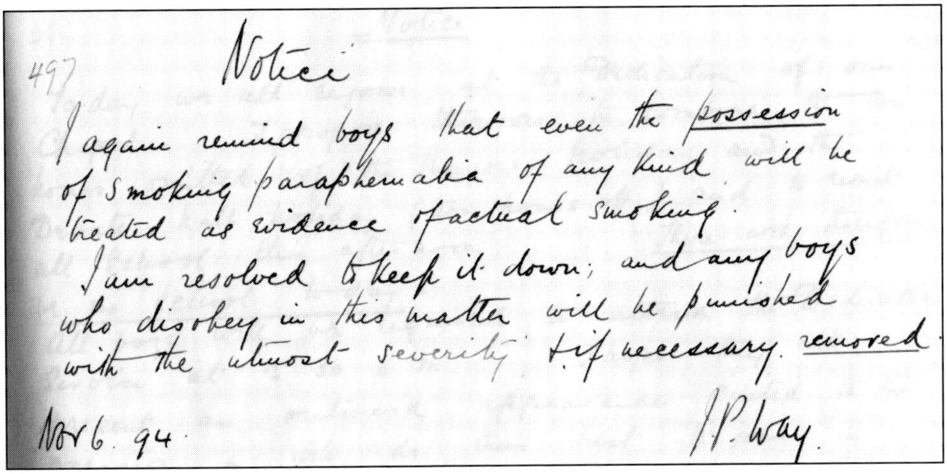

JP Way's 1894 diatribe on smoking from the Master's Book, Volume 1.
(Warwick School Archives)

I again remind boys that even the *possession* of smoking paraphernalia of any kind will be treated as evidence of actual smoking. I am resolved to keep it down; and any boys who disobey in this matter will be punished with the utmost severity and, if necessary, *removed*.

Nov 6, 1894

I must forbid snowballing before Chapel for obvious reasons. I must add too that at any time it would be more noble for members of School House to assail fellows as big as themselves rather than to attack the members of the Junior House.

Feb 1, 1895

I must make it clear to everyone that *Golfing* is forbidden on the School field. This includes all use of Golfing Clubs or irons & Golf balls.

June 1, 1895

I am informed that last Sunday one of our boys was maltreating the sheep on a farm close by. On Wednesday the same, or others, repeated this misconduct. The farmer concerned has, with great moderation, asked me to say a word on the subject. It is always a matter of doubt whether the boys who do such things are amenable to the reasoning that appeals to boys of good & refined natures, but I hope they will listen to this warning. If they do not, I shall ask the farmer to take what measures he likes to protect himself.

June 7, 1896

JP Way's relationship with his neighbouring Chairman of Governors, the Earl of Warwick, is revealed in a fawning letter, dated March 24th, 1894, from the Warwick Castle archive. It concerns a boy who was caught poaching in the Castle Park but who does not seem to have been named, for no disciplinary action was recorded in the Master's Book:

> Our boys have been guilty of trespass before but I have never known them violate the game laws. I doubt if the boy in question was clever enough to have caught anything: at the same time, to attempt to set snares was an outrageous act and I cannot wonder that strong measures were thought necessary. I desire to thank your Lordship for sparing the boy from the Police Court & talking so kindly to him when he came up to the Castle.

> I am sure that the main mass of the boys have a right feeling on the subject but we have over 150 boys of whom well over 100 are resident at the school. Out of so many *one* now and then is sure to do some reckless deed despite all our efforts. We do all we can to influence or restrain by appeals to their good feeling, by instruction to Prefects to prevent trespassing, by making our games compulsory & by declaring in our rules all the Castle Park to be out of bounds & by punishing most stringently any who are caught.

> I am most grieved that we have already proved ourselves a nuisance to your Lordship & regret much that we should have caused you so much trouble.

> I am, dear Lord Warwick, Yours faithfully, JP Way

A delicious sequel to this incident occurred about 80 years later, according to Mr Robert Hudson (who was a young member of staff at the time), when a later Earl of Warwick telephoned Headmaster Pat Martin at the school and complained that two boys had been cycling in the Castle Park: "As the owner of the land, Headmaster, I have to tell you that they had no right to be there and I have confiscated their bicycles." Retorted Pat Martin: "And as a Justice of the Peace, My Lord, I have to tell you that you had no right to confiscate their bicycles."

Another County Record Office document sheds considerable light on what the school was like in late Victorian times – a valuation drawn up on Way's departure in 1896. The governors sold (or rented at 10% of the total value per year) the contents of the headmaster's house and School House to every new headmaster, and a professional valuation was made each time. The 1896 valuation included certain minor items such as curtain rods throughout the buildings, but the grand piano (valued at £40) in the Music Room in School House raised the bill considerably. The valuation very helpfully lists the rooms of the resident masters – Mr Liddell, Mr Rivington, Mr Gaussen, Mr Davies and Mr Forbes – and there was also a Lady Matron's room, an Undermatron's room and a Lady Housekeeper's room.

Outside, in addition to the cycle shed, the five greenhouses and the orchid house, every row of vegetables and fruit trees was individually valued. The garden produced winter greens, celery, leeks, lettuce, parsnips, carrots, onions, beet, potatoes, artichokes, rhubarb, greens and asparagus, and there were 23 apple and pear trees and "2 doz goose-berry trees". The remains of the headmaster's orchard can still be seen to this day beside the Guy Nelson Hall. The wondrous leaning mulberry tree, which unfortunately blew over late in 2002, does not seem to be mentioned in the 1896 valuation, but the "range of piggeries" and the 73 chickens certainly were. The total value of the transferable contents of the school was £308 1s 11d, equivalent to a modern value of about £20,000.

The building of the brand new Grammar School on the Myton Road in 1879 seems to have prompted the Earl of Warwick to consider what to do with the farm-land surrounding it, all of which he owned. In a plan from Warwick Castle archives, which seems to date from the mid-1880s and which was discovered in the County Record Office in November 2003, the Earl of Warwick's land is divided up into count-less building plots, which would have completely surrounded the new school with houses, and roads would have been driven across the present playing fields to serve them. The development of what would have become a completely new suburb of Warwick, south of the river, would have prevented any expansion of the school, even though it might have provided pupils for it. One wonders whether the Earl of Warwick was acting in his own or the school's best interests – he was, after all, the Chairman of Governors. As it happens, Warwick School sat at the southern edge of the town for the next 100 years, before an industrial park extended its boundary and enclosed the land in question. There is no direct evidence that JP Way knew anything of the Earl's plan, although it is clear from an architectural drawing of the new 1889 Junior House in the County Record Office, entitled "Plan of a Master's Boarding House for the Revd J. P. Way", that it was to be sited on a corner, and that one of the Earl's new roads, referred to as "projected New Road", which was never built, is drawn just east of the building. It would have turned off the Myton Road almost exactly where the exit from the Junior School car park is now.

The complete set of governors' minutes for this period, also preserved in the County Record Office, shows that by 1893 they had increased the summer holiday from six weeks to seven and the Easter holiday from two weeks to three. The Christmas holiday remained unchanged at four weeks. The minutes also describe what seems to be the start of the teaching of physics in 1891, and the setting up, in 1893, of a "dark room in one corner of the large Lavatory for the use of boys engaged in Photography".

From our viewpoint, 100 years later, it would seem that Way left a school in sparkling good shape, heaving with boys, financially sound – but perhaps he was just extremely lucky to get out when he did. Maybe he had his ear remarkably close to the ground of vicious local politics. At all events, the ten years after JP Way left were the worst years in the school's history, and events conspired to defeat totally the next two headmasters. JP Way, as his successor pointed out, had tried to create a public school called Warwick School out of a sleepy historic town grammar school, and within a dramatically short time it turned out that the town did not want it.

CHAPTER 12

Rev Robert Percival Brown

Any discussion about Rev Robert Percival Brown usually starts with more questions than answers. It can certainly be seen now that the six years of his headmastership were, in retrospect, ones of severe crisis. Quite simply, the school ran out of pupils. In theory, this should not have happened, for, on paper at least, Percival Brown was a highly qualified and experienced headmaster. Born in Peckham, he went to St Paul's School and then Trinity College, Cambridge, where he secured a First in Classics. After very short teaching spells at Marlborough and King William's College on the Isle of Man, he was appointed Headmaster of Kendal Grammar School at the age of 25 in 1887, and of the Royal Naval College, Eltham, in 1891, aged 29. Coming to Warwick at the age of 34 in 1896, he had already been a headmaster of two very different schools for nine years. He himself chose to use the double surname, and it must have irritated him immensely that no-one else accorded him that privilege!

The first historian of Warwick School, AF Leach, avoids commenting on the crisis by a neat side-step:

> Mr Brown's time is too recent to be made the subject of history. For reasons which it would be difficult to set out, if indeed they are exactly ascertainable, the school experienced a serious decline in numbers under him. School House, which was full with 70 boarders in 1896, with 55 day boys in addition, had fallen to 35 in 1902. At the Junior House, there was an even more serious drop to 4, and the day-boys also declined in proportion.

It was in the summer of 1902 that the governors finally lost patience with their headmaster: there were only 62 boys in the entire school. The reasons for this are, as Leach suggests, varied and complex. In 1896, the King's Middle School in the Butts, Warwick, had become a School of Science. The fees there were two-thirds of the day-boy fees at Warwick School. In 1899, a dynamic young scientist, HS Pyne, had been appointed the Headmaster of the Middle School, with a new set of staff and excellent local press coverage. One of Pyne's successes at this time was to get the local press solidly behind the Middle School at the expense of the Grammar School over the river, which was seen as aloof and insular. Although the two schools were in the same Foundation, the governors saw the Middle School as a local school for local boys and

Rev Robert Percival Brown, taken around 1902.
(Warwick School Archives)

didn't give the rival Grammar School (Warwick School) enough support. One partic-ular complaint, which is probably justified, is that money from the 1875 Charity Commission scheme was unfairly distributed in favour of the Middle School and the new King's High School for Girls, and that Warwick School was expected to get by on the profits from its (rich and out-of-county) boarders.

Percival Brown's personality didn't help either, and he was seen as severe, with too much emphasis on teaching the Classics. Evidence has come down to us that he was not a very pleasant man, and, quite simply, he lost the confidence of those parents who could easily afford to transfer their sons – the profit-producing boarders – to other schools.

Percival Brown's achievements must not be overlooked, however. He wrote a great deal in Volume II of the Master's Book, so it is possible to discover, in enormous

The dining room in 1901, showing the brand new oak tables still in use over 100 years later.
(AF Leach)

detail, how he ran the school. He changed the public examination system from the single examination of the Oxford Delegacy to include the Higher Certificate of the Joint Board, the "recognised standard for the Sixth Forms of the best Schools". JP Way had only once offered this examination, in the golden year of 1885, when Wilfrid Gibson and three others won the Higher Certificate. Percival Brown built the main Common Room staircase, a better wash-house and lavatory (the current laundry), and a large new "bicycle house" (on the site of the modern Tuck Shop), which he felt was important enough to be opened by the Countess of Warwick in April 1901. He organised the manufacture (in 1901-2, in the school workshop) of new oak tables for the dining room, fifteen of which survive and are still in everyday use.

It was Percival Brown who encouraged the formation of the Old Warwickian Club, which was announced in *The Portcullis* of July 1898, and which held its first dinner in Holborn in January 1900. It was trumpeted as follows:

> It is with great pleasure we announce that the long talked of scheme has been brought into execution, thanks to the efforts of Mr Norman W Brown. Ever since the idea was started at the Old Warwickian dinner held in London some years ago, an Old Boys' Club has been the constant theme of speeches at the Break-up Supper and Speech Day, and now it is at last in process of being carried out.

The general object of the Club is to unite OWs in perpetual fraternity on the basis of loyal devotion to the school.

Life membership was set at £1 10s.

Percival Brown formed a Camera Club in 1901, with 20 boys, and organised a photographic competition. He provided rather elegant cast-iron lecterns in the chapel, some of which survive, and carried on the scheme of completing the chapel started by JP Way. He organised the building of six studies alongside Big School, which were completed just after he left in 1903. These studies became known as Prefects' Corridor and disappeared when the new dining hall was built. It is remarkable that only one surviving photograph, taken from the far side of the field around 1912, shows these studies. It is to Percival Brown that we have to give credit, also, for the formation of the "House" system in January 1897. He may have been rather unimaginative in calling them 'A', 'B', 'C' and 'D' houses, but the idea was to encourage a competitive and corporate spirit, and in that the system worked, and has survived, albeit with changes of name, for over 100 years. Grundy had called the dormitories 'A', 'B' and 'C', but they were age-differentiated. Percival Brown deliberately created, as he himself wrote, "three parallel divisions" out of School House, and the fourth, or 'D' house, was for day-boys.

Percival Brown did not ignore technological advances either. On June 9th, 1899, he invited a certain Herr Slapoffski to demonstrate the "Edison-Bell Phonograph-Graphophone" to the school. Eighteen months later, he wrote:

It is officially announced that Her Majesty the Queen died at 6.30 this evening.

Jan 22nd, 1901, 8.30pm   R Percival Brown HM

From surviving records, it is clear that the school did not acquire a telephone until 1903 (the school's number was "Warwick 42"), and for Percival Brown to be able to record the passing of Queen Victoria within two hours of the announcement is rather astonishing. In all probability, the message was rung through to Warwick Castle and then passed on by messenger.

A year after Percival Brown came to the school, a 15-year-old Cadet called Thomas Lister died after an accident on Field Day at the Public Schools Camp at Aldershot in August 1897. Almost his final words are reported to have been: "Hard lines on Warwick, isn't it, Sir?" The lack of further detail about the accident in *The Portcullis* suggests that he may have been accidentally shot, and, in fact, the Roll Book (pupil admissions register) records: "Thomas Lister: died of an accident in Public Schools Camp through mishandling his carbine."

A month later, his father donated the sturdy altar (still in use) in the chapel "as a memorial of his son's confirmation".

Within his first year, Percival Brown found that it was necessary to introduce two forms of punishment not previously recorded: pupils were gated, some quite regularly, for "exceeding bounds", and eventually one of the worst offenders was suspended for the rest of the term. He also makes a rare mention of corporal punishment in a written notice that is perhaps indicative of his high-handed way of dealing with a parental complaint:

> While I am on the subject of punishment I ought perhaps to add that I received an enquiry a short time ago concerning caning in the school based on a statement that caning on the hand was employed by some Master. I informed my correspondent of his mistake & informed him of the principle we follow – that a boy can be caned only by the Head Master or his House Master.
>
>   Oct 7, 1897   R Percival Brown

Disciplinary matters continued to bother him: he set up (or confirmed an existing arrangement for) a "Punishment Drill" on Wednesday and Saturday afternoons by the west wall of the gymnasium, which was taken by the Drill Sergeant of the Cadet Corps. Another punishment he used quite widely was the withdrawal of "bicycle leave" – that is, permission to bring a bicycle to school. Between 15 and 20 boys had this privilege in the late 1890s, and many of them were day-boys who cycled in from Leamington. In 1899, Percival Brown was able to announce that a "special school tram" was available for the journey from Leamington, with the following timetable:

Victoria Terrace	8.20 am
Warwick Street	8.25 am
Milverton Station	8.33 am
All Saints Road	8.39 am
St John's	8.43 am

One reason why bicycles became so popular at Warwick School at this time may well have been the dramatic growth in the bicycle manufacturing industry in nearby Coventry. The Coventry Machine Company (having started out by making sewing-machines and then "bone-shaker" bicycles in the 1860s) became Swift Cycles in 1896, following the development, in rapid succession, of the penny-farthing (the "ordinary" bicycle), the tricycle and, finally, the "safety bicycle" with its two equal-sized wheels. Tandems were available in 1882, and Dunlop's pneumatic tyre ten years later. The "free wheel" was developed in 1897, and the three-speed rear hub in 1903. It is doubtful, however, whether penny-farthings ever saw the light of day at Warwick School, headmasters naturally inclining, one presumes, towards allowing only bicycles which were equipped with effective brakes!

There is ample evidence that Percival Brown was very strict as regards punctuality. For example, he noted in 1898 that it was "positively scandalous" that 31 boys were late for chapel on one occasion and reminded Masters that "the School Clock is kept by Greenwich, and is the standard of time by which the bells are sounded." Boys

The earliest surviving photograph of Big School, taken around 1900, complete with its
Victorian furniture, and set out for teaching.
(AF Leach)

were to be in chapel before the hour was struck: "the first strike of the clock was to be
the test of the hour being reached". There is evidence that the "School Clock" used
to be in the main entrance lobby, and an arrangement might have been made for it to
strike the bell in the tower several floors above. Despite his uncompromising attitude,
it is interesting to note that Percival Brown excused four boys permanently from
chapel in 1898, owing to a "Conscience Clause". They may have been the first four
Catholics at the school because, in 1902, Percival Brown categorically states that "the
Conscience Clause has never been invoked in my time in favour of any of the
numerous Protestant Dissenters."

Despite being given considerable freedom, at times, to roam during the day, boys
were literally locked in at night. The time of "Lock-up" varied almost weekly, from
dusk in winter to 6.40pm at the height of summer. Percival Brown very helpfully
published the evening schedule for boarders in the summer of 1899:

6.40	Lock up
6.45	Tea
7.15 – 8.45	1st Preparation
8.45	Prayers and supper
9.00	2nd Preparation

On Sunday evenings beginning tomorrow, June 4th, the back door only will be unlocked from 8.20 till 9 o'clock to allow of a quiet stroll on the Pitch in the cool of the evening.

Presumably in response to AF Leach asking for information about what the school had been like in previous generations, and no doubt encouraged by Percival Brown, a remarkable series of articles started to appear in *The Portcullis* of June 1900 and lasted until March 1901. Largely anonymous, they are nevertheless extremely valuable in giving us a pupil's eye view of characters and events at the King's School in the nineteenth century. Excerpts have been given earlier in this text. It was at this time, too, that the governors grudgingly guaranteed to purchase 250 copies of AF Leach's book – and bitterly regretted their decision when the book was finally published five years later, coinciding, as it did, with the school's economic collapse.

The centre panel of the east window in the chapel is a memorial to a 12-year-old boy, Cecil Meiggs, who died (presumably in the sanatorium) from septic pneumonia in 1902, towards the end of Percival Brown's time; the headmaster dealt with the whole tragic affair extremely well. Cecil's funeral was in the chapel, and afterwards the boy's mother, who paid for the window, wrote a most wonderful letter:

My dear Boys.
I wish it had been possible for me to tell you how much your loving tribute helped to comfort me in one of the saddest moments of my life. The tokens of love and devotion to my boy will for ever be treasured by me as some of my most hallowed memories.

And you, dear Cadets, whom he loved so, may you leave behind you when your "last post" sounds, the memory of a blameless life, the highest tribute to your God, your Parents, your Masters and your School mates.

Yours ever gratefully, Gertrude Meiggs

Cecil was, apparently, a star treble soloist in the chapel, and he was also the only Junior School pupil ever to have been allowed in the Rifle Corps.

Just before he left the school, Percival Brown arranged an impressive ceremony in which two oak trees were planted by Miss Hill, one of the daughters (which one is not recorded) of Rev Herbert Hill, the Headmaster of the King's School from 1843 to 1876, to mark the coronation of King Edward VII on 10th November, 1902. It was, at first, difficult for the author to identify exactly where these were planted, but it is now certain that one of them is the tree (alleged in 2003 to have been killed by summer pollarding in earlier decades) that stands forlornly on its own grass island

The earliest surviving photograph of the prison-like back of the school, taken in 1897.
The Limes are ten years old.
(Warwick School Archives)

outside the Tuck Shop. This small triangle of grass was formerly called the Prefects'
Lawn, and stepping onto it, if one was not a prefect, usually earned the miscreant
several whacks of a slipper. The oak was planted at the end of the avenue of trees
formerly called "Jubilee Avenue" – now known as The Limes. This avenue, planted in
1887, of which ten trees survive, was probably originally sixteen trees long. At least
one tree had to go when the new dining hall was built, for otherwise it would have
been in the doorway, and its two neighbours were perilously close to the 1910
Engineering Shop. The two lime trees at the Tuck Shop end of the avenue are not in
line with the rest, and this may have been the start of an attempt to build a grand,
curving avenue all the way to the Myton Road. Percival Brown's successor, Rev WT
Keeling, used to hold roll-calls "by the Coronation Oak". The other Coronation Oak
is outside the 1957 Science Block and was planted when the cricket pavilion was
nearby. It has done rather better than the "Scotch firs planted to the left of the
pavilion which have been destroyed by sheep and cattle", as reported in 1901. It is
amazing to discover that in 1953 a later headmaster, AHB Bishop, was still
complaining that "cattle straying from Myton Road cause constant damage to our
playing fields."

A fascinating sequence of entries can be discerned in various copies of *The Portcullis* at this time:

1899: Horse (for roller and mower) – £4 10s 0d. Hay for horse – 4s 0d.

In 1901, the school horse was accused of having "a rather thoughtful demeanour of late" and, in 1902, of "moulting".

1903: In spite of numerous obituary notices, the school horse continued his existence undismayed until a few weeks ago, when his demise really took place as the result of drinking cold water when over-tired.

A new horse was purchased in December 1903 for £7 1s 0d and was paid for by the governors.

1904: Expenditure on horse: £10 0s 0d. Paid to hay-makers: £4 9s 0d. From sale of hay: £17 0s 0d.

1909: Expenditure on horse and harness: £6 0s 0d.

1910: From sale of hay and grass: £8 0s 0d. From sale of horses: £7 5s 0d.

Horses were no match, however, for modern technology:

1937: Purchased, a "Trusty" 4½ hp tractor. It does the work of two horses and ploughs an acre of ground in 3½ hours.

The rear of the school, pictured around 1900. This is the only surviving photograph of
JP Way's pavilion, on the far left.
(AF Leach)

Team games, particularly rugby and cricket, were immensely popular, and, despite the falling number of boys at the school, Percival Brown fielded three cricket teams in 1900: the 1st XI, the 2nd XI and – a new feature – the U14 XI. A rare photograph of this U14 XI has survived. It is also interesting that a triumphant note was sounded in a *Portcullis* from 1902, when "all the goal-posts were put up in 14 days", which was a record. With such a small number of boys in the school, it is not, therefore, a surprise to learn that staff frequently played in 1st XI and 1st XV fixtures. Even JP Way, the headmaster from 1885 to 1896, played one innings in a school cricket fixture (but not at first team level) in 1891 and scored 22 not out. WT Keeling, the headmaster from 1903-6, batted for two first team innings in the summer of 1904 and scored 13 runs in total. Later, in 1908, HS Pyne played in an OW match versus Budbrooke Barracks – and was bowled out for o. Fixtures with other schools largely depended on there being a suitable rail link. Schools against which regular fixtures were held as long ago as the 1890s included Trinity College, Stratford; King Edward's School, Stratford; King Henry VIII's School, Coventry; and King Edward's School, Birmingham. Inter-house fixtures provided the mainstay of sporting activity, and in *The Portcullis* of December 1902 we are given the new names of the six houses in the school: School, Liddell's, Davies', Tomas', Sill's and Town.

As regards team photographs for the 1st XV and 1st XI, the first of these seem to have been taken in 1888, and the corresponding prefect photographs in 1890. The Headmaster appears in prefect photographs from 1891 onwards; the Second Master, from 1955. Virtually all of these photographs have survived, but the earliest ones have not been on display for several years. While on the subject of sport, it is interesting to read that the lightest pupil in the 1st XV of 1910 weighed 8st 12lb (56kg), and the heaviest (the "giant of the team") weighed 11st 10lb (74.5kg). Comparable weights for the 1st XV of 2003-4 are 10st to 15st (63.5kg to 95.5kg). Changes in diet over the past 100 years have had a lot to do with the speed with which boys grow – it is on record that the average age of puberty in 1870 for boys was 16.5 years. Sixth-formers (and even, perhaps, players in the 1st XV) with unbroken voices would have been a normal occurrence at this time!

In May 1901, Percival Brown attended the opening of new buildings at the Middle School and was outraged at many things he heard. "The whole circumstances of the function were remarkable," he said. The Chairman got off to a bad start by declaring that the Middle School (set up in 1875) "dated from Saxon times". Grammar schools had had their day, and the way forward was science. "The contempt expressed by Dr Oliver Lodge for schools such as this," wrote Percival Brown, "was greeted with tumultuous applause, in which I had the mortification of seeing members of my Governing Body participating." Dr Lodge was Principal of the newly-chartered University of Birmingham, and a leading physicist. If Percival Brown was an official guest at the Middle School function, then it was a particular snub to be informed from the platform that "we are determined that this shall be the School of Warwick."

By 1902, the losses made by the school (and by Percival Brown, who claims his salary went down from £942 in 1896 to £518 in 1901, that is, an equivalent reduction from £60,000 to £32,000 in 2003 values) were becoming so severe that in June that year the Clerk to the Governors "was requested to see Mr Brown and if possible arrange for his retirement at the end of the summer term". Percival Brown resigned in August, and in October the governors "unanimously resolved that Mr Brown's resignation be accepted". He was sent the following letter by the Clerk: "The Governors desire me to accept the resignation of your office as Head Master of the King's School and to express their regret that the financial condition of the school obliges them to take this course. I am also desired to forward the enclosed memoranda in reply to certain parts of your letter." Percival Brown's letter was, in fact, a spectacular, printed, 44-page booklet, in which he said to the governors:

> You have closed my career as a schoolmaster. I have spent on your school 6 years of mature work, and have done all I knew to advance its interests in every way. And now my reward is to be hustled out of office. You have not only written me down a failure as a head-master, on what I believe to be utterly insufficient grounds, but by asking for my resignation in advance of my obtaining another appointment, you have made it possible and perhaps inevitable for posterity to surmise that some moral obliquity of my own was your unavowed motive.

He also implied that the governors were not devoting sufficient time to the school; the governors were particularly incensed at this, and minuted: "It is hardly within the province of the Head Master to decide as to the amount of time and interest which it is necessary for the Governors to devote to the School, but we may point out that for 20 years before the advent of Mr Brown, the school was successful under their management."

In his final speech to the boys on December 19th, 1902, Percival Brown said that he had not succeeded in doubling the numbers at the school, as his previous successes had led him to expect, owing to "a combination of adverse circumstances". In the hour of danger, he had not deserted Warwick, but Warwick had deserted him. His maxim had always been, "Aim high", and he could leave no better advice to the school. He thanked the Senior Prefect, "who had so generously expressed the loving gratitude of the school" towards himself at the House Supper on the previous evening. Perhaps he was being a little hypocritical, for, in his monumental resignation booklet, he complains about the boys (who took "an abnormal delight in outwitting Masters"), the governors, the prefects (one of whom "diverted himself with the society of the maid-servants, and took them to Church on Sunday"), the food, the pro-Middle School press coverage (even Percival Brown refers to it as "propaganda"), the "practical helplessness of the staff to cope" (ie, 7 staff for 160 boys), the conflicts between day-boys and boarders, and even a maid-servant, who was "dismissed summarily for putting a note under a boy's plate". Elsewhere in the booklet, he quotes a report that said that he was "the ablest Head-Master the School has ever had". He mentions that the boarding fee was £40 per year, that JP Way had allowed boarders in at a substantial discount without telling his successor of the fact, and that it had taken himself many

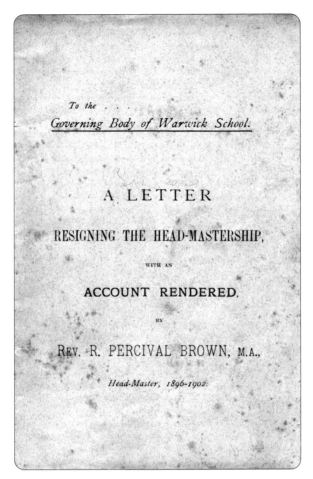

To the . . .
Governing Body of Warwick School.

A LETTER

RESIGNING THE HEAD-MASTERSHIP,

WITH AN

ACCOUNT RENDERED,

BY

REV. R. PERCIVAL BROWN, M.A.,

Head-Master, 1896-1902.

Rev R Percival Brown's resignation booklet of 1902.
(Warwick School Archives)

years to whittle away the number of boys on this unofficial discount. Like his exact contemporary at Ipswich School, PE Raynor, Percival Brown felt compelled to supplement staff salaries from his own pocket, and this he did to the tune of just over £280 during his six years at Warwick School – the equivalent of £18,000 in 2003 values.

The December 1902 issue of *The Portcullis* contains a good deal of sycophantic material – even a gushing poem – about Percival Brown's departure, much of which he must have written himself. He was right in that the whole affair had finished his career as a schoolmaster. He became a vicar, first of all in Stirling in 1905, and then, during the First World War (in which he acted as a temporary Chaplain to the Forces), in Kirkby Lonsdale in Cumbria, from where he retired in 1933 to Worthing, Sussex. A few years before his retirement, he published a book, *Edward Wilson of*

Nether Levens (1557–1653) and his Kin, published by Wilson in Kendal in 1930. Preserved in the school archives is a tatty letter written by Percival Brown to the new Headmaster of 1933, Eric Percival Smith, offering back to the school a small copy of John Owen's Epigrams – a collected edition of 1622 – which Percival Brown says he bought "at some expense", but which he felt ought to be back in the school library. In typical waspish style, he declares that, after "shivering through the volume I expect you will agree that the 'English Martial' was much overrated" – he didn't think much of 17th-century Latin humour, obviously. Neither, incidentally, did the satirist Ben Jonson, who described Owen as "a pure Pedantique Schoolmaster sweeping his living from the Posteriors of little children, having no thinge good in him, his epigrames being bare narrations". It would be extremely interesting to know what Percival Brown said when he returned to the school on 27th May, 1934, by invitation, to preach in the chapel.

It is fascinating to note that, in 2002, the vicar of Kirkby Lonsdale was able to inform the author that one very elderly parishioner still remembered Percival Brown as "not a very convivial person", and also that bits of bottles are still being dug up from the vicarage garden – the remains, apparently, of a huge dump dating from the Percival Brown years. He is recorded in the parish history as a man who could not easily communicate with the parishioners. It is also interesting to note that Percival Brown reveals very, very little about his personal life anywhere, although he lets slip in his monumental booklet of complaint of 1902 that he had daughters at King's High School (and it was presumably one of them, Hilda, who became headmistress of Doncaster High School in 1925), and a *Portcullis* of 1897 laments that Mrs Brown (who died in 1940) was recovering from "a simple fracture of the leg in a bicycling accident". Percival Brown himself died in 1944 – aged 92, according to a brief entry in *The Portcullis*. He was, however, 82, and a full obituary never materialised.

In November 1902, the governors appointed Rev WT Keeling as the next Headmaster – he won on the third round of voting. In January 1903, the governors wrote: "The committee proceeded to consider a rejoinder of the late Head Master to the reply sent by the governors to his letter of resignation and also a report by the Clerk as to certain statements therein. It was resolved that the Clerk acknowledge the receipt of the rejoinder and that in the opinion of the governors no good purpose will be served by continuing the discussion." Six months later, they dismissed out of hand a letter from Percival Brown's solicitor demanding compensation for his "lost" salary and, apart from reimbursing him to the tune of £8–10s for a dining table he had left behind, they thereby washed their hands of Rev Robert Percival Brown.

CHAPTER 13

Rev William Theodore Keeling

Rev William Theodore Keeling was another young headmaster, appointed when he was not quite 32. Born in 1871, he was himself the son of a headmaster (Rev William Hulton Keeling of Bradford Grammar School) and was educated at Jesus College, Cambridge. He taught at Liverpool College, Epsom College and Weymouth College, where he spent one year as Deputy Headmaster, before coming to Warwick in January 1903. In his short time at the school (his was the second-shortest headmastership on record), he tried very hard to modernise it, and his Science Block of 1905 was his main building achievement. That Science Block was converted to the teaching of history and geography in the 1950s and is now the Music Block. Keeling stated in 1904 that his ambition was to make the school the chief secondary school "for both town and district". His very act of modernising destroyed what for us nowadays would be fascinating material: for example, he threw out all the old heavily-carved Victorian desks as soon as he came to the school, but not before Big School in its original guise had been photographed for posterity. This photograph of Big School, taken around 1900, shows clearly the intended effect of building a lantern on the roof – light floods down from it. The lantern is still there but was sealed off when Big School was converted into the school library early in the 1970s.

Whether by accident or design, Keeling caused to have published the first complete list of the staff in 1904: as well as himself, there were Messrs Davies, Liddell, Richardson, Tomas, Beaven, Howlett and Bott, as well as the Bursar, Mr Riches (an unfortunate choice of name, given the financial state of the school!). A bicycle club outing to Henley and Stratford in the summer of 1904 was "spoiled by a nasty accident to the bursar" – from which he fully recovered, however. The earliest staff photograph in existence dates from 1903, but it is not possible to tell in all cases which teacher is which: for one thing, every single man on the photograph has a moustache!

Keeling must have realised early on that unless he dramatically increased the number of pupils at the school, he would be destroyed by the same market forces as his predecessor, and in his second term at the school, the summer term of 1903, he commissioned a series of professional photographs, taken by Messrs Elliott and Fry, which were marketed as postcards – a very early attempt at publicity. The master

Rev WT Keeling and the teaching staff of 1903.
(RH Thornton)

copies of the photographs, presented to Rev Keeling in a handsome album, have survived, as has just one of the postcards. Further publicity photographs were added to the collection the following summer.

Keeling supervised the filling in of the east window of the chancel of the chapel with stained glass by Henry Holiday. In 1904, he wrote to the governors: "I am glad to hear the 2 new lights are liked so much" and that the final 2 "are in an advanced stage." He would, however, like to be paid: "I do not think the Governors will expect me to wait a third year; the total amount being £114–4s." Henry Holiday had, in fact, visited the school in 1901 and had proposed that he be commissioned to supply a window for the new chancel. In due course, this became the Cecil Meiggs memorial window (Cecil Meiggs being the 12-year-old boy, mentioned previously, who had died at the school in 1902). Henry Holiday is remembered these days for being the illustrator of Lewis Carroll's *The Hunting of the Snark*.

Keeling enlarged the concept of extra-curricular activities and encouraged the formation of Cycling and Chess Clubs and a School Fire Brigade, as well as maintaining the very popular Natural History Society, the Photographic Society and the Shakespeare Society. He welcomed OWs back to the school for a few days before

The sole surviving 1903 publicity postcard, showing a cricket match in progress.
(Warwick School Archives)

The interior of the chapel, photographed in 1903 and showing the centre light only –
the Cecil Meiggs memorial window.
(RH Thornton)

Christmas 1904; they were "housed, as usual, in the Sanatorium"! One innovation Keeling tried in 1904–5 was to publish the termly calendar in *The Portcullis*. From this we learn, for example, that the autumn term of 1904 ran from September 18th to December 21st, with a one-day half-term holiday on October 31st. The Shakespeare Society met every Saturday; there were three meetings of the Debating Society; and every Saturday, the 1st XV played teams from Stratford, King Edward's School, Birmingham, Bromsgrove, Reading School and St Edward's School, Oxford, among others. The term ended with a Carol Service on the Sunday, a House Supper on the Monday, an Entertainment called "Past and Present" on the Tuesday and departure on the Wednesday. Similarly, the summer term of 1905 stretched from May 5th to July 31st, with another one-day half-term holiday on June 19th (marked by a Bicycle Club Run). The Athletic Sports were held on May 13th, having been postponed from the previous term, owing to the death of the Matron. After the third week of term, the 1st XI played twice a week, and the Under 14 XI got two fixtures against Arden House – one at home, and one away. The Natural History Society had two expedition days, the Cadet Corps met sporadically, as did the Camera Club, and there was a Choir Picnic late in July, as well as a Swimming Competition, and an Entertainment on the final Saturday of term. Hidden away amongst all this activity are two entries – July 14th:

The carpenter's shop on the far side of the gymnasium, photographed in 1903.
(RH Thornton)

Examinations for Higher Certificates, and July 24th: Examinations for Lower Certificates. The experiment in publishing the calendar in *The Portcullis* was not carried on past 1905, and the earliest surviving card calendars in the archives date from the early 1930s. It was only in 1934 that the modern-style Blue Book was first published.

In the same issue that gives the summer term calendar of 1905 – *The Portcullis* of June 1905 – can be found a last-minute appeal for information prior to the publication of AF Leach's *History of Warwick School*:

> All OWs willing to give any further information to the Editor of the History of Warwick School, are invited to send in their names to the Secretary of the OW Club. Mr Leach is still anxious for more material, especially for the years 1880–1885.

It is perhaps refreshing to read an extraordinary series of entries in the Master's Book, Volume II, in which WT Keeling is faced with what seems an inexhaustible supply of inventiveness as regards bad behaviour on the part of the boys.

> I wish to remind boys that the desks in the Classrooms are for books and are not intended to be used as larders for jam or birds' eggs. (May 25th, 1903)

> I see that there are drawings, initials etc on the walls and doors of some of the closets. (May 26th, 1904)

> I notice that the entries in the Punishment Book are far more numerous than it is possible for Carter conscientiously to work off. There have been 360 entries during the last 17 days. It seems to me that Drill is made a panacea for all ills. (Oct 18th, 1904)

"Carter" was the school caretaker and laboratory assistant, but his military rank of Sergeant presumably made him an ideal candidate for running WT Keeling's punishment drills. James Lycett Carter's grand-daughter, Pam Harris, was able to prove in

The earliest surviving photograph of the Cadet Corps, taken in 1903.
(RH Thornton)

March 2004 that his first daughter, her aunt, was born in the school sanatorium in 1905 – a rare event in a boys' school! It is thought that JL Carter is the tall man in the back row of the 1903 Cadet Corps photograph. He may have been the only employee of the school to survive the 1906 crash, too, for he appears in a newspaper list of the new employees for September of that year.

More bad behaviour followed:

A custom has grown up of flicking wet blotting paper against the walls and ceilings in the Classrooms, especially the Upper 3rd room. (Nov 25th, 1904)

It has been reported to me that boys are in the habit of hitting stones with their hockey sticks over the Gymnasium. Several of the slates on the Bicycle Shed have been broken. It is also very dangerous for men working in the field behind the Gymnasium. (March 4th, 1905)

I wish especially to point out to the School the desecration of throwing anything whatever against the walls of the Chapel, which is a sacred building both inside and out. I see that at the present time there is a wicket on the Chapel roof, and I am told that it is a common practice to throw stones, coal etc against the board on the south side of the Chapel, or even at a target placed above the board. (June 6th, 1905)

I notice that the practice of throwing darts in the Big School Room has begun again. (March 10th, 1906)

It is interesting, in the light of what WT Keeling wrote about the south side of the chapel, that film exists from the 1950s showing boys playing tennis against the wall of the south transept. Indeed, in 2004, a painted white line, representing a tennis net, is still clearly visible!

In addition to this plethora of misdeeds, the economic problems which consumed Percival Brown had not gone away. The school gradually got into deep financial trouble, existing solely on the profits brought in by the boarders. Initially, indeed, a large influx of boarders caused the total number of boys at the school to rise from 62 to 94 within a year of Keeling's arrival, and academic results were outstanding: two Warwick boys were first in all England in Scripture and Greek in the Oxford Local Examinations. However, the continuing spectacular rise of the King's Middle School (also known as the King's County School) under HS Pyne, aided and abetted by local politicians and the press, and also by very favourable charitable financial contributions at the expense of Warwick School, caused a massive loss of confidence in the school by local parents, and increasing calls for the two schools to be amalgamated.

Carefully-drafted documents outlining the crisis, which were circulated to the governors in May 1906, have survived, as has the Earl of Warwick's response to them. The splendid gold-embossed letter to the Vice-Chairman, Michael Lakin (who was to succeed him as Chairman of Governors in 1919), and signed merely "Warwick", shows that Francis Richard Greville, 5th Earl of Warwick, had not only completely

The earliest surviving photograph of the interior of the 1890 gymnasium, taken in 1903.
The boys changed in the gallery at the far end.
(RH Thornton)

The school library, photographed in 1903.
(RH Thornton)

misunderstood the documents, but also confirmed his dislike of the school he so seldom visited in his official capacity:

Warwick Castle, May 30th, 1906

Dear Mr Lakin.

I have read with alarm and dismay the papers which have been sent to me as one of the governors of the King's School, and the report from the Board of Education. In that report the statements are absolutely untrue that the Middle School has received more than its share of the Endowment to the disadvantage of the King's School. The proposal of the Board of Education practically means the extinction of the Middle School, for the sake of bolstering up the King's School which in my opinion cannot be a success.

   I did my best on the deputation with you to the Board of Education to express these views.

   I wish now to say that if their scheme as proposed is carried out, I shall at once tender my resignation as Chairman, and request the Mayor at once to call a town meeting to explain my reasons.

   Forgive this hurried letter which I beg you kindly to read at the meeting in the event of my attendance through camp duties being impossible.

   Yrs very truly, Warwick

The King's Middle School was situated just north of where King's High gymnasium is now – a very cramped site indeed. Nothing exists of it these days except a portion of the outer wall of its school-yard, which passes along The Butts, and the original entrance gate-way, near to which was the famous ilex tree (evergreen oak) – beloved by generations of school children until it fell in 1949. The Middle School functioned between 1878 and 1906, and records from it are extremely rare. In Warwick School's present-day archives are its admission books for 1899 to 1906 in HS Pyne's own hand, two whole-school photographs, dated 1901 and 1902, and a local newspaper of February 1904, folded by Pyne into a scrap-book and overlooked for 100 years, in which is printed a laudatory article – and a line-drawing of the school. Contemporary photographs of the buildings (designed, like the Grammar School, by John Cundall) do not seem to have survived, or perhaps were never taken. When the Middle School closed in 1906, the neighbouring King's High School was able to use some of the buildings, and the King's High Junior School, or Kindergarten, which many Warwick School boys attended, moved in from the Eastgate at the end of the First World War. The buildings, renamed St Mary's Hall, were severely damaged by fire in 1970, and the remains were finally demolished in 1981. Pyne collected in his scrap-books every single statistic, article and newspaper letter about his own and the rival school. He must have seen it as ripe for a takeover – the failing school over the river with plenty of space and a brand new Science Block.

A newspaper drawing of the King's Middle School, also known as the
King's County School, published in 1904.
(Warwick School Archives)

Indeed, it is tempting to speculate that he had this takeover in mind for several years, and that he was encouraged in this by his board of governors.

At the Grammar School, Keeling shed staff in order to try to cope, but to no avail. One of them, WP Richardson, the Head of the Junior House, did not go quietly at all: he published the entire correspondence between himself and Keeling, trying to drum up massive parental support in his own favour, but he still had to go – his departure eventually softened by a grudging admission from the governors that, although it was the headmaster's perfect right to dismiss anyone, it was actually done purely for financial reasons. This does not seem to have been explained very well to the poor man at the time.

In 1905, a desperate modernisation programme was attempted. The governors adopted a new scheme for the recognition of the school as a Secondary Day School and sanctioned the building of the necessary science buildings, as well as raising the maximum boarding fee to £60 per year (worth £3,700 in 2003). The new Science Block cost about £2,500 (£150,000), of which just over £1,000 (£60,000) came from the County Council.

In the middle of this intense crisis, a huge festival was being arranged – the

The scene from the Warwick Pageant of 1906 representing the founding of the
King's New School of Warwick. The schoolmaster leading the boys is Robert Davies.
(Warwick School Archives)

The first performance of the school song, *Floreat Domus*, at the Warwick Pageant of July 1906.
(Warwick School Archives)

Warwick Pageant of 1906, in which many Warwick School pupils took part. The music master of the King's Middle School, Allen K Blackall, wrote most of the music for the Pageant. Blackall was to become the music master at Warwick School from 1906 to 1927 and the Principal of the Birmingham School of Music (now called the Birmingham Conservatoire) from 1934 until 1945. At the age of almost 70, he embarked on a third career – as the first sub-warden of the new Royal School of Church Music at Canterbury, from which post he resigned in 1947. He was the organist of St Mary's Church until 1945, and his portrait still hangs in the vestry there. It may be either a final relic of the idea that music was not an important academic subject (which seems to be reinforced by the paltry salary offered), or that Blackall was easing his way out of Warwick School by accepting lecturing work in Birmingham well before he left in 1927, but it is a sad fact that his departure, after 21 years at Warwick School, merited only two lines in *The Portcullis*. It is somewhat illuminating to discover that, somehow, Allen K Blackall managed to write his own entry in the Staff Register (normally the prerogative of the headmaster only) and, in the space reserved for "Particulars of retiring allowance, if any", has merely written "!!". Blackall died in 1963 at Canterbury.

An item from the 1906 Pageant has passed into common usage as the second Warwick School song – *Floreat Domus*, with words by Keeling himself and music by Blackall's rival, James Haworth, the music master at Warwick School from 1905 to 1906. It was performed at the end of Episode VIII of the Pageant, to celebrate the re-founding of the King's New School of Warwick in 1546 (through a simple historical error, they got the year wrong). It was preceded by a march by Blackall, for which the cue was: "Enter the King's School with a Master at their head." A pencilled note on the back of a contemporary photograph states that the boys were "dressed in brown and yellow costumes". The school owns Blackall's autograph manuscript orchestral parts for this Pageant March, and the piece was reconstructed in the summer of 2003 by Gervald Frykman, thanks to RE Hawkins (Warwick School 1937–43) and his late father, who not only saved the orchestral parts from destruction but also provided a copy of Blackall's piano reduction of the piece. This was vital, since the surviving orchestral parts clearly did not represent the original total orchestration.

In the introduction to the Pageant script, Louis N Parker, the Master of the Pageant, wrote: "The Rev WT Keeling, Headmaster of Warwick School, has written a Latin Carmen, which I expect the School will be singing centuries hence." *Floreat domus* means "May the house flourish." In the middle of each verse is a refrain, *Floreat Scola Warwickensis*, meaning "May Warwick School flourish", which is somewhat ironic considering that Keeling wrote it when it the school was on the verge of collapse! Indeed, events were already overtaking the preparations for the Pageant. In February 1906, the governors requested "that the Clerk draw the attention of the Head Master to the fact that the period of 3 years during which it was understood that the school should be carried on by him in the hope of a successful result had

The cover of the 1906 School Song, *Floreat Domus*.
(Warwick School Archives)

already expired, and inform him that at the close of the current year should further loss be incurred it will be necessary for the governors to consider their position." Keeling needed no further hint; he resigned and became Headmaster of Grantham Grammar School at Easter 1906, leaving the school to be run by the Deputy Headmaster, Robert Davies. The governors, perhaps grateful to get rid of Keeling so easily, agreed, after a lengthy discussion, to pay his salary for a further term but then tried to get him to continue to be responsible for the chapel services – and from Lincolnshire! Keeling wrote to the Clerk to the Governors: "I am afraid I cannot undertake to make myself responsible for the Sunday Services in Chapel. It is possible that Mr Davies may find a man in Holy Orders. Failing that the boys had better go to St Nicholas." The governors minuted that they "decline to release him from the

Rev WT Keeling (centre) and the chapel choir of 1903. To the left of the
headmaster is Robert Davies.
(RH Thornton)

obligation to provide for the Chapel services", and that they "will be obliged to
engage some one to perform the duties and deduct the cost from Mr Keeling's
salary". Keeling presumably shrugged his shoulders – and continued to hand over
his salary to Robert Davies, who was paid his normal salary as well!

The accounts for 1906 show a huge deficit – £1,267 19s 7d (about £76,000 in 2003
values). Just how many pupils and staff were left in that summer term of 1906 is
partially revealed in a 1907 *Portcullis* – probably 4 staff and 50 boys. In response to
this sorry state of affairs, the governors decided to put into effect, from September
1906, the long-discussed amalgamation of the school with The King's Middle School
and to appoint Pyne as its head – allowing him, quite extraordinarily, to take over
'lock, stock and barrel', with his own pupils and staff, without re-appointing any of
the previous staff, including Robert Davies. During what must have been an
extremely difficult summer term, Robert Davies did his best to carry on as normal,
but he obviously felt under enormous strain – if the decidedly shaky handwriting in
the Master's Book is anything to go by. He managed to get to the penultimate page
before he and all his colleagues lost their jobs when Pyne took over.

This savage act of Pyne's caused howls of protest from the OWs, and they soon organised a testimonial presentation of two pairs of silver candlesticks and a cheque for £56 17s to Mr Davies. It is not known whether he received any form of pension, but at the dinner in his honour in April 1907 (R Percival Brown and JP Way contributed to the testimonial, but WT Keeling and HS Pyne did not – the latter "sent a kind message of good wishes... over the telephone") a good deal was revealed about the previous twenty years at the school and, in particular, the cataclysmic events of 1906. Firstly, OW Secretary WVP Hexter spoke about the troubled interregnum of 1885:

> Mr Davies came to Warwick School in September 1885. Mr Way saw to it that he would be at some trouble to discipline the 80 or 90 young colts whom his predecessor had left behind – so he made overtures to Mr Davies to come to Warwick – and Mr Davies appeared on the scenes, being the only new master that term. Mr Davies at once set to work to reduce us to order, and I am afraid he at first found it a difficult and thankless task, for many of us were pretty rough and ready fellows, particularly the Fifth Form, which contained the majority of the Football XV. So far

The exterior of the chapel, taken from the Myton Road in 1903.
(RH Thornton)

The front of the school, photographed in 1903. Many of the young trees pictured are
still there, over 100 years later.
(RH Thornton)

as I can recollect, Mr Davies' cure-all was 300 consecutive lines of Virgil for the first
offence. There was no second offence, as a rule.

Then he spoke of the events of the summer of 1906:

> A year ago, deserted by half its boys, and left practically without an official head, the
> school found a loyal and ever self-sacrificing leader in Mr Davies. There were few
> who knew what a term was the Summer Term of 1906 – a struggle against adversity
> from beginning to end – a term of sleepless nights and anxious hours. But right up
> to the last that remnant of 50 kept up the old traditions manfully and played the
> game, thanks to Mr Davies. At the Warwick Pageant few sights could have been
> more touching than that of Mr Davies and his boys marching into that arena, with
> happy faces, but alas! heavy hearts.

It is very interesting that Davies' carved subscription panel in the old dining room
does not have a leaving date – as if no-one would dare carve it. These panels were
available for anybody to purchase, at 10/6 per panel, plus 2d per letter, but were
particularly aimed at pupils whose "names being absent from scholarship panels and

The headmaster's garden, photographed in 1903. It is assumed that the lady seated in the chair
is the very heavily pregnant Mrs WT Keeling.
(RH Thornton)

sporting photographs ... would otherwise fade from history". Perhaps staff thought
that they might also "fade from history", because a great number of them purchased
panels, and these staff panels form one of the best set of records that we have of the
teaching staff from the 1880s to 1906. The only way of distinguishing pupil panels
from staff panels is that the staff have their degrees carved, as well as their names
(except, for example, the first Music Master, AG Warren, who didn't have a degree).
The names of all the headmasters from MacMichael to Percival Brown are carved by
the fireplace, too, but most have been covered up since 1958 by a portrait of the Queen
Mother. Robert Davies himself died in 1940. His long stay at Warwick School was
the exception rather than the rule: most staff did not stay more than two or three
years at this time.

A unique, and somewhat harsh, comment on Keeling's time at Warwick School
has come down to us in an annotated copy of AF Leach's *History of Warwick School*,
now owned by Antony Randle (Warwick School 1939-45). Its former owner was Rev
Ralph Fitz-James Sawyer, who attended the school from 1891 to 1898, and who later
served as a Chaplain and housemaster at Wrekin College. In 1945, he wrote:

This HM completely failed on personal grounds... The "Middle" School then moved in with its HM and boys – lock, stock and barrel; and the character of Warwick became entirely changed.

Keeling stayed at Grantham until 1910, when he paid a brief return visit to Warwick School on Speech Day, and after one further short headmastership at Cordwalles School, a prep school near Maidenhead, he emigrated to British Columbia, Canada. He became a lecturer in Theology at St Mark's Hall in Vancouver from 1913 to 1920, and finally Dean and Professor of Hebrew and Old Testament and Patristics at the Anglican Theological College of British Columbia, North Vancouver, until 1927. In his "retirement", he held the post of Rector of St John's Church, Vancouver, from 1928 to 1941. He came back to Warwick School in 1930, to attend, somewhat bizarrely, the Debating Society's Annual Dinner (for 100 pupils and staff) in the old gymnasium, and he presided over Holy Communion in the chapel the following morning. He also presented a set of four different-coloured stoles for use in the chapel, and this set has survived almost intact. On his return to Canada, he was appointed Chaplain and Classical and Modern Language master at St George's School, Vancouver, and held those posts from 1941 to 1945, thereby extending his varied working life to virtually 50 years. Thus he finally stopped teaching at the age of 74, but did not enjoy a long retirement: he returned to England and retired to Bournemouth, where he died the following year.

CHAPTER 14

Howard Seymour Pyne

Howard Seymour Pyne was certainly different from all the headmasters before him – the first non-Oxbridge man, the first scientist, the first non-clergyman. He had a very long headship: 22 years at Warwick School, preceded by seven years at the Middle School, which he regarded as continuous employment – as in effect it was, being under the same Foundation. Pyne was a ruthless man and a dynamic physicist. He was also devious – and perhaps not even totally honest by the end of his time at the school. Complacency had also set in by then, and he left his successor more problems than he had bargained for. He was certainly an opportunist, and his opportunity was the complete takeover of Warwick School in the late summer of 1906 on his own terms: none of the existing staff, no compulsory Latin, a preponderance of day-boys (at the start, at least) and generous financial terms.

HS Pyne attended Lancing School and obtained all his subsequent degrees externally (a total of five: from London, the Royal University of Ireland and Trinity College, Dublin) while working full-time. He taught first in London for two years, followed by King William's College on the Isle of Man for 14 years. In 1899, he was appointed to be the Headmaster of the King's Middle School in Warwick – and had all the existing staff there sacked before he started. Very soon, the Middle School became a Centre of Scientific Excellence. This was not its original purpose, which was meant to be the education of boys for commerce. An official complaint was made by the Board of Education in 1905 that not only was Pyne taking in boys of sixth-form age but, quite incredibly, he was also taking in boarders in his own home – and, what is more, had been doing so, as had other staff, since 1900, despite the fact that the school was officially a day-school. The Board reported that "there is evidence of a deliberate intention on the part of the authorities of the Middle School unduly to compete with the Grammar School."

Unlike his Victorian predecessors, Pyne has left very little written record of his time in the town of Warwick. Two exceptions are his scrap-books for newspaper cuttings, which stop in 1906, and his Staff Register, which was started in 1899 and is still being continued, many volumes on. He published a couple of theses, presumably for two of the external degrees he obtained at Trinity College, Dublin, as a mature student, and the school owns copies of these. He maintained his great friendship with

An informal group of teachers, probably from the King's Middle School, taken around 1906.
The three staff on the right are HS Pyne, AK Blackall and MM Clark.
(Warwick School Archives)

Sir Oliver Lodge of Birmingham University, and spent at least one summer holiday at the university, conducting research. In one thesis, he laments that he was unable to carry on, since Birmingham University had been turned into a military hospital in the First World War. However, he carried out the work for the second thesis at Warwick School, and a physics laboratory was named the Pyne Room and kept that name until 1957, when the new Science Block was built. Pyne's skill as a scientist extended to photography, too: he used to give lantern slide lectures to the boys in Big School with his own colour photographs, particularly of his travels abroad, from 1915 onwards. It may have been Pyne's love of photography which caused him to arrange the first in a series of whole-school photographs that have been taken at intervals of a few years ever since. The earliest surviving whole-school photograph is dated March 1920. Staff photographs have not fared so well, and we have only three such photographs surviving from this era – those dating from 1903, circa 1906 and 1927. It was to be another fifty years before the next one was taken.

Pyne spent the summer of 1906 (with his former pupil HE Cullis's help, it is said) transferring the contents of his laboratories from The Butts to Keeling's new Science Block, south of the river, and in the autumn there was virtually a completely fresh start for the school – headmaster, boys and staff. On 19th September, 1906, 220 boys

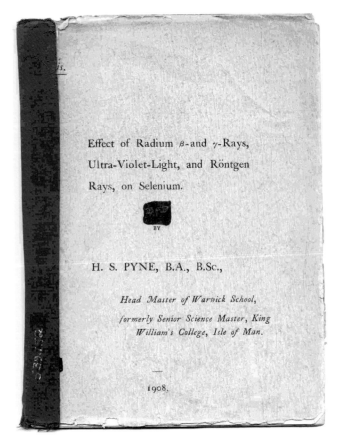

Effect of Radium ß-and γ-Rays,
Ultra-Violet-Light, and Röntgen
Rays, on Selenium.

BY

H. S. PYNE, B.A., B.Sc.,

Head Master of Warwick School,

formerly Senior Science Master, King
William's College, Isle of Man.

1908.

HS Pyne's thesis of 1908.
(Warwick School library)

were enrolled – term started at 10am, and an entrance examination was held an hour later. It has to be said that the lack of confidence that the existing parents of pre-1906 pupils had in Pyne meant that only 13 boys from the old grammar school signed up to the new regime.

It is significant that in the December 1906 edition of *The Portcullis*, an issue which very much tries to 'pour oil over troubled waters', Pyne's appointment is said to be "without prejudice", and the implication is that it would be reviewed by the governors after one year. Right from the start in 1906, numbers rose steadily, so Pyne could afford to employ more staff and even embark on a new building programme. Since it was largely on account of the poor number of pupils that his two predecessors lost their jobs, there seems to have been no more discussion about whether Pyne's job was temporary or not! In fact, the governors quietly appointed him "formally, without advertisement" late in 1909.With plenty of local authority money, and day-boys in rapidly increasing numbers, he was soon able to appoint more staff to teach them. Two members of staff who came over the river with Pyne stayed with him for the whole of his Warwick School career – Allen K Blackall, the musician, and Marmaduke Musson Clark, the Second Master and Bursar. Between 1906 and 1927, the teaching staff expanded from 12 to 25. MM Clark stayed on, and on, long after most men would have retired. At the age of 71 in 1946, he officially retired but was kept on for three years as "Honorary Bursar", perhaps so that he could claim a total service of fifty years. Dying early in 1955, Clark had a prodigious memory and could recount any pupil's details, such as his school number, and even that of the pupil's father, long after that pupil had left the school.

Pyne started in 1906, therefore, with 220 boys and twelve teaching staff, six of whom he brought over from the Middle School. In addition, there was a "Drill instructor to the Cadet Corps" (Sgt Fell) and a "School and Laboratory Assistant" (Sgt Carter). The two or three "non-academic staff" (teachers of music, art and woodwork) did not rate as being important enough to be on the stage for Speech Day. Pyne was able to appoint six more staff by 1908, and, thanks to his meticulously-kept Staff Register, we also know the salaries of these early members of staff, and how different subjects merited dramatically different wages. It should be borne in mind

The canal bridge on the Myton Road, pictured on a postcard dating from 1906.
(WCRO)

that HS Pyne was allowed to keep any profit he made on the boarders, in addition to his official salary. £100 in the following table of 1906 salaries would be worth about £6,000 in 2003 values:

HS Pyne (Headmaster)	Divinity, physics, chemistry	£200 + £120 capitation
TJ Lewis (Second Master)	History, French, geog, Eng Lit	£155
JD Day	Chaplain, OTC, Head of English	£205
AH Doherty	Head of Classics	£180 resident
MM Clark	Junior maths, geography, Bursar	£149
FR Tutton	English	£115
CR Beechey	Head of Mathematics	£100 resident
F Bromwich	Woodwork	"as per WCC"
AK Blackall	Music	£40

Some of the following early Pyne appointments show a similar wide variety of salaries, and even, dare one say it, an extraordinary favouritism towards his own son:

Eva Walker (1907)	Eng, Arith, Fr, drawing (Junior School)	£70
F Holte (1908)	Art	21 guineas
W Morris (1911)	PE	£25
AH Pyne (1914)	Drawing	£120

Boys relaxing between lessons, taken around 1912. The photograph clearly shows the newly-built Engineering Shop (on the extreme left) and, next to it, what became Prefects' Corridor, joined onto the side of Big School.
(Warwick School Archives)

The outdoor swimming pool in use, photographed around 1920.
(Warwick School Archives)

The school was being modernised almost from the start of Pyne's time. Electric lighting was installed during 1910, and teaching rooms dedicated to just one subject were being developed, starting with history in 1910. The long-awaited outdoor swimming pool was ready for the first school swimming sports in 1912, but it never got its cover. This led to certain unhygienic conditions, to say the least – the old joke that "the P is silent as in bathing" was definitely rumoured to apply, as well as "the outpourings of ducks and gulls, the remains of foot plasters, and an inevitable colony of mosquitoes"! The new boiler-house was started in 1911, with the promise of – at last – sufficient hot water for bathing and heating. At the same time, a 40-foot well was sunk, just to the east of the Engineering Shop (Pyne's first building), to ensure that the school was independent of the town's water supply.

Other innovations were also happening at this time. Warwick School Orchestra's "inaugural concert" was in December 1915. The orchestra consisted merely of five violins, a cello, a piccolo, a piano and two drums – but it was a start! A previous attempt at a "school band" had been made in the 1880s, with a similarly motley collection of instruments – "two pianos, violins, 'cello, drum and triangle". The year 1916 saw events being organised which involved both Warwick School and King's High School for Girls. In March of that year, there was a joint debate (the return trip, a more adventurous exercise, perhaps, was made in 1920), and, in what must have been an electrifying show, in April 1916 "a team of girls gave a display of physical drill and club-swinging" at a gym competition. Pyne seems to have started the tradition of the

The interior of the Engineering Shop, pictured around 1920.
(Warwick School Archives)

An engineering session in progress, photographed around 1920.
(Warwick School Archives)

yearly visit of the Town Crier – in 1912, it is recorded that the visit was taking place "according to custom" – but there is no mention of it in the Master's Books before 1906. It may be that the Town Crier visited the Middle School while Pyne was head there, and that he brought the tradition over the river in 1906. Another innovation, apparently started in 1916, was the annual Science Exhibition – a feature of school life, on and off, for the next fifty years or so. In October 1918, there was even a demonstration baseball match on the school fields by two visiting American teams.

At Christmas 1912, an extraordinary event occurred in which a full fox-hunt invaded the school ground – and presented the "mask" of the late fox to the headmaster, who promptly put it on display. This was shortly after the whole school had paraded to St Mary's Church, banners included, for a service "to perpetuate and revive the bond of connection" between the two institutions. The modern annual Carol Service in St Mary's might, therefore, be said to derive from this 1912 revival. The installation of electricity in the school allowed films to be shown in Big School, and these events, particularly in the "silent film" era, were hugely popular. Music was provided to accompany the films, and it is worth pointing out that the celebrated composer and organist of Christ Church Cathedral, Oxford, from 1955 to 1970 (and, before that, of New College, Oxford), Dr Sydney Watson, who was a pupil at Warwick School under AK Blackall from 1914 to 1921, 'cut his teeth' accompanying silent films in Big School.

The first building which Pyne can be credited with, as mentioned earlier, is the Engineering Shop of 1910, which is still used for its original purpose. All too soon after it was built, though, the Engineering Shop was being used to help produce munitions in the First World War – shell-cases and then shell-caps – and the Junior Boarding House was even used to give a home to displaced Belgian refugee children from 1914 to 1915. It re-opened for use by the school in 1915. Pupils who won school prizes were awarded a certificate instead of books, the money being sent to the Red Cross for "the alleviation of the suffering of our wounded soldiers". At the same time, military drill became compulsory for all boys in the school.

Crises all of a sudden hit Pyne, starting in 1913 when, having been given an incorrect mark of zero for a pupil's Greek paper by the exam board, he awarded the valuable Fulke Weale exhibition to the wrong boy. Legal action was averted only when the governors awarded the wronged candidate a university scholarship of equal value – which, nine years later, he had still not claimed fully, on the grounds that he was "employed in Iraq"! Hot on the heels of that came, in May 1914, an appalling sanitary report on the whole school from the Medical Officer of Health. Worse was to come: in December 1914, just after the start of the war, HM Inspectors of Schools produced a severely critical report, and Pyne was given until May 1916 to remedy "serious defects in the organisation of the school" and "unrest among the Staff" – or lose his job. Pyne's protests that "there are no suitable Masters to be had; a few old men are willing to fill up gaps for a term or two" may have convinced the Inspectors that the timing of

The Officers' Training Corps of 1914, one of the first pictures ever published in *The Portcullis.*

their visit, when virtually all the young staff were on military service, may not have been ideal! The re-inspection was continually postponed, and when it finally occurred in 1921, the report stated that, despite problems in English and mathematics, "the Headmaster was to be congratulated upon the social life of the School, the tone and discipline of which was good." However, the headmaster was getting old, and "the time was arriving when the School would require increased vigour and drastic reorganisation", part of which was a reduction in the number of teaching staff – "the present number of 22 full assistants is a very liberal allowance," said the report!

In addition to all the other difficulties, the supply of food to the school during the war was also becoming a problem. In 1917, in response to an official circular, the land bordering the "Football Field" was dug up, and boys started growing crops of food, with varying degrees of success. Just over half of all the boys in the school did voluntary agricultural work in the holidays, and there was even an agricultural camp near Salisbury in the summer of 1918, at which Warwick School pupils were hired out (for 2s per day) to local farmers. By 1915, all the Officer Training Corp's rifles and bayonets had been called in by the War Office. Nevertheless, that same year, the OTC and its band marched up to Stoneleigh, "playing throughout the entire length of the Parade". The OTC was actually on camp the day the First World War broke out in 1914, and the camp had to end early because "mobilisation deprived us of most of the cooks." Within a term, "the corps, masters and some boys" had subscribed to "200 dozen boxes of Safety Matches", which were to be despatched to the 1st and 2nd Battalions of the Royal Warwickshire Regiment.

The First World Word had a significant impact on the school in other, more sombre, ways. Hundreds of former pupils endured the horrors of the Western Front and beyond, and nearly ninety lost their lives. The war provided its own share of tragedy for the Pyne family. Their son Eric, so often pictured in half profile (which was not normally allowed in team photographs) and looking a touch arrogant, was killed when his ship was torpedoed off Italy in 1917. The Pynes erected the west window of the enlarged chapel in his memory; the window and the vestry were the gift of the headmaster in 1925, and the young designer FH Spear was commissioned to fill the three extra windows involved. As well as including the "unauthorised" school crest already discussed, Spear included in the main west window some personal quirks, such as spiders' webs and flies. Pyne read out from the altar steps each November 11th the names of all the fallen, but with the added poignancy of having to include the name of his own son. The names of 90 members of the school are inscribed on the First World War memorial in the chapel, which originally formed a parapet along the front of the balcony. Eighty-eight names are those of pupils, and two are of members of staff. The memorial was moved to its present position on the south wall in the early 1930s, "to enable boys in the gallery to be entirely seen from the chapel". Bad behaviour in the gallery is obviously not a modern phenomenon! It is also alleged that whenever a pretty girl among the guests in the balcony stood up and appeared above the stone parapet, the whole congregation of boys would turn and stare – in unison.

The figure of 90 names on the war memorial is extremely high, and this is because the school provided officer material, by and large, rather than rank-and-file soldiers. We are told that the average life expectancy of a junior officer on the Western Front was only a few weeks: they were the first to go "over the top" every time. This figure

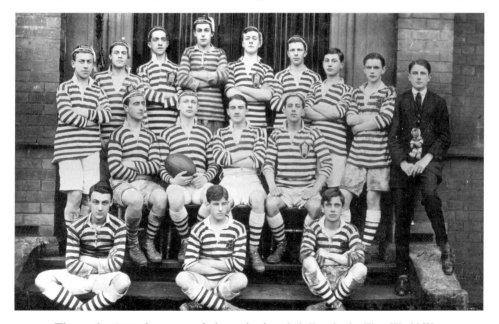

The tragic 1st XV of 1912-13, of whom nine lost their lives in the First World War.
Seated in the centre at the front is the headmaster's son, Eric Wilfred Pyne.
(Warwick School Archives)

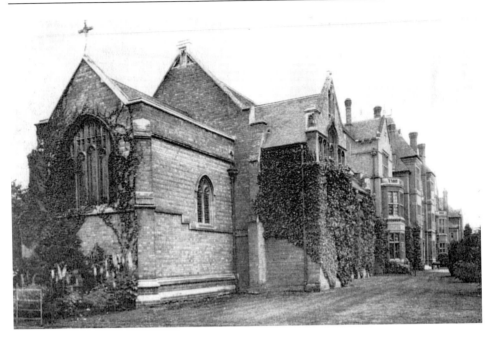

The chapel and east wing, photographed around 1920.
(Warwick School Archives)

of 90 pales into insignificance, however, compared with Rugby School's war memorial, which has nearly 700 names on it. There is, apparently, a rule of thumb that the number of names on a school's First World War memorial is approximately equal to the number of pupils in the school in 1914, and this certainly holds good for Warwick School. One of the most poignant photographs at Warwick School is that of the 1912-13 1st XV: nine of the players did not survive the conflict. Neither should we forget the five old pupils of the school who died in the South African War, whose memorials, dated 1900 and 1905, are now on the wall of the chapel balcony.

At the end of the First World War, the Old Warwickian Association started raising funds for a statue of Edward the Confessor. This statue was eventually purchased (for a sum of nearly £40) and unveiled in 1924 by Sidney Flavel, and it still occupies an important niche in the entrance lobby of the school. The connection between King and School is somewhat tenuous, and the phrase "Chartered by King Edward the Confessor" has been quietly dropped from official literature, but his name is still used as the basis for several chapel services in the Michaelmas term each year. As the current Chaplain, Rev AW Gough, says, this is on the grounds that, almost alone amongst English monarchs, he was a truly worthy Christian.

Despite the "few old men" on the staff and the various crises besetting Pyne, the school thrived as never before during the war. Pupil numbers rose to 200 in 1916, and towards the end of the war this rate of growth accelerated to such an extent that the

Big School, pictured around 1920, showing the new interior decoration,
including Honours Boards.
(Warwick School Archives)

school doubled in size, to over three hundred. It can be seen from the complete set of
governors' minutes from this period (kept not by the school, but by the County
Record Office) that, starting in October 1914, "Elementary School boys who had
been successful at the examination held by the County Council" were awarded scholarships equal to the full value of the day-boy fees – 11 guineas. There were eight such
free-place boys in 1914, rising to 26 by 1919. The grant from the County Council
increased in proportion: it was raised from £900 to £1,200 in 1912, and by 1918 to
£2,200. The awarding of free places at the school continued for the next 60 years or
so: up to half of all entrants by 1957 were free-place boys, and this practice did a great
deal to alter the social mix of the pupils. The change to include the working class
during the First World War is reflected in the parental occupations listed (in MM Clark's
shorthand) in the admissions books. Pressure on space meant that new classrooms had
to be built quickly, and in 1918 the governors granted £400 towards a range of
ramshackle buildings, named "New Buildings", which were erected on the end of the
Engineering Workshop. This row of buildings suffered the indignity of a hole ("The
Wynd") being knocked through it in order to gain access to the 1957 Science Block,
and was only finally demolished in 1974.

At the same time as the post-First World War influx of pupils came the introduction of the Burnham Scale of staff salaries, which had the immediate effect of consid-

erably increasing the wage bill. As a direct consequence of this, there was a serious financial adverse balance (of £5,701) in 1921.

Pupil reminiscences from this period of the school's history are extremely rare. One pupil from this time who did contribute was CH Chattaway, who attended the school from 1919 to 1923. Just before he died in December 1997, he wrote:

> I started at Warwick in 1919. We had to wear a school uniform of a black jacket, long grey trousers and a small navy blue cap with a badge comprising a portcullis in silver braid with a crown on top. The prefects had a gold braid portcullis. All boys under sixteen and below five feet six inches in height were required to wear an Eton Collar outside the jacket. It was high and wide and extremely uncomfortable in hot weather.
>
> The examinations we sat, the Oxford Junior and Senior certificates and Matriculation, which was essential for admission to a university, required passes in all subjects. Attendance at school rugby and cricket matches was compulsory, with prefects taking a roll call beforehand. The games were usually on a Saturday afternoon following morning school. Boys were forbidden to go to the Warwick Mop, a fair held in the Market Square in the autumn, but many of us did go, disguised to avoid being seen by masters on patrol.
>
> I especially enjoyed my three years in the school's Officer Training Corps, often being chosen as "scout" on field days. I also recall when the OTC was part of the guard of honour in Warwick for the visit of the Prince of Wales (later Edward VIII) on a day when the temperature was in the eighties and he was over half an hour late.

The dining room, pictured around 1920, showing the completed oak subscription panels.
(Warwick School Archives)

The chapel gallery, as originally designed with the War Memorial along the balcony,
photographed in 1925.

We happen to know quite a lot about the late 1920s at Warwick School through the
efforts of another OW, Dennis Castle, who, in 1983, set down in print what he called
"an unpublishable history of Warwick School" and gave it to Simon Wheeler, then
Head of History. Dennis Castle's recall of events, locations of rooms, names of pupils
and names of staff is truly excellent, and his good memory enabled him to become a
professional actor in later life. He was a boarder at the school right at the end of Pyne's
reign and the very beginning of Riding's, and although he was only at the school for
fewer than three complete years, he was very proud of it, eventually becoming
President of the Old Warwickians. The exterior of his work, a shabby yellow folder, is
fairly unpromising, but the interior is packed with photographs, reminiscences, bills,
his chemistry exercise book – and some allegations that were the reason he called his
account unpublishable. It has been very difficult to prove that much of what Dennis
Castle wrote is actually wrong, so we have to assume that the vast majority is right.
He describes life as a boarder as being dominated by food – or lack of it. "Spinach
with everything," he says – and, indeed, so much spinach was grown at the school
that the plants were still thriving in the headmaster's kitchen garden 50 years later.
Bread and butter was called "scratch", he tells us, precisely because that's exactly
what Mrs Pyne, supervising the cooks, did with the butter. Chapel was, for him, a

dreary place of worship on winter nights. He managed to get the job of organ-pumper, which meant that he could hide and read a book during the interminable sermons. When he arrived in 1926, the practices of issuing free midday beer for the senior boys, and fagging, had only just been stopped, although they had been going on for at least the previous 50 years. Pipe-smoking was quite popular among the senior boys (in their studies), but the junior boys had to be content with going behind the Red Barn for their Woodbines – except for away matches, when some of them lit up with a vengeance:

> Away matches for the Under 15 rugger side were happy memories. In the charge of a master we would visit Coventry, Wolverhampton and other venues, by rail of course. There, after the match, we would be allowed to go to a cinema and return to Warwick in time for lights out. Some bolder than myself would wear trilby hats, smoke in the carriage, usually with the master's full knowledge, and act like little Humphrey Bogarts, even to using strange dialogue. Hats seemed to change their personalities. Frankly they looked what they were, dressed-up schoolboys, but the hat was supposed to lure the girls – which I cannot remember ever meeting beyond cinema usherettes who would treat us as the kids we were. We were, of course, aping the first team, who all wore trilbies on away matches – but they could get away with it, with Oxford bags to match, pipes and cigarette holders. They always returned long after lights out!

Dennis Castle records that between 1927 and 1928 the school was over-run with rats: "They came along the hot water pipes, ate the tongues from your boots and shoes and scurried about the dormitories to cheers from the boys." The rat-catcher who was called in caused rats to die in all sorts of unfortunate, inaccessible places, including under the masters' seats in chapel. The smell was appalling, apparently.

Apart from the Engineering Workshop, the most obvious structural legacy of Pyne's time at Warwick is the pavilion. JP Way's pavilion was destroyed by fire in December 1924, having been moved from its original location at the end of the First World War. It was then discovered that the pavilion had not been insured, so a new one was built, by subscription, in 1927. It came complete with a fine turret-clock, made by Evans of Birmingham, and a 1-cwt bell, dated 1693, which used to be Warwick Market bell, and which still rings out today. The complicated system of wires, pulleys and underground metal pipes necessary to get a clock designed for use in a church tower to operate in a single-storey wooden pavilion has to be seen to be believed! As well as having a new pavilion built, Pyne also dramatically enlarged the playing fields.

In 1926, Pyne arranged for Big School to be equipped with a stage, allowing dramatic productions to be given on the premises rather than in the towns of Warwick or Leamington. A very successful run of performances of *Richard II* in the County Theatre (which was situated at the far end of St Nicholas Church Street, Warwick) in

The Birmingham-made Evans turret clock in the pavilion.
(GN Frykman)

1924 must have convinced him of the benefits of having proper drama facilities at the school, and performances of Shakespeare plays continued to be a regular feature in Big School, with younger boys playing women's parts. Pyne had encouraged the performance of these plays right from the start of his headmastership and produced several of them himself. In 1927, he appealed for money to equip the roof corbels of Big School with busts, "about two feet high", of famous people, at a cost of five guineas each. The list is surprisingly eclectic: Beethoven, Chatham, Cromwell, Dante, Descartes, Goethe, Kepler, Lincoln, Mazzini, Michelangelo, Plato, Wellington and Wycliffe. These were to join the busts of Garrick, Livingstone, Newton and Shakespeare which had already been installed.

Staff turnover under Pyne was, at times, fairly high. This was especially true during the First World War, but it seems that very few staff stayed for their whole career. Mention has already been made of MM Clark and AK Blackall, but seven other Pyne appointees deserve inclusion here for their very long service on the staff. AD Hainworth, a Classicist, ran the Junior House and served from 1907 to 1938. TH Bumpus, the Head of Modern Languages, who started in 1911, also retired in 1938. KStC Carruthers, the Senior Science Master, served from 1915 to 1939, and his departmental colleague, Rev HE Cullis (a pupil under Pyne at the King's Middle School from 1898 to 1905), taught science and mathematics from 1921 to 1954 and was appointed Honorary Chaplain on his retirement. He had the misfortune to suffer

The staff of 1927.

Back Row: Major DG Pearman, CT Freeman, AS Adams, Rev HE Cullis, RAF Mears
Middle Row: AS Wolstencroft, JL Lees, unknown, HF Browne, T Nichol, WD Canham, JW Holmes,
LH Robinson, PNG Whitlam, HE Gibbs
Front Row: AK Blackall, Miss E Roberts, JA Bingham, TH Bumpus, MM Clark, HS Pyne, AD
Hainworth, KStC Carruthers, Rev RGE Bowers, Rev WN Thomas, ER Jones
(DSV Castle)

a serious injury involving concentrated sulphuric acid in an explosion in the chemistry laboratory in 1946. AS Wolstencroft taught languages from 1922 to 1958, and Major DG Pearman (who had seen service at Gallipoli in the First World War, and who had been ADC to Lawrence of Arabia) ran PE and games from 1923 to 1957. Mention must be made of the Curator and physics technician, Philip Noel Garvey Whitlam, who worked at the school for a magnificent forty-four years, from 1920 to 1964, and whose nickname graduated from "Pissy" in the 1920s to the more polite "Peewit" as he got older, and the rather less prominent Skelsey, the chemistry "lab boy" and Tuck Shop manager, who was finally granted the honour of being described as Mr Skelsey when he had completed fifty years' service to the school in 1970.

Despite the presence of an increasing number of archives from this period, it is extremely difficult to determine what was actually taught, or when. Dennis Castle very helpfully quotes his 1927 L4b timetable, which is worth reproducing in full:

Monday	Fr	Science	Geom	Arith	Div	Gym	Maths
Tuesday	Lit	Singing	Eng	Hist	Alg	Fr	OTC
Wednesday	Geom	Grammar	Practical sci........		Rugger............................		
Thursday	Fr	Literature	Gym	Sci	Hist	Arith	OTC
Friday	Alg	Lit	Woodwork..........		Draw	Fr	Geog
Saturday	Music	Gram	Rep	Geog	Rugger...........................		

Mr Arthur Skelsey, who completed 50 years service to the school in 1970, serving boys
in the school Tuck Shop in 1963.
(Photo-Reportage Ltd)

By the 1980s, Castle had forgotten what "Rep" meant, but it seemed to be an all-
encompassing weekly test, supervised by MM Clark – perhaps it stood for "repetition". The heavy emphasis on mathematical subjects will be noted, as will the absence
of compulsory Latin for this year-group. There is no mention of a mid-morning
break, although there probably was one, and Castle was set 15 pieces of homework
per week.

A tantalising glimpse of what was taught at Warwick School at this time can be
gained from an extraordinary set of internal examination papers, donated to the
school in 2002 by the sister of John Swift, the boy who took them in the upper fourth
(Year 8, boys aged 12 to 13) in the summer of 1922. Sample questions (spelling
mistakes included) are given below:

Algebra: Simplify $\dfrac{3x^2 - 7x + 2}{2x^2 - 5x - 3} \times \dfrac{x^2 - 9}{9x^2 - 6x + 1}$

How many lbs of tea at 1/6 and at 2/6 a lb must be mixed to make a
box of 200lbs worth altogether £18?

Arithmetic: Find the cost of fencing a square field of 22½ acres at 3s 6d per yard.

Find the available Assets in an Estate where the Liabilities are £1120.9.4 and the Dividend paid is 8/9 in the £.

Some articles are bought at three pence a dozen and sold at sixpence a score. What is the gain or loss per cent?

Geometry: Prove that the angle at the centre of a circle is twice an angle at the circumference standing on the same arc. AB is an arc of a circle subtending a right-angle at the centre of the circle, and P is any point on the arc AB; find the size of the angle APB.

French: Write out ten lines of French repetition.

Give the French for (1) an hour ago (2) it is raining (3) to take shelter (4) 15 years old (5) in spring (6) to know by sight (7) the elbow (8) the finger (9) the ear (10) I have a sore throat.

Physics: What do you mean by unit of heat, specific heat? 200 gms of copper (sp. ht. = 0.1) is heated to 100°C & placed in 100 gms of alcohol at 8°C contained in a copper calorimeter weighing 25 gms & the temp rises to 28.5°C. Find the specific heat of the alcohol.

Chemistry: How would you prove the hydrogen and oxygen are in water?

Name & discribe each of the substances in the equation
$NaOH + HCl = NaCl + H_2O$
What sort of reaction is this? What do the symbols & the equation convey to you?

Divinity: Narrate the Parable of the Sower.

Give the speaker, place and occasion of the following questions:
(a) Why reason ye because ye have no bread?
(b) Tell us when shall these things be?
(c) Why, what evil hath he done?

Literature: Describe in detail the Casket scene in "The Merchant of Venice".

Describe the character of Shylock and give illustrations from the play.

Write short notes on:
(a) The Lass of Lochrozan (b) Sir Patrick Spens (c) Lady Clare (d) "Diverus" and Lazarus.

The chemistry laboratory as it existed on the ground floor of the original 1905
Science Block, pictured around 1917.
(Warwick School Archives)

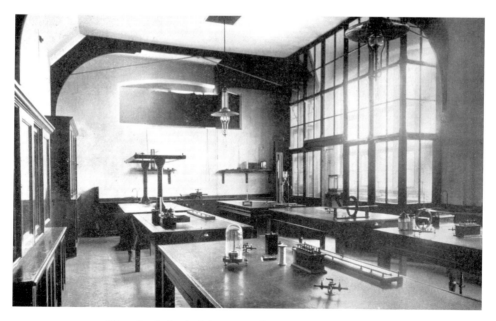

The school physics laboratory, photographed around 1917.
(Warwick School Archives)

WEMK Allander, who joined the school from Ireland as a boarder at the age of eight in May 1926, and who left in 1932, gave his recollections of Pyne in a letter to the author in April 2004:

> To me he was a remote figure, although our dormitory was in the top of his house. He seemed to rule with the cane. Every Monday the "cosh list" came round, of those he wanted to see whose work was unsatisfactory. Prefects were allowed to cane for breakfast lateness.

The financial system used by the school from 1906 onwards seems to be that the day-boys paid their fees to the Bursar and were subsidised by the Charity Commission and by grants from the Education Department, while the boarders paid their fees, which were five times that of the day-boy fees, direct to the headmaster. Day-boy fees in the 1920s were £18 per year (worth less than £1,000 in 2003), while boarding fees were £72, plus the £18 tuition, per year (between £4,000 and £5,000 with extras). It seems certain that Pyne did very well financially from this arrangement – rather better than he was prepared to let on. There were, for example, 146 boarders in 1921, and figures show that the headmaster was allowed to keep £54 of the £72 boarding fee – so the less he fed the boarders, the more profit he could make.

The front of the school, pictured around 1920.
(Warwick School Archives)

Dennis Castle (on the right) and a friend, WJ Bourne, sitting on the horse-drawn roller in May 1928. The height of his friend gave him the freedom not to wear the hated Eton Collar.
(DSV Castle)

As early as 1910, Pyne wrote to the governors that he was "desirous of avoiding if possible the necessity for submitting to the Governors accounts showing the expenses of the Boarding Establishment and the amount of profit resulting from the Boarders", on the grounds that they were inextricably linked to his own domestic expenditure. There is the distinct possibility that, for Pyne, the money just poured in, with very little checking by the governors, despite his telling them as late as 1927 that he made "practically no profit on the boarders". He made so much, in fact, that, before he retired, he commissioned an architect-designed Tudor-style retirement mansion, Sheen Lodge, opposite Sheen Gate, Richmond Park, "complete with ingle-nooks, a vast hall and a musicians' gallery" – and two acres of land. We know this because the architect's son was none other than Dennis Castle! In one of the lantern slide shows which Pyne used to give, he inadvertently included a shot of this mansion, which was ready well before he retired, and covered up his mistake by saying that it was a shot of an old Surrey manor house. Unfortunately, Dennis Castle's father, the architect, was also in the photograph... Young Dennis's squeak of recognition must

HS Pyne (left), AHB Bishop (centre) and the Senior Prefect,
NT Clarke, at the 1940 Prize Giving and Speech Day.

have seriously alarmed Pyne, who was desperate to keep the secret of this property
from becoming known. Indeed, in 1933, the governors minuted: "The Governors
should reserve the right of seeing the Headmaster's annual Boarding House profits."
Pyne never lived in the house, but sold it – it was later occupied by Rudolf Nureyev,
among others. The original Sheen Lodge, incidentally, had been given by Queen
Victoria to Sir Richard Owen, the scientist who coined the term "dinosaur", in 1852.

Dennis Castle alleges that Pyne's departure from Warwick School was a little
earlier than planned, following a disagreement with HM Customs after a weekend
visit to France. The disagreement, he said, concerned goods (probably antiques) that
Pyne had in his car and which he shouldn't have had! At all events, Pyne gave his
notice to the governors in the summer of 1927 to leave that Christmas but then asked
for, and was granted, an extra term in office. To the public, he announced his retirement in *The Portcullis* of December 1927 and left at Easter 1928. He moved to
Warwick Cottage, Hythe, Kent, where he had a stained-glass window inserted,
featuring a caricature of him "treading the long road to Richmond" – his lost
mansion – as well as other Warwick memories. He came back in 1940, very much as
an elder statesman, to present the prizes, and again, in 1949, to oversee Alderman
Southorn presenting the portrait of him in Big School. He died in 1950.

16. A commercial Frith photograph of the River Avon in 1892, showing some of the new school buildings. (WCRO)

17. Francis Frith's 1892 photograph of the King's Grammar School. (WCRO)

18. The chalice and ewer given to the school on the occasion of the
completion of the chancel in 1893 by JP Way. (AW Gough)

19. Rev JP Way and Mrs Gertrude Way, photographed around 1895. (WCRO)

20. HS Pyne, the teaching staff and pupils of the King's Middle School, The Butts, in 1901. MM Clark is to the right, and AK Blackall two places to the left, of the headmaster. Mrs Pyne and the three children are looking out of an upper window. (Warwick School Archives)

21. The King's Middle School in 1902. Some of the staff and boys are those who transferred to the merged school south of the river in 1906. (Warwick School Archives)

22. An original colour photograph taken by HS Pyne of his wife, Hannah Huxley Pyne, around 1911. (Warwick School Archives)

23. Dennis Castle's school bill for the Lent term, 1927, showing the boarding fee paid directly to the headmaster. (Warwick School Archives)

Telephone No. 42.

Warwick School

To WARWICK SCHOOL

(Cheques to be made payable to H. S. PYNE).

Board and Tuition		30	0	0
Cab Fares, Railway Fares				
Luggage		4		
Cricket Flannels, Boots				
Football Jersey, Knickers, Boots				
Bathing Costume				
Gymnasium		10		
Chemist		6		
Boot Repairs				
Boot Laces				
Tailoring		2	6
Hair Cutting		3	4
Pocket Money			
Medical Officer and Sanatorium		10	6
	32	4	1

24. The chalice given to the school by AM Patrick in 1928, complete with its error-ridden Latin inscription. (AW Gough)

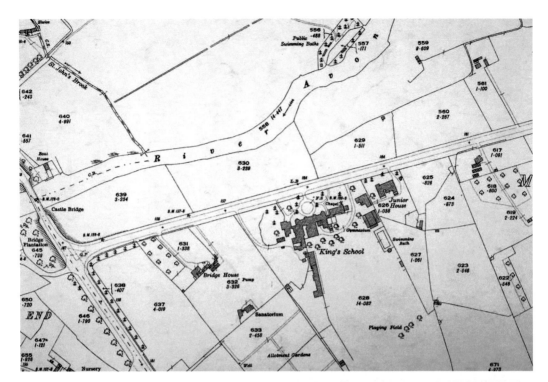

25. Part of the 1925
Ordnance Survey map of
Warwick, showing how the
school had developed since
the first such map in 1886.
(WCRO, photographed by
PJ O'Grady)

26. The east window of the
chapel, the centre light
being the 1902 memorial to
Cecil Meiggs.
(GN Frykman)

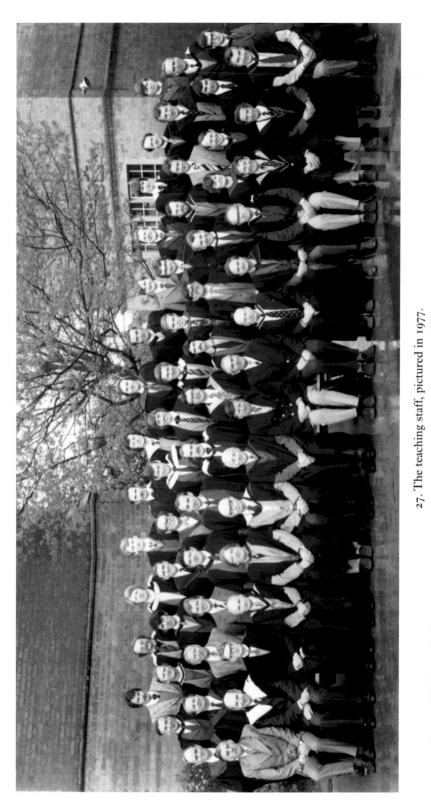

27. The teaching staff, pictured in 1977.

Top row: GK Jaggers, D Pirie, JA Cooper, P Smythe, WG Adams, PR Wales, AGM Parkes, A Wilkins, G Eve, C l'Anson, R Webb, JJ Rider, RJ Howes
Second row from the top: T Belton, Rev MM Robinson, AJ Reilly, TA Pritchard, DW Stooke, SH Woodward, C Aldred, D James, CG Daniel, R Hudson, PA Johnson, S Briton, IB Moffatt, RP Usherwood
Second row from the bottom: B Hornsby, D Keighley, H Robinson, B Emmerson, AH Hughes, D Nichols, MJ Green, J Haine, PJ O'Grady, JPC Bannerman, HE Collis, R Johnson, C Byfleet, AM Sparks, D Dews
Front row: PB Waterworth (bursar), PA Adcock, E Blackshaw, BW Young, RH Thornton, IJ Beeching (2nd master), PW Martin (headmaster), J Swindlehurst, J Marshall, H Sheppard, R Heaton, KG Brocklehurst, KW Freeborn, HE Owen, GJ Lane

28. The teaching staff, 1989.

Back row: Mrs H Barber, J Freeman, FAF Daniell (bursar), N Tully

Second row from the top: S Tidball, J Huitson, SR Letman, Mrs LM Haines, Rev J Davy, DJ Shield, P A Johnson, D Jones, S Morris, P Ashworth

Third row from the top: M Rodham, GR Ogdon, RR Cousins, I Setterington, S Wheeler, G Ward, GN Frykman, PA Snell, BT Meatyard, CH Watmough, RM Howard, Mrs J McBrien

Third row from the bottom: MM Fry, R Flintoff, RW Fair, EJ Kennett, JA Cooper, PJ O'Grady, JW Clift, Mrs EM Freeman, CJ Marshall, GS Wilson, LG Grimes

Second row from the bottom: WG Adams, JJ Rider, IB Moffatt, SH Woodward, DW Stooke, HE Collis, MJ Green, CG Daniel, JPC Bannerman, R Hudson, C I'Anson, AGM Parkes

Front row: TA Pritchard, D Nichols, AM Sparks, PS Heelis, PJ Cheshire (headmaster), GJ Lane, RH Thornton (2nd master), KW Freeborn, AH Hughes, B Emmerson, D James

(Gillman and Soame)

29. An exciting moment during the 1990 Junior School Activity Weekend. (GP Sainsbury)

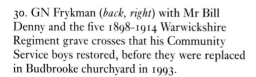

30. GN Frykman (*back, right*) with Mr Bill Denny and the five 1898-1914 Warwickshire Regiment grave crosses that his Community Service boys restored, before they were replaced in Budbrooke churchyard in 1993.

CHAPTER 15

George Albert Riding

According to Dennis Castle, George Riding was brought in rather hastily in the summer term of 1928, but he had, in fact, been appointed before Christmas. It is perhaps astonishing to learn that there were 65 applications for the post. Riding had been a housemaster at Rugby School and before that had studied at Manchester Grammar School, Queen Mary's School, Walsall, Manchester University (where he read English) and, after the First World War, at New College, Oxford, where he secured a First in Modern Languages. He started his teaching career as Senior English Master and games master at Penarth County School, Wales, and spent a year at Mill Hill School before war service with the Northumberland Fusiliers. According to his Curriculum Vitae, in 1917 he was wounded in the right shoulder in France as a Lieutenant and in the same year became the first non-medical Registrar in the country at the King's Lancashire Military Convalescent Hospital, where he was "responsible for the organisation of 3,000 beds". The contrast with Warwick, where, he said, "I have a boarding house with 70 boys," must have been profound. Of his war service, he said (in a radio broadcast in 1948), "I myself, schoolmaster turned soldier, saw men vomiting with fear, chattering with fear, unable to hold the contents of their bodies with fear. Time and again my own heart stood still with fear and I told myself honestly that I would give my right arm to be selling newspapers in Piccadilly Circus." Dennis Castle states that one of the consequences of Riding's war wound was that he flogged boys back-handed.

Riding was a literary specialist and a linguist, but, certainly by the end of his career (he was headmaster at Aldenham School for 16 years after he left Warwick), his main strength seems to have been oratory – some say that he was something of a relentless preacher. Indeed, in his CV he records that "I was the first lay-reader to be asked to preach in Coventry Cathedral" – his sermon in 1929 was on gambling. He undoubtedly saw himself as 'a new broom sweeping clean' and, according to Dennis Castle, seems to have been obsessed with the idea that boys engaged in vice at every opportunity! One of his first actions was to sweep away the boarding cubicles in order to create large, military-style open dormitories, with the new main dormitory being called the Elstow wing. This action did not go down well with the boys, who undoubtedly valued the small amount of privacy that their cubicles provided. Dennis Castle

The remarkable photograph, taken by Sydney Jennings (a sixth former) in 1923,
showing the Victorian boarding cubicles.
(Warwick School Archives)

remembers that the cubicles contained a wash-stand, a flap for a dressing-table, a bed and a chamber pot, and a red curtain could be drawn across the entrance. One extraordinary photograph of these Victorian cubicles has survived. It was taken by a pupil, Sydney Jennings, by flash-light in 1923. Although Sydney was only at the school for some of his sixth-form studies, he went on, among other things, to be President of the Veterinarian Society – and to marry one of MM Clark's daughters! An anecdote provided by Mr Christopher Riding, George Riding's elder son, in November 2003, gives another side to the sleeping arrangements. Apparently, on his first tour of the dormitories, accompanied by the Matron, the new headmaster spotted trunks underneath the beds and suggested that a more suitable place for them would be in a box-room. "You can't take the trunks out from there, Headmaster," said the Matron. "They're holding the beds up!"

Riding's own diaries (kindly loaned by his son Christopher in 2003) record that he made many visits to the school early in 1928, before taking up the post of Headmaster at Easter, and several entries are significant. Riding seems to have been in conflict with WW Vaughan, his headmaster at Rugby, almost to the day he left. His diaries reveal all too dramatically the run-down state of the school he was about to take over:

> 22 Feb, 1928: Went to see Pyne, but he could not do with us. Decided to buy the School House gear, & abolish the 10% basis: it seems the only way of getting the thing straight. Went over the building with Harcourt Ashford, General Wiggin and Mr Bailey, all governors. All disgusted. Went to see Clark.
>
> 20 Mar, 1928: Vaughan says I ought not to go to Warwick again this term.
>
> 31 Mar, 1928: Had the Boat Race broadcast in my English lesson – and got rent by Vaughan for it.
>
> 3 Apr, 1928: Off at 9-15 to Warwick, where we spent the day: some of the time with Pyne, handing over, some with Dean & the electrician & Miss Bamford. Very thrilled by the house & the garden.
>
> 5 Apr, 1928: Spent a hectic evening with Clark – a dreadful state of things revealed.
>
> 7 Apr, 1928: Arranged for a £1,000 – £1,500 overdraft.
>
> 10 Apr, 1928: Left Rugby for Warwick. Paid bills most of the morning. Spent the night & dined with Sir Michael Lakin, in great luxury.

As mentioned previously, incoming headmasters could rent from the governors the contents of the boarding house for 10% of their total value per year. The "disgust" of the governors may have been a response to the rat infestation.

Riding's first term, as, indeed, the whole of his time at Warwick, had its fair share of incidents. He had had set up for himself an accounting system – the school's first? – but found after a term that the accountant "was stinging me badly." These diary extracts give what must be a rare outlook on the busy and varied life of any head-master, let alone one from Warwick:

18 May, 1928: I found Mr Patrick waiting for me in my study with a very lovely silver chalice & paten. Went to see the Doctor again who is quite pleased though he says the slight murmur persists.

21 May, 1928: A masters' meeting which went very well, I think. Fortnightly reports coming in.

11 June, 1928: Beat Coulson, reported by Bailey, for using bad language. In the afternoon went with A[ideen] to the Girls' Sports where she gave away the prizes and made a speech, badly dithering.

18 June, 1928: One of the maids, being given notice, drank half a bottle of poison, but recovered.

26 June, 1928: A rampagious day. Took Bumpus's French and found that he had set next to no prep & that this was badly done. Had them in at 4-30 & gave B. a dressing down for it.

Aideen Riding's extraordinary contribution to the history of Warwick School is discussed further below. TH Bumpus was no junior member of staff – he was the Head of Modern Languages! AM Patrick's gift of the chalice to the chapel, as well as the turret-clock which he had given for the new pavilion the previous year, is still in regular use, but, when examined closely in 2002, the Latin inscription on the chalice was found to be somewhat imperfect: indeed, as Mr Robert Hudson has remarked, there is an error in almost every word! Around the rim are etched the words: *Calicim salutaris accipiam et nomini domini in vocabo*, which Robert Hudson says should read: *Calicem salutarem accipiam et nomen domini invocabo*. The words come from the Catholic Latin mass, and mean: "I will take the cup of salvation, and I will call on the name of the Lord." It is astonishing to discover that this chalice was exhibited at the Royal Academy before being given to the school – maybe it did not have its inscription then, or perhaps the Royal Academy was devoid of Latin scholars!

Right at the start of the new school year, in September 1928, the headmaster's house was burgled, and the Ridings lost all their silver.

Dennis Castle's suspicions about Riding's attitude towards behaviour in dormitories are perhaps confirmed by a diary entry later that term:

1 Nov, 1928: Lloyd reported his dormitory for filthy talk. Beat Dickon, Ryter, Gilks & Wood & gave Capper a thumping imposition [lines].

Riding's concerns about the financial state of the school were soon much reduced, when MM Clark was able to give him, in November 1928, "wonderful figures about the heating and lighting for the last six months – a reduction from £240 to £90". Two months later, in February 1929, he was told that there was a profit of £313 on the previous term. "I raise Matron's salary to £100 a year," was his pleasing response.

The most dramatic period of Riding's headmastership came late in 1930, as his own diary reveals:

The open-plan Elstow dormitory created at the start of GA Riding's headmastership in 1928.
(Warwick School Archives)

8 November 1930: Wakened in the dark at 6.30 by crashing of glasses and boys
dashing about. Found the school on fire – all the Elstow dorm wing. All the boys
out safe. School brigade put it out and then the Town Brigade finished it off.
Breakfast in the gym only 5 mins late & piping hot. School as usual – except for
my lessons – police, insurance, newspapers &c. Assessors satisfied that fire due to
normal causes. A great thrill for everyone & everyone capital. Got the family
across to the Junior.

9 November 1930: Armistice Day Service at St Mary's. Some of the OTC in mufti,
uniforms being burnt.

10 November 1930: Wakened at 1.0 again by a fire alarm. This time left the family
in bed & dressed a bit. Boys all safe again; fire in Masters' Room & a second one
in Clark's room, quite independent. Dirty work suspected by self, Police and
Brigade. Table in middle of room burnt. Clark's key missing. Back to bed by 5.0
Breakfast & school an hour late. At breakfast began to make enquiries & suspected
Paul who was sick. Got all the evidence possible. From 2.30 till 11.0 Supt Wake
making investigations, & at 10pm got an admission of accident from Paul.
Everyone very jumpy & some boys in the san. Many enquiries.

What seems to have happened is that the boy took advantage of being sick in the "san" in order to wander around freely at night, stealing keys and causing multiple fires, including a giveaway blaze on a table in the middle of MM Clark's room. *The Portcullis* states that the boy (who was not named publicly at the time, his identity only becoming known to the author from the diary entry above in 2003) received immediate psychiatric care. With hindsight, Riding might have been able to foresee trouble: in March 1929, he had received a "beastly letter from Mrs Paul about her boy's illnesses" and, the following day, "saw Mrs Paul and spent an hour arguing pointlessly with her." George Pantry, who was at the school from 1928-1936, recalled the fires in an interview with the author in April, 2004, and mentioned, in particular, seeing the Warwick OTC boys march up the High Street without their uniforms the following day. He says that when the identity of the arsonist became known, other boys recalled that it was the very boy who had been spotted ringing the tower bell in alarm in the early hours of that Saturday morning. He also says that the boarders had been entertained by a film featuring a fire-raiser the previous evening.

The roof of the school had also caught fire in November 1910, but on that occasion the blaze was quickly put out by the School Fire Brigade, and the cause was found to be an over-heated flue.

Riding was responsible for a great deal of modernisation at the school. Being concerned about the physical fitness of the boys, he instituted compulsory whole-school 15-minute physical jerks every afternoon, "to rectify stooping and bad carriage", and was accordingly delighted at the corresponding increase in chest measurements of the boys. The extraordinary rise in the popularity of boxing as a school sport was also a feature of the Riding years. There was an appeal in an 1889 *Portcullis* which suggests that it had featured, to some extent, in Victorian times:

Pugilists who desire to revive boxing should make a start for themselves.

WT Keeling offered a "Boxing Class" in September 1905, and for years OTC cadets seem to have taken part in competitions whilst on camp, but it was only in 1930 that the sport featured officially at Warwick School. At first, inter-house competitions were organised, and then came fixtures against other schools, for example, a "boxing and shooting match" against Solihull School in 1934. Riding's successor, Eric Percival Smith, must have approved of the sport, since he extended it to the Junior School. The weights of contestants in the 1935 Junior School inter-house boxing competition varied from the heaviest section (over 6st 7lb, or 41kg) to the lightest (under 4st 7lb, or 28.5kg). There was only one competitor in that ultra-feather-erweight section, who therefore won without having to hit anybody!

Further progressive actions taken by Riding included re-founding the school orchestra and organising the official granting of the present school badge. Half the chapel choir was sacked, and he auditioned every boy in it. Pyne's habit of promoting every boy up to the next form over each summer was discontinued, and the school

The school Boxing VIII of 1935. On the left hand end of the middle row is DPR Scarr,
the fifth-form head boy appointed by Eric Percival Smith.
(Warwick School Archives)

reverted to the Victorian idea of promotion being dependent on academic merit. Riding started the tradition of Gilbert and Sullivan operettas being performed every few years, which lasted until the mid-1980s. In 1932, he built the toilet block and changing rooms (now the Bursary), and created a terrace by the swimming-pool for prefects and sixth-formers, soon to be known universally as "the Altar" – because on it "one becomes a burnt sacrifice," said Dennis Castle. Prefects were given gold braid to put on their caps; and monitors, or sub-prefects, received silver braid. Riding also created a new Tuck Shop out of Percival Brown's "large old bicycle shed". He founded a Scout Troop for 11- to 12-year-olds and created new houses in the Junior School – Drake, Nelson and Scott. He established Confirmation classes in the chapel, a Biology Garden and a "suitable uniformity of dress", by which he meant the abolition of Eton collars for the boys, and its substitution by a soft-collared blue jacket and waistcoat, with grey flannels, for weekday wear, and a totally blue suit for Sundays. During the mid-1930s, the school blazer with Riding's new badge on the front pocket came into use, and this has remained unchanged in design ever since. The original intention was to have the blazer just as summer wear, but since the Second World War blazers have been worn all year round. Riding encouraged the formation of the OW Rugger Club and compensated the members of the boarding house for the loss of their cubicles by "the provision of studies for all the boys in it". The number of boys in the school rose from 250 to over 300 during Riding's headmastership – but Pyne had managed to squeeze in nearly 400 only a few years before.

Harold B Robinson, who joined the school as a pupil in 1930, ending up as head boy, came back to teach in the Junior School from 1961 to 1982, latterly as Deputy Headmaster. Three years before he died (his funeral was held in the school chapel in 2002), he wrote:

> Hardly anyone came by car, many by bus, but the majority by bicycle. There were enormous bicycle sheds. Many of us cycled home for lunch. Every boy wore school uniform including a school cap, even the Upper Sixth wore a cap. On the last day of one's final term, it was traditional to throw one's cap into the river as one crossed Castle Bridge for the last time.

The first aerial photograph of the school, taken in 1931.
(Aerofilms Ltd)

"Nobby" Clark was not only Second Master, he was also the Bursar and ran the tuck shop and second-hand clothing store and taught shorthand after school for anyone interested in journalism. He had a perpetual rasping voice and was always clearing his throat.

George Riding was a tyrant. He made great use of the cane and was feared by almost everybody. In those days we had three-weekly orders. Assembly was held in Big School and the bottom boy in all the lower forms was caned before the whole school. Quite often it was the same boy time after time.

It is said that in order to keep the Earl of Warwick happy, the Bursar had to go to the castle weir after the end of every summer term and fish out as many caps as he could with a long pole. It is certainly true that no really old school caps seem to have survived – the donor of one of the two caps in the school archives told the author that it was his own particular act of rebellion against the school that he did *not* throw his cap into the river! From a different era altogether in the school archives is another rare survivor – a straw boater dating back to 1908.

Rev Bill Allander (Warwick School 1926–32) recalled the early years of Riding's headmastership in April 2004:

> Riding brought a much needed new discipline to the school. Trousers had to be a uniform grey. I remember coming back after a holiday with a lovely baggy light grey pair and was promptly told to go and change them.

George Pantry (Warwick School 1928–36) recalled that boarders from this time, if invited home to a day-boy's house for a meal on a Sunday, would "almost eat the table as well as the food". He also commented on the use of corporal punishment, particularly for bad behaviour on trains. It was apparently a Warwick School custom to slice off the leather straps holding the railway carriage windows in place, and repeated caning of "train boys" by the headmaster did little, he said, to stop the habit. The school secretary would go round on certain mornings with a list of boys the headmaster wanted to see, and this list was inevitably known, as it was in Pyne's day, as the "Cosh List".

In terms of administration, Riding started the General Purposes fund in 1928, which all headmasters since have used to finance items which don't fit into any other category. He applied for the school to become a Direct Grant school, but this was refused. He started the idea of entrance scholarships, re-introduced Greek and started "a museum of items directly connected with the school". Late in 1932 came the gift of "a complete outfit of crockery bearing the new school crest", some items of which have survived into the 21st century and are on display in the headmaster's house.

Riding felt strongly about the original school song and its rather dated Victorian words, and set about introducing the 1906 Latin *Floreat Domus*. Dennis Castle says

The December 1928 performance of Shakespeare's *Julius Caesar*.
This was one of the earliest productions on the new Big School stage.
(DSV Castle)

that after the Christmas 1928 school play, Shakespeare's *Julius Caesar*, the school sang the Latin song, as instructed, but the furious OWs who were present stuck to the 1892 English song, which they sang at the same time, and Riding was apoplectic with rage. He changed tack, however, re-wrote the words of the 1892 song and had large numbers of cards printed with his version of the words, marked *GAR 1931*. It is this version, rather than the original one (reproduced in this book), that OWs were singing at their dinner as late as 2003.

Earlier in the same term, the future Poet Laureate, John Masefield, was the guest of honour at the annual prize-giving. Riding relates the story proudly in his diary entry for that day:

> 20 Nov, 1928: My first Prize Giving. A glorious day for it & otherwise a complete success, I think. Spent the morning getting ready for it. School ended at 10-45, after which an assembly & rehearsal. Commemoration Service in the chapel at 2-15 after having the Governors to lunch in the School Dining Hall. John Masefield came to chapel & gave a wonderful address. Tea for all afterwards. All went swimmingly, except that some had to be turned away; & I had a gift of £100 for my Scholarship Fund.

Dennis Castle hints at events being fairly riotous on this occasion: "There were protests and Edward the Confessor was crowned with a chamber pot in his main hall niche." The protests may well have been due to the number of people not allowed into Big School – Masefield attracted a full house – rather than anything else. Masefield is reputed to have said, "I hope all you boys are happy here. I wasn't – I ran away!" However, his grand-daughter told Dennis Castle that it was not strictly true that he ran away: "They never caught him, because instead of taking to the road, he stole a punt and went down the Avon."

It was under Riding's headmastership that the first school trips abroad took place: in 1929, an expedition was mounted to Dunkirk, Brussels, Bruges and Ghent. After a similar trip in May 1930, however, it seems that the idea of school trips abroad was temporarily abandoned. Whether this was on account of the collision, in thick fog, between the ship carrying the Warwick School party and a German oil-tanker, or the subsequent, and supposedly more shocking, incident in which a boy was offered a "bière" instead of his "billet" in a café, is not made clear in *The Portcullis*. Pupils had to wait until 1935 for the next chance of a school trip abroad – and that was to some of the First World War battlefields.

George Riding – unwittingly, perhaps – stirred up a huge controversy when remarks he made at a meeting of the Church of England Men's Society, late in 1930, were widely interpreted as an accusation that padres in the First World War were guilty of cowardice. He rather lamely complained that he did not know that a reporter would be present, but the upshot was that columns of furious letters appeared in the local press just before Christmas that year. Even more controversial, as it was to turn out, was his marriage to Aideen Rolleston, daughter of TW Rolleston, the Irish author, and grand-daughter of Stopford A Brooke, poet and literary critic. Aideen was considerably younger than her husband, but the headmaster seemed to be bliss-fully unaware of the effect that she had on the boys. As their son Christopher related in 2003:

> Several old Warwick boys commented to my father in later years that they didn't at all mind being caned by him because the chair over which they were asked to bend was positioned in such a way that, as they received their punishment, they were able to study his photograph of my mother who was, after all, only a few years older than themselves as well as being extremely good-looking!

Apart from her duties in the boarding house, Aideen Riding became much more involved in school life in December 1929 when, aged 25, she acted in a school play, Shakespeare's *Twelfth Night*, having stepped in to replace a boy who was ill. Officially-sanctioned females were in very short supply, of course, and boys used to take women's roles, as in Shakespeare's own time. This performance must have been one of the first at Warwick School to have a real woman playing a woman's role, but, sadly, no photographs of this production seem to have survived. The 17-year-old boy who played Sebastian opposite Mrs Riding's Viola, Francis Gilbert Macaskie, went as

Mrs Aideen Riding on holiday in the early 1930s.
(C Riding)

far as publishing a love poem to her in the December 1929 edition of *The Portcullis* –
but did not, of course, put his name to it at the time, only admitting to his authorship
several years later. It is not clear when the headmaster realised the nature of the poem,
but by 1932 he was insisting that *The Portcullis* should have a permanent editor who
was a member of staff, an arrangement which persists to the present day.

"Cat" Macaskie went on to be Senior Prefect in the boarding house, Captain of the
1st XV and Captain of the 1st XI, and left the school in the summer of 1931. As a
Lieutenant Colonel during the Second World War, he was imprisoned by the Nazis
in Greece and condemned to death for spying, but managed to escape. After the war,
he became political adviser to the Regent of Greece, and was appointed to be the

The headmaster, GA Riding, and the senior prefect in the boarding house,
FG Macaskie, on the 1931 prefects' photograph.
(Warwick School Archives)

Balkan Correspondent of *The Times* in 1948, but, unfortunately, he died of sandfly fever at the beginning of 1952.

It has been claimed that Macaskie's relationship with Mrs Riding was more than a schoolboy crush, but, as Christopher Riding points out, Macaskie remained on friendly terms with both of his parents until he died, which makes the substance of the claim less certain. It is also true, however, that even while Mrs Riding was pregnant in 1930, "schoolboy tittle-tattle", as remembered by George Pantry in April 2004, meant that about 300 pairs of eyebrows were being raised, and direct comparisons were being made between events at the school and the astonishingly similar plot of John van Druten's initially banned play, *Young Woodley*. Written in 1925, this was eventually published in 1928 and was turned into an early "talkie" film, starring Frank Lawton and Madeleine Carroll, in 1930. The original ban was brought about due in part, it is claimed, to the fact that it was seen as an attack on the Public Schools of the day, but mainly because of the scandalous nature of the story-line – the relationship between a poetry-writing prefect and the young wife of his much older house-master.

A unique aspect of the Riding years was the appointment of a female Chair of Governors late in 1931. Elfrida Marjorie, Countess of Warwick, served in this capacity until 1933. She was the sister of the future Prime Minister, Anthony Eden, and the daughter-in-law of Frances, Lady Warwick, the Socialist wife of the 5th Earl. In the official biography of Lady Warwick, who died in 1938, Marjorie (as she preferred to be known) is described as "a sour and waspish woman", which cannot have gone down too well with the governing body or the headmaster. One of the governors' principal worries at this time was a feeling of loss of independence from the County Council, having surrendered the Board of Education's Substantive Grant in 1926. A particular concern was the issue of free places to local Elementary School pupils. About six Elementary Minor Scholarships per year were awarded, but, in an extraordinary statement, the governors minuted: "This has meant that the school has had to find, from the very inferior remnant of material, entrants up to the number of 25%. This means, of course, that the school is heavily weighted with inferior material." Figures were produced to show that boys were leaving at 17 or earlier, having stayed, on average, four years at the school. In 1932, the governors applied for a Direct Grant and tried to get the number of free places reduced to 15% and the fees raised to £25 per year (£28 outside the county), but all of this was rejected by the Board of Education.

The 1933 OTC inspection. PNG Whitlam is on the extreme left, with the headmaster, GA Riding, looking on. The inspecting officer, General Archibald Wavell, was to achieve considerable prominence in the Second World War.

Whether it was for personal reasons, whether because his naturally combative style was beginning to grate within the school and in the towns of Warwick and Leamington, whether it was reaction to his extraordinary habit, for a headmaster, of taking a nap after lunch, or whether it was that he merely regarded his tenure at Warwick as a stepping-stone, George Riding was soon applying for posts at larger, more prestigious institutions. In his application for the headmastership of Cranleigh School in 1931, he quotes Sir Michael Lakin Bt (his Chairman of Governors at the time) as saying: "He has shown himself to possess great organising power and an unbounded energy which has enabled him to do very much for the improvement of an ancient school." In a similar vein, the Bishop of Coventry said: "I have seen the school change from a lethargic institution into a vigorous and bracing place." When he applied for the headmastership of Felsted in 1932, and Wellingborough School early in 1933, his new Chair of Governors, the Countess of Warwick, signing the testimonial in a somewhat masculine way as "EM Warwick", said: "I must whole-heartedly support his application, even though his success will deprive us of the best headmaster Warwick School has had in the memory of any of the governors." Later that year, he was successful in his application for the headmastership of Aldenham School, and the family left Warwick in the summer of 1933. After an extremely active retirement in Mevagissey, Cornwall, during which he maintained an enthusiastic correspondence with JA Strover, Headmaster from 1977 to 1988, George Riding died in February 1982, at the age of 93. Aideen Riding lived to a similar age, dying in 1997.

CHAPTER 16

Eric Percival Smith

Eric Percival Smith was Warwick School's shortest-serving headmaster – he stayed only three years (1933–1936). He was educated at Tonbridge School and Gonville and Caius College, Cambridge, where he studied Classics and history. After teaching at Rossall School, he became Headmaster of Bolton School before coming to Warwick in 1933. Being unmarried, he installed his mother to look after the boarding house. He had serious health problems, even while at Warwick (he was absent for the whole of the Lent term, 1934), and died in 1938.

There are very few written records from Percival Smith's era, but we do know that one of his head boys was Arthur Godfrey Kilner Brown, later a member of the winning 4 x 400 metres relay team at Hitler's 1936 Olympic Games and eventually a headmaster himself. Godfrey Brown's self-written "Valete" ran to one whole column of the December 1934 *Portcullis*. Incidentally, it seems an extraordinary coincidence that not only did Godfrey's son John lecture the author in physical chemistry at Oxford in the mid-1970s, but he was also working for a PhD at Cambridge a few years earlier with the author's Head of Department, Bob Fair.

Also mentioned in the December 1934 issue of *The Portcullis* is the creation of a new form – The Remove. It was classified as "a superior upper fifth" but was abolished four years later, only to re-surface after the war. Almost as soon as Percival Smith arrived at the school, he changed Riding's "fortnightly marks" into a "half-term order" – an arrangement which has basically persisted to the present day. In addition, internal exams were to be taken at Christmas rather than Easter. In contrast to his predecessor, who appointed (and therefore replaced) sixteen members of staff in his five years as headmaster, Percival Smith's reign must have seemed somewhat more peaceful, for he only appointed two.

Percival Smith was different from his predecessor in many ways, not least in his forward-looking habit of using boys' first names. George Pantry said in April 2004 that boys were completely unprepared for this – it was unheard of in the 1930s. George was also somewhat taken aback, when watching a cricket match in Canterbury in 1934, to spot his headmaster returning from a holiday in France with a 14-year-old pupil of the school.

There are several more aspects of this short headmastership which are memorable. Bill Grimes, who was at the school from 1930 to 1938, said in 2003 that Percival Smith created a sensation when he appointed a boy who wasn't a sixth-former to be head boy. Douglas Patrick Renforth Scarr, the pupil in question, left form Va in 1936, aged 19, only managing his School Certificate, but he was a fine athlete and boxer. In 1936, the school acquired a ciné camera, and some remarkable 16mm footage was shot. The man who shot most of the film that is still in the school archives was PNG Whitlam, the physics technician, who was officially called the Curator (his predecessors having been called upon to look after the school museum). Mr Whitlam shot mostly outdoor scenes, especially athletics, swimming and school CCF camps; about 90 minutes of footage dating from 1936 to 1940 have survived, followed by about 2½ hours of footage from 1947 onwards. One of the most striking features of the footage from the late 1930s is an attitude towards health and safety that is apt nowadays to cause gasps of astonishment from modern viewers – boys standing in the path of javelins being thrown, pole-vaulting with a mere sand-pit to land in, one boy standing on another's shoulders while diving into the pool from the spring-board, and so on. In 1939, Whitlam managed to acquire some 16mm amateur colour film, which he used to striking effect until it was used up at Easter 1940. The camera was last used in the early 1970s by Alan Reilly, to film two educational Mediterranean cruises.

PNG Whitlam's successful floodlighting of the chapel in 1935, to celebrate the silver jubilee of King George V.

Headmaster Eric Percival Smith at the 1935 OTC inspection.
The inspecting officer is Lt Gen Sir Arthur Phayre.
(Warwick School Archives)

Technological advances seemed to be the province of the forward-looking Wireless Society, led by PNG Whitlam, which, although it complained that AC mains (necessary for easily transforming voltages) was not yet available at the school in 1935, reported at the end of 1934 that "some successful reception of Television has taken place." By 1935, the Chess Club had 52 members, the OTC had 152, and the Scouts had 18. Culture was very much to the fore in the mid-1930s, as a result of the presence in the school of two pupils, Eric Hope and Denis Matthews, who went on to become internationally-renowned concert pianists. The school's experiment, in the summer of 1935, of broadcasting the whole of the Commemoration Service from the chapel to a crowd in Jubilee Avenue (The Limes), and then holding Speech Day out of doors, was no doubt aided and abetted by the electronic wizardry of PNG Whitlam – and totally ruined by a violent and drenching thunderstorm.

Percival Smith actively encouraged boys to have some sort of political awareness, and he very much supported the "League of Nations Union", formed in 1932, which had attracted 200 boys as members by 1935. A whole series of outside speakers was brought in, and social events no doubt lightened the atmosphere somewhat. To reinforce the study of politics, a large party of boys visited some of the First World War battlefields in April 1935. Political debate must have intensified when Percival Smith allowed a long article in defence of fox-hunting to be published in the December 1935 *Portcullis*. Membership of both the LNU and the OTC was encouraged and was not seen to be contradictory; the OTC reported a total of 140 members in 1934. Out of this political hotbed came Fred Mulley, a pupil at the school from 1929 to 1936 (and both Chairman of the LNU and a member of the OTC) and later a Labour Minister for Aviation, Defence Minister, Minister of Transport and Education Secretary. Fred Mulley's moment of glory, at least according to the media, came in 1978 when he was photographed, apparently asleep, while seated next to the Queen during an RAF fly-past! Another keen member of the LNU, but of a completely different political persuasion, was JCC Jordan, a pupil at the school from 1934 to 1942. Better known as Colin Jordan, in 1959 he was appointed National Organiser of the neo-fascist British National Party, and in 1962 he was imprisoned for organising a paramilitary group, losing his job as a Coventry schoolteacher. He was still politically active as recently as 2001, when, aged 78, he was reported as objecting unsuccessfully to the creation of a multi-faith sanctuary in the remote Scottish village where he lived.

One of the longest-lasting effects of Percival Smith's reign is that he started production of the Blue Book, which has continued uninterrupted ever since. Indeed, apart from its thickness and the fact that it is a bit faded, the first of Percival Smith's Blue Books, dating from September 1934 and trumpeted in *The Portcullis* as "a veritable gold mine of information", looks remarkably like those published 70 or so years later. Confusingly, the school calendar, printed on card, seems to have been called the Blue Book before 1934, and is referred to as early as 1899, when it seemed to contain certain school rules – perhaps for games fixtures. The publication of termly Blue Books was halted in September 2003 in favour of a yearly issue, with termly calendar inserts. Another continuing activity, which began under Percival Smith in 1935, is the playing of badminton as a school sport. When Percival Smith left the school, he donated a magnificent carved oak organ screen to the chapel in memory of his mother. This complemented splendidly the new oak benches for the front seats in the chapel, which had been put in place in 1934.

CHAPTER 17

Arthur Henry Burdick Bishop –
The First Ten Years

Arthur Henry Burdick Bishop grew up in Cornwall and attended Callington Grammar School. He then served in the army in France, Egypt and Palestine from 1917 to 1920, before going up to Jesus College, Oxford, where he took First Class Honours in Natural Science in 1924. He was a very able chemist, and his two published text-books (*Introduction to Chemistry* and *An Elementary Chemistry*, both written with GH Locket) were widely used throughout the country. His teaching career started at Westminster College, Oxford, but he was soon appointed to the post of Senior Chemistry Master at Radley, and thence to the headmastership of Magdalen College School, Brackley.

In 2003, Bill Grimes (Warwick School 1930–1938) recalled that Bishop said in his first assembly in Big School in 1936: "All my life I've wanted to be Headmaster of Warwick School, and now I've got here, I'm going to stay here!" This remark made more sense when it was discovered that Bishop had applied for the headmastership when it fell vacant in 1933, but had lost out when Percival Smith was appointed. He was certainly not expecting the chance of applying again quite so soon. Like his two predecessors, Riding and Percival Smith, Bishop was offered a salary of £800 (a sum worth about £41,000 in 2003), together with whatever profits he could make from the boarding house. Almost his first action was to use the Junior House, which had been closed in 1935, as additional classrooms and cloak-rooms. Also in his first term, he gathered the whole school together to listen to the funeral of George V on the wireless in Big School. Within two years, he had arranged for the front of the school to be flood-lit – a short-lived improvement in view of the proximity of the Second World War.

By the following year, he had modified the school telephone network (which still had the number Warwick 42), so that it had five extensions, and had a call-box installed (Warwick 292) "for personal calls for the convenience of Masters and boys". In 1953, a separate internal telephone network was installed, and this system lasted until the mid-1980s.

In 1938, the Junior House was re-opened as a preparatory school, although, it has been suggested, there had been an unwritten agreement that Arnold Lodge would be

1277   WARWICK SCHOOL   PAN-AERO PICTURES
                                                         KINGSTON-ON-THAMES

An aerial photograph of the school, taken in 1937.
The vegetable garden to the west of New Buildings is clearly visible.
(Warwick School Archives)

the feeder prep-school – the reason given for the closure of the Junior House in 1935. There were 70 new boys in September 1938, mostly in the Junior School. Junior boarders arrived in January 1939.

The threat of war led to the formation of an ARP committee in 1938, and boys "volunteered" to help assemble huge quantities of gas masks in the Corn Exchange in Warwick – for which effort a handsome certificate (which still survives) was awarded to the school. As is made clearer later, the boys had a choice of sorts – either assemble gas masks or dig the air-raid shelters!

School trips abroad continued in the late 1930s, as did exchanges of pupils. Finnish, Danish and German pupils spent some time at Warwick School throughout the 1930s, at least until the war started! In April 1937, there was a school excursion to Norway, and the following year there was a trip to Switzerland.

Early in 1939, Bishop was elected to the Head Masters' Conference (HMC), and a young man called Felix Dugdale was appointed to the staff, as Head of Modern Languages. He served as Second Master from 1954 to 1969 and retired in 1970, although he had been suffering from angina for some time before this. He died in 1991, aged 83.

In 1938, according to reminiscences from Roger Smith (Warwick School 1937–1944) in 2004, the whole school lined up, by arrangement, to view an army unit called

The Corps, led by Major DG Pearman, marching out of the White Gates in 1939. The original frontage of the biology laboratory can be seen, as well as the lean-to Tuck Shop.

The holiday camp run by AHB Bishop on the school field in August 1940.
(Bishop family photo)

Major DG Pearman (centre), Lt PNG Whitlam and the Officers and NCOs of the 1939 OTC.
(Warwick School Archives)

"The Modern Army" – Bren Gun carriers, small tanks, and so on – which was slowly parading past, along the Myton Road. At the same time, a postman, who had been emptying the box opposite the school (the post-box is still there), stepped out into the road, and the whole school saw him get run over and killed by a lorry that was overtaking the military convoy. The Head of School House, RTC Worsley, was called to give evidence at the inquest.

Roger Smith made some further pertinent observations on the early years of Bishop's time. For whatever reason, be it the legacy of Percival Smith's benevolence or otherwise, bullying of junior boys was unpleasantly rife, and Bishop had to expend a great deal of energy on stamping out initiation ceremonies such as throwing new boys into the swimming pool – irrespective of whether they could swim or not. Roger Smith also commented on corporal punishment: official canings by the headmaster for serious offences were still part of the normal life of Warwick School, but other staff – T "Scotty" Nichol was mentioned, along with his "blood-stained blackboard compass" – saw fit to assault boys in a way that would now render them liable to prosecution. Prefects were allowed to administer three whacks of a slipper, without the offence or the punishment being recorded. Roger Smith also revealed a canny way of involving boys who were useless at games in compulsory sports sessions: they were given a whistle and told to walk round and round the pitches, looking skyward for enemy aircraft! These boys were referred to as "Jim Crows", and they were trained in aircraft recognition, but it is doubtful whether they ever blew their whistles for real. Life as a schoolboy in the war had many distractions, he said:

> At home, we accommodated a family which had been bombed out of their home in Birmingham, and they had a mentally retarded child whose tantrums affected my ability to concentrate on my homework. My father was an Air Raid Warden and my mother was a Fire Watcher in addition to her WVS duties, and this meant that they were always on duty when the air raid siren sounded. Because of this, I became an ARP messenger, also turning out during alerts.
>
> The arrival of Bishop's buns at the tuck shop (Bishop being the name of the Leamington baker, not the headmaster!) always created a stampede for the queue. Buns cost 1 penny each, and rock cakes and custards 1½d each. Lunch was almost equally divided three ways: some had school dinners, some had sandwiches in the tuck shop and others went home. If sausages were on the menu it meant a meat content of no more than two per cent (what the other 98% was, no one dared to enquire). Even fruit was not too plentiful, as bananas and oranges were completely unobtainable, as were other imported fruits.

Portents of things to come can be seen in some touching 16mm film shot in 1939: Major Pearman is seen supervising boys somewhat dangerously constructing the school's huge air-raid shelter system, which consisted of concrete-lined trenches, designed for a total of 700 boys, around the area where the Junior School car park is now. The boarders had their own air-raid shelter in one of the fives courts – now the site of the laundry room and Medical Centre. Although Warwick was not a military target, Coventry and Leamington were. Birmingham was considered to be in especial danger from air-raids, and, in an extraordinary arrangement, the whole population of Birmingham's King Edward VI School, Camp Hill, was moved to Warwick in September 1939 during the Phoney War. Their pupils and teachers used the premises in the afternoons, and Warwick School used them in the mornings. The Camp Hill Headmaster, TF Rogers, was allocated the school library as his study, and the boys were billeted locally, including a substantial number in Warwick Castle. The scheme foundered in 1940 when the pupils drifted back to Birmingham – several of them had been going back to Birmingham to see their parents at weekends, anyway! The apparent lack of danger from enemy bombers was used as the excuse for the ending of this scheme, but the danger was proved to be all too real later in the war, when Birmingham was heavily bombed – and Camp Hill School was hit. A congenial group of over 20 former Camp Hill evacuees was entertained at Warwick School in July 2003; for most of them, it was their first visit to the school for 63 years.

Also caught on film – in colour – are the unusually severe weather conditions of the period shortly before Easter 1940: "the great freeze-up", as it was called, resulted in an extra week's holiday at half term. The frozen ground held up progress on the vast air-raid shelter trench system. Huge pitched snowball battles took place, not only due to the presence of so much snow, but also because two rival schools were sharing the same premises. Sixty-three years later, it was grudgingly admitted that Warwick probably won these battles, but only because they had the advantage in terms of numbers, and also because they had all afternoon to assemble ammunition, ready for the bombardment of the Camp Hill boys at 6pm, when they were released for the day.

From 1940 onwards, a medical examination was insisted upon for all new pupils – an endurance exercise very much part of the tradition of Warwick School to this day. In August 1940, a school camp was held on the school field, to "make up for boys not having a holiday". The invitation was extended to all local schools, including elementary schools, and Bishop enthusiastically took part. Before this, in June 1940, a party of exhausted soldiers, who had just been rescued from the beaches of Dunkirk, rested for an hour on the headmaster's lawn, where they were fed copious quantities of cake and given cups of tea. Despite being shattered, they passed an envelope round and collected some French coins for the headmaster's four-year-old daughter, a kindly act which the girl in question, now Mrs Ros Partridge, remembers to this day – and she still has the coins.

The day-boys' air-raid shelters were not used very much, because most enemy planes flew over at night. One day-time incident, concerning AHB Bishop and MM Clark, was recounted in 2003 by OW Graham Morris (who explained that it was useful to know that Spitfires were single-engined, whereas the Dornier, a twin-engined plane, looked completely different):

> I happened to be going over to the shelters as a result of a day-time air-raid warning, and caught up with "The Bish" and "Nobby" Clark, who were going there, too, at their customary half trot. At this point an aircraft appeared overhead. "Look, Bursar, a Spitfire!" boomed The Bish. Seconds later the Dornier bomber seriously damaged the Lockheed factory in Leamington.

On another occasion, when the Lockheed factory was once more a target, a German bomber circled the school with its bomb doors open, but the school was on holiday at the time. In November 1940, the air-raids became much more serious. Mark Thomas, who was at the Junior School at the time, and who left in 1943 to go to Bloxham, wrote:

> We were at school during the Coventry blitz, and spent an uncomfortable night trying to sleep on suitcases laid on the floor of the downstairs passages. The dayboys from Coventry and Kenilworth appeared next day having apparently spent the night in their own beds! My parents saw the glow of the fires from their Vicarage in Chipping Norton.

He goes on:

Things that stand out are Wings for Victory Week, when the school "bought" two Spitfires by subscribing for National Savings stamps at various shows and Exhibitions including a scientific Conversazione. I hasten to say that I was a mere onlooker. We were then challenged to buy a third Spitfire, the reward being an extra day at half term, and were successful, helped by a large contribution from a parent.

The "Conversazione" was a triumph of the newly-formed Science Society, which held its inaugural meeting on May 8th, 1942, chaired by the Head of Science, FA Fisher. The first Conversazione was held on July 25th, 1942, and involved demonstrations of scientific experiments, utilizing about 80 boys. The name soon changed, but the annual Science Exhibition, which Pyne had started during the First World War, became once again a prominent feature of Warwick School life until the 1960s.

By June 1940, some 50 boys were spending their afternoons at farms. On two occasions, a dozen boys cycled 14 miles to a farm, worked for 5 or 6 hours, and then cycled home again. They were paid 5d per hour (if under 16) or 6d per hour (over 16), which

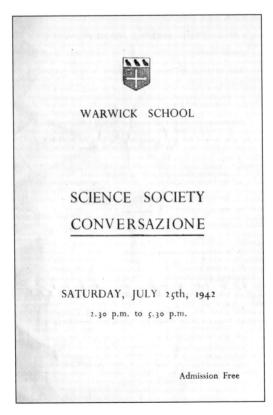

WARWICK   SCHOOL

SCIENCE   SOCIETY

CONVERSAZIONE

SATURDAY, JULY 25th, 1942

2.30 p.m. to 5.30 p.m.

Admission Free

The front cover of the programme for the 1942 Conversazione,
or Science Exhibition.
(Warwick School Archives)

is about £1 in 2003 values. One form per week was to live under canvas at Evesham, helping with fruit-picking and haymaking. Agricultural work became very popular amongst the boys for three reasons: they were allowed to miss afternoon lessons; they were excused homework; and they were paid. In Roger Smith's view, the whole agricultural economy of the country at this time depended on school-children.

This whole scheme was thrown into jeopardy by an accident on 6th July, 1940 (a Saturday afternoon), at Charlecote, in which Robert Camkin, aged 14, lost an eye. A clod-throwing riot had gone on for half to three-quarters of an hour: "A boy called Mackareth became annoyed with another lad called Ball and threw a clod of earth at him. Ball 'ducked', the missile went on, and struck Camkin in the eye," states a contemporary newspaper report. A court case was brought in March 1941 at Birmingham Assizes, with Bishop being sued for damages. The pupil was awarded £750 damages, and his father £64, on the grounds that Bishop had failed to exercise proper supervision. Camkin was a boarder but had not got permission from his parents to do the work – he "forgot to ask". Nevertheless, Bishop had allowed him to do the farm work "until a reply was received". The geography master, Mr Reeve, who was in charge of farm placements, attracted some criticism, but the defence "had not dared to put him in the witness box".

The huge damages, and the implication that boys had to be supervised at all times, led Bishop, "with the untiring support of the Secretariat of the Headmasters' Conference and Association, with the full sympathy of his staff, and with encouragement from his Governors, but against some weighty legal and actuarial advice", to appeal. In July, 1941, the case was summarised at the Appeal hearing as follows:

> On their half-holiday, a number of boys from a school were allowed by the headmaster to help a farmer by working in a field. As a result of horseplay among some of the boys, the infant plaintiff was struck on the forehead by a clod of earth, and one of his eyes was so badly injured that it had to be removed. In an action for damages for negligence against the headmaster, it was contended that he was under a duty to arrange for the supervision of the boys while they were doing the work.

The Court of Appeal heard that the headmaster had the duty of a careful parent, and such a parent would have said, "Go off and have a good time – and be useful to your country." The Court ruled: "In the circumstances of this case, the headmaster owed no duty to the infant plaintiff or his father to provide for the supervision of the boys." The boys regarded the farmer as being in charge, and there was no requirement to have a prefect or a master supervising them. The Appeal Court judges suggested that Bishop's two-hour cross-examination had been "most improper". A public school, or any school, for that matter, is not a crêche, they said: "Can you imagine a party of boys going out on their bicycles on a Saturday afternoon, and behaving like plaster angels all the time?" The judges ruled that the whole action should never have been brought and set aside the original judgment.

The boy's father wrote a letter to the *Warwickshire Advertiser and Leamington Gazette*, saying that his action on his son's behalf "carried no reflection whatever on Warwick School or the headmaster", and that he had tried to settle the whole matter amicably, but that his son "apparently has no redress for a grievous injury for which he himself was in no way responsible." Mr Camkin added, "We lose our case but we respect the law, with the utmost goodwill to the other side." The case of *Camkin v Bishop* became important in case law, particularly with regard to the insurance of pupils, and was still being quoted in legal text-books forty or fifty years later. An editorial note to the original case notes reveals why the case was considered to be so important:

> The provision of supervision in schools is a matter in which the practice of head-masters varies very considerably, with the result that it may have become a question whether the meticulous practice of some headmasters in this regard has placed a duty on others to provide more supervision than they normally would. The obser-vations in the Court of Appeal herein will, therefore, be of considerable assistance to headmasters and those called upon to advise them.

Incidentally, JA Strover (Headmaster 1977-88), in retirement at Yetminster, Dorset, said in 2003 that Bishop's late son Andrew (a former colleague of his at Harrow School) had told him that his father was so delighted about finally winning his case that he went out and bought all his children new bicycles, although it has to be said that his elder daughter, Mrs Ros Partridge, born in 1936, denies that she ever got a new bicycle until her teens! It must be realised that the damages would have been about £32,000 in 2003 values. The bicycle – or bicycles – must have seemed cheap in comparison!

Robert Camkin went on to have a successful career as a caterer, at one point running the "Charlecote Pheasant", very close to the scene of his unfortunate acci-dent. Later on, when Bishop's daughter Ros wanted to join a potato-picking party from Kingsley School, her father, "normally indulgent, absolutely forbade it"!

One aspect of the war which Bishop was very keen to keep secret was the plan by the Regional Offices of the Ministry of Health in Birmingham to make Warwick School a "reserve hospital in the case of a grave emergency". By 1942, Ministry offi-cials were pressing Bishop to provide plans of the school so that they could "re-survey in the near future the accommodation which we may need to take over." It is perhaps a consequence of the piecemeal development of the school buildings over the previous sixty years that Bishop had no idea what plans existed – or maybe this was his own way of stalling the "Men from the Ministry".

In 1942, an attempt was made to set down in writing the way that Warwick School boys were expected to behave. The resultant *Warwick School Code* was "not so much a list of rules as a useful guide to conduct and behaviour". Each boy was then given a small, green-covered copy to keep with him at all times. Some extracts from the first edition of 1942 (by courtesy of JL Randall, who preserved his cousin's copy) are given below:

Behave well, but naturally. Walk briskly, don't slouch, don't eat in the streets. Take trouble to speak well, and be courteous. On the pavement, give the inside to women, elders and children.

Dress smartly, wearing regulation School clothes and cap (not at an angle) to and from school. Be well groomed, with hair short and well brushed, neat nails, shoes shining and in good condition, and clothes well brushed and without stains, tears or missing buttons.

Cap properly visitors (use discretion), masters, full prefects and other Warwickians if they are with adults. (You should be capped back.) When in uniform, salute, or if you are on a bike give "eyes right (or left)."

Accidents may well have prompted the last instruction to be revised in a later edition: On a bike do *not* cap or salute.

Firearms and catapults are forbidden. Never throw things so that they might hit others.

Smoking, swearing, drinking and vulgar conversation are forbidden.

In later editions, "all forms of gambling" were also forbidden.

Be economical and avoid all waste. Don't leave spaces in exercise books, don't mark text books with ink, except for your name. Spare electricity. Save waste paper, and don't drop litter on the floor. Avoid damage and breakages.

Walk smartly, with hands out of pockets, and swing your arms. Caps must always be off indoors. Don't rush in or out of classrooms.

Form rooms and School buildings (excepting Stores) are out-of-bounds during Break. Don't loiter, rag or be noisy in classrooms.

Bad behaviour in the Tucker is an offence, punishable by exclusion.

The following are out-of-bounds:
1. Baths Enclosure, subject to bathing rules.
2. Gym, except with a master.
3. Fives Court Roof, outside the railings.
4. Stage, except with the Stage Manager's permission.
5. Air Raid Shelters, except during alerts.
6. Groundsman's sheds (including machines).
7. First XI Ground, for cricket, football or band, unless supervised by a master.
8. Pavilion, Altar, Main Gate, Entrance-hall doors, Exit doors in Big School, except for the Elders*.
9. Boarders' common rooms, dormitories, bike-shed and the Booter – these are for boarders only.

10. Dining Hall (except for meals). Music Rooms (except for official practice). Unorthodox use of any piano is forbidden.
11. Biological Garden – except for members of the Biological Group.

Cycle with both hands on the handle-bars. Books, coats etc., should be in, or on, a proper carrier.

It is a major offence to tamper with another boy's bicycle, or to borrow it without his free consent.

No one is excused Chapel, except those exempted on religious grounds. The latter will assemble quietly under the senior boy in Big School.

This extraordinary instruction was amended within two years to "under a senior boy" and much later altered to "those exempted, together with bus and train boys who are late for Chapel, should go to the room detailed."

Lateness: Morning school begins at 8.55am. Afternoon school begins at 2.15pm. If you arrive after these times without permission, you will be considered late, and should bring a note of explanation from your parents next day.

*The Elders are Prefects, Sub-prefects, members of 2nd year VIth; and Colours of 1st XI, 1st XV, and Athletics.

The "Altar" mentioned above as being out-of-bounds was nothing to do with the chapel, but was, in fact, the terrace created in the 1930s against the end wall of the gymnasium, with benches overlooking the outdoor swimming pool.

In the 1942 Prospectus, the tuition fees for Warwick boys are given as £5 per term (the 2003 equivalent of £145), and the separate boarding fee as £23 5s per term (£675). Boys from Leamington and beyond had to pay £6 per term. By 1950, as will be seen later, the basic day-boy tuition fee had risen to £18 and the boarding fee to £30 per term, which, with post-war inflation taken into account, were equivalent to £350 and £600 per term in 2003. The tuition fee in 1950 was, in real terms, less than 20% of its value 50 years later. The most likely explanation for this lies in the low salaries paid to teachers at the time and in the fact that the boarders were still subsidising the day-boys.

Losses in the war continued to mount, and the pages of *The Portcullis* are full of obituaries at this time. One particularly poignant obituary from 1943 is that of Claude Falkiner, who can be seen on some surviving 16mm-film footage of a mock ceremony, cheerfully cycling out of the school gates onto Myton Road (on which the traffic consisted of just one slow-moving lorry!) in the summer of 1940, after a jocular farewell from a fully-gowned headmaster, prior to pedalling all the way down to Boscombe, near Bournemouth. This film was used as the centre-piece of the school's Remembrance Service on 9th November, 2003, and it was particularly fitting that one

Field Marshal Sir Bernard Law Montgomery inspecting Ian Painton's bugle on
the third anniversary of D-Day, 1947.
(I Painton)

OW present at the service, Roger Smith, was captured as a small boy on the 1940 film;
he remembered the occasion well, recalling that Bishop had pressed 1d (one old
penny) into Claude Falkiner's hand as he bade him farewell – "for subsistence
expenses"!

In 2003, Ian Painton, who was the bugler for Field Marshal Montgomery's visit in
1947, wrote to the author. His letter prompted Mr Pipitone, the Regimental Sergeant

Major, to look for the original bugle. He found not one, but two suitable candidates! Ian Painton was delighted, and wrote:

> During the war, one Sunday afternoon an American army film unit drove into the quad. In spite of being completely unexpected, they were welcomed particularly as they gave out packets of chewing gum. They took pictures of the school buildings, and at their request we demonstrated (on film) the different rough and tumble games we played in those days.
>
> During the War it was a Sunday night "treat" to watch films. The early school scenes, like those shot in 1936–7, were regularly shown alongside Russian wartime propaganda films and others such as "Dig for Victory" – how to cultivate vegetables in your back garden. Riveting! In the days before TV we'd watch anything.

Further astonishing revelations come from RPS Jones, who was a boarder at Warwick School from 1941-6 (although he only came from Banbury), and who submitted his reminiscences in 2003. In describing life at school as a boarder during the war years, he revealed that, on entering Senior House, all boys were given a sex lecture by the headmaster:

> This consisted of a "tea-party" held in the HM's house by way of introducing and explaining the mysteries of sex. Despite the fact that the HM had given this lecture on many previous occasions, his delivery nevertheless was stilted and extremely nervous. His introductory theme began with the "birds and the bees" as an example of nature in action. This progressed to the embarrassing inclusion of himself and wife, Olive, as living proof of reproduction "de facto". During this era, any relationships with girls for boarders, in particular, were absolutely forbidden, and any attempt to introduce or include the opposite sex in any school social events or activities was solidly rebuffed. It was during half term, when I decided not to return home for this brief holiday, but to meet a young lady from King's High School instead. As I innocently walked hand in hand with my new girlfriend round the perimeter of Warwick Castle, I had the misfortune to meet Mr Bishop on an outing with his two children. I was instantly ordered to return to the HM's study, awarded six of the best and sent home immediately with a letter of explanation to my father, who was more amused than annoyed.

Ron Jones also elaborated upon the deprived circumstances in which boarders had to survive at school during the war. The range of foods was both limited and basic, and the quality invariably poor. One particular feature continued to rankle sixty years later, and that was the egg allocation – which amounted to one boiled egg per month. He claims that the serving of this ration always coincided with the boarders' only free monthly afternoon off, when the staff knew that hardly any boys would be there. An alternative view, as given by Bishop's daughter Ros, is that the monthly egg allocation was normally used up in cooking and baking, and the monthly egg treat for the few boys left behind was, in fact, a voluntary and kind act, the eggs coming from the head-master's own hens.

More information about Bishop's sex education lectures comes from John Randall, who was at Warwick School from 1944 to 1952 as a day-boy. He writes:

> Early in my first term at the school – it may even have been at the end of the first week – I found myself herded into Big School with all the other first year boys for a sex talk from the headmaster. This was the one and only time we were addressed on this topic, apart from the very formal purely biological information imparted during biology lessons at a much later stage.
>
> We sat in hushed silence as "Bish" delivered his talk. He stressed the fact that women are physically weaker than men and suffer pain and physical discomfort during the birth process. Therefore, females should always be treated with the utmost kindness and courtesy.
>
> After the talk we had time for questions. We had been told about the pain suffered by the mother during the birth process, but what about the baby? Did it, too, suffer pain while it was being born? I was told that nobody bothered much about the baby as long as it was alive and kicking; it was simply laid aside while attention was given to the mother. This seemed to me to be grossly unfair.

RJ Taylor (who joined the school in 1935) recalled, in a letter to the author in 2003, some of the staff he encountered:

> T "Scotty" Nichol: A dour Scot who fired up from a very short fuse. He used to wield a huge blackboard compass in a very menacing fashion. We used to quake as we waited to go into his classroom, and nervously ask the boys coming out: "Is he in a sweat?"
>
> HE "Hector" Cullis: The epitome of a country parson – a gentle, kindly person. In September 1940, when we really thought that invasion by the Germans was but hours away, the atmosphere was electric. I was cycling home through Emscote when I came up to a road block. There was Rev HE Cullis and a companion sporting tin hats and armbands, checking identity cards. Quite what effect his presence there would have had on the enemy landing on the South Coast, I leave to the imagina-tion.
>
> CCC "Pin" Lewis: Very slim build with a small head, hence the nick-name Pin. I remember him cycling through Barford one winter morning on an old "sit-up-and-beg" bicycle en route to Exeter for his Christmas holiday. Can you imagine it? I do not know whether he biked back as well.
>
> AHB Bishop: In assembly one day, he announced in suitably sepulchral tones his extreme displeasure at an occurrence he had recently witnessed. He had seen two boys in Leamington, in school uniform, walking along the street eating ice creams.

Bob Taylor also recalled the Munich Crisis of 1938:

The "A" side of the school spent a week up in the town assembling civilian gas masks. The "B" side drew the short straw, and dug ARP trenches in the school grounds. When the crisis blew over, we diggers bemoaned our luck to Major Pearman regarding our wasted efforts. His reply was along the lines of: "If not this year, then next year we will need them."

Mrs Ros Partridge, Bishop's elder daughter, remembers the same staff: Scotty Nichol was on his own for much of the war, his wife and son being prevented from leaving Southern Rhodesia; HE Cullis ("Hector the Rector" – or "Science Director" or even "Sanitary Inspector") found a second wife amongst the staff of the Junior School, one of a "spate of in-house marriages in my father's time"; CCC Lewis "horrified my father by growing a beard". She also recalled that one war-time directive had been that there should only be 4 inches (10cm) of water in any bath, and all the baths in School House had a black line painted at this level. Concerning eating in the streets, her sister, Mrs Caroline Sterratt, recalls:

I remember Dad saying the 11th Commandment was "Thou shalt not be found out." I think it was probably easier for him if the boys kept that one, but he had to act if they didn't. Of course I did it as well, but I probably got away with it, possibly because my friends and I used to go to a back-street chip shop in the dark!

"Pin" Lewis's "magnificent black beard" was the subject of an extraordinary incident during a morning assembly in Big School at this time. As Dick Mann (Warwick School 1935-1944) related in April 2004:

AHB Bishop was giving one of his short addresses, with all the masters sitting behind him, so that he could not see them. He said he was very dissatisfied with the personal appearance of some of the boys – some didn't even brush their hair or black their boots. "It is really a disgrace," he said. "What would you think of me if I came here one morning and had not shaved?" At that moment Mr Lewis rose up and walked off the stage. At this the whole school roared with laughter, and the headmaster had not the faintest idea of what they were laughing at.

One particular aspect of the war years was the difficulty in obtaining non-geriatric staff, and it must have been a huge shock to the 'status quo' when the first female member of staff, ironically called Mrs German, was appointed in 1942, to replace a man on active service; she stayed until 1946 – and taught Latin. According to John Randall, Mary German was the first wife of a nephew of the composer Sir Edward German, and although she was a very competent musician as well as a classicist, more than one Old Warwickian has described her as being somewhat tough on small boys. Not all temporary staff were geriatric – or female! One man, Martindale Sidwell, who was temporary music master from 1943 to 1946, went on to be a celebrated London

The JTC Band of 1944.
(RPS Jones)

organist and choirmaster before his death in 1998. His successor at Warwick School, CPP Burton (known as Peter, but whose full name was Claud Peter Primrose Burton), was appointed organist of St Alban's Cathedral in 1949, and died tragically, aged 41, during an outing to Hemel Hempstead baths in 1957, while attempting to save the life of a choirboy who he thought was drowning. At the inquest, it was found that he had chronic tuberculosis in both lungs, and it is probable that he should never have gone swimming. CPP Burton was also organist of St Mary's Church, Warwick, and was the first holder of the title of Director of Music at Warwick School. His memory lives on in a couple of published hymn tunes, one actually named *Warwick School*, which was written to accompany Sabine Baring-Gould's stirring hymn *Onward, Christian Soldiers*, and first performed, to the great excitement of the headmaster, in 1946.

Change was inevitable as the war came to an end and Warwick School embarked upon what can be seen as its modern era. The 1944 Education Act signalled changes that lasted for decades and represented a significant challenge to the school. That this challenge was foreseen by Bishop and the governors did not diminish its potential threat to the school's continuance as it sought to survive and develop as an independent institution. The formal description of the school was to be "an independent school associated with the state system of education", and this enabled a degree of co-operation between school and LEA for the next two decades. It would need to ensure sufficient finance to offer the curriculum needed by its pupils; to attract "custom" at an affordable price; to pay and motivate the teaching body; to add to its building-stock; and to retain its local reputation. Mrs Ros Partridge wrote in 2004:

> From the time Labour won the 1945 General Election my father was seriously worried. He knew that Direct Grant status was likely to be turned down. Warwick was made a test case in the Commons, spoken for by Anthony Eden. It was referred to disparagingly by Ellen Wilkinson (Education Minister) as "Mr Eden's pet school". I remember my father being constantly in conference with the governors – all very aware that going independent was a great gamble. After having done so, about five or six Midlands schools followed suit, including Bablake and Solihull, but Warwick was the trail blazer.

It is useful to remember that the sister of the Conservative MP for Warwick and Leamington between 1923 and 1957, Anthony Eden (Prime Minister 1955-1957), was the Countess of Warwick, who chaired Warwick School's governing body at the beginning of the 1930s.

The issue of affordability came to a head in 1946, when the governors' application for the school to become a Direct Grant School was, indeed, turned down: the school was to become independent. However, even Guy Nelson, Chairman of Governors at the time, admitted that the word "independent" was "not very appropriate" owing to the degree of co-operation with the LEA:

> In the past a very considerable part of the expense of maintaining the school has been borne by the Local Education Authority, and that Authority has been reimbursed a proportion of their grant by the Minister of Education. This arrangement enabled parents to send their children to the school for a fee very greatly less than the cost of the education received.
>
> The governors have little choice but to declare the school to be an Independent School, but at the same time to make it perfectly clear that they desire the school to take its place in the general Scheme of the Education Act, 1944, and to provide Grammar School education for pupils without payment of fees.

A public meeting was held on 6th May, 1946, at which the announcement was made that the tuition fees would have to rise to £16 per term – that is, more than triple. This is equivalent to £420 per term in 2003 values. The Local Education Authority declared that it would nominate a total of 45 pupils each year (that is, half of the yearly three-form intake) for "places at the school carrying total exemption from tuition fees", irrespective of parental income. Furthermore, it would institute a fees remission scheme for existing pupils so that "no fees should be paid in cases where the parents' income is below £7 10s 0d per week." This sum is equivalent to an annual salary of £10,000 in 2003. Finally, the governors themselves would fund ten free places for boys from Warwick itself, but, they admitted, this would probably be at the rate of two per year.

One potentially catastrophic consequence of the transfer to independence in 1946 was that the staff would lose a serious proportion of their pensions when they eventually retired. This situation took at least a couple of years to resolve, and Bishop and the governors took their responsibilities in this matter extremely seriously. The larger salaries that had to be offered in compensation for loss of pensions led to continual upward pressure on tuition fees: roughly two-thirds of fee income was paid out in staff salaries at the time, a figure virtually unchanged even in 2003. Teaching staff were paid between £230 and £480 per year in 1946 – that is, between £6,000 and £12,500 in 2003 values, and therefore approximately one third of modern staff salaries in real terms.

PART TWO
The Post-War Era

The main corridor, pictured in 1961. Every morning it would be lined by pupils waiting for an inspection by AHB Bishop before they went into chapel.

(RF Wilmut)

CHAPTER 18

AHB Bishop – Post-War Independence and Growth

There were 450 boys at the school at this time of fundamental change in 1946, and while it is certain that some boys were withdrawn because their parents felt that they could not afford the increased fees, numbers did go up, and eventually significant building developments could be financed, largely thanks to the Memorial Endowment Fund, which began its appeals in 1945. A priority was the creation of the War Memorial tablet in the chapel – some 59 names were to be inscribed. In the immediate post-war years, improvements were smaller scale. The removal of blackout and repainting of the lower corridor had great psychological benefit, and the asphalting of the area under The Limes up to the Junior House had been long awaited; facilities for science and in the Staff Common Room were improved some-what, as were those for sport and changing; the Orlits buildings were set up in part of the Biological Garden (where the 1996 History and Geography Block is located); improvements to the swimming pool and to the school's facilities for tennis were completed by 1951, as well as the start of the change from DC to AC mains; and a new science wing (the bulbous protuberance on what is now the Music Block) was ready for occupation by 1952, in which year the front of the school was floodlit.

The school had virtually doubled in size in 15 years, without much extension of buildings or fields. Fortunately, these needs were about to be addressed, with plans for a completely new Science Block, gymnasium and changing-room area outlined in 1954. By 1957, these plans had been implemented, largely, but not totally, from the Memorial Fund. A grant of £27,000 (nearly £400,000 in 2003 values) from the Industrial Fund for the Advancement of Scientific Education in Schools went a long way towards paying for the new Science Block, which was to consist of two lecture rooms, five laboratories for physics and chemistry, plus work- and prep-rooms. More building was needed as numbers of pupils grew year on year. In 1947, the Junior and Senior Schools numbered 585 (130 of whom were new boys), and there were 29 staff. Originally, Bishop had set a notional limit of 600, but this figure was rapidly exceeded. By the time he retired in 1962, he had 742 pupils and 44 staff.

The Junior School was, by this time, taking in some 45 to 50 new boys a year. Fittingly, it was the Junior School which benefited from the final "wave" of major

The front of the new Science Block, pictured in 1957 before the biology laboratories were added.
(WCRO and Leamington Courier)

The rear of the new Science Block, photographed in 1957, showing the magnificent Coronation
Oak of 1902, and also the heap of coal behind the Orlits building which AHB Bishop was at great
pains to hide from the Queen Mother in 1958.
(WCRO and Leamington Courier)

The brand new chemistry (ground floor) and physics (top floor) laboratories, pictured in 1957.
(WCRO and Leamington Courier)

The new physics department, photographed in 1957.
(WCRO and Leamington Courier)

building that marked the end of Bishop's reign: an extension to its teaching facilities and to the Junior Boarding House, along with the creation of a music school over the changing rooms by The Limes. The large music room and individual practice rooms were absorbed by the Staff Common Room in the 1980s.

Bishop's attitude towards the Junior School was the same as that of his predecessor, JP Way, who had set it up seventy years previously – at his own expense. In October 1959, in proposing a new wing and substantial improvements, Bishop addressed the governors as follows:

> In 1935 both House and School were closed down, and it was noticeable that recruit-ment of boarders and fee-paying boys dropped considerably. I asked the governors soon after I came to re-open the Junior Boarding House and Junior School, but they were not in a position to do so. Because I was convinced of their vital importance I then asked if I could re-open them myself on a private basis, and this was done in a modest way and on modest fees in 1938. When the school became independent in 1946 I asked the governors to consider taking over both boarding houses and in due course they agreed. At the same time I asked them to accept the Junior School as a going concern including furniture and goodwill, as my contribution to independence.
>
> Since then these two ventures have never looked back. There are now 125 boys in 5 forms with a staff of six teachers in the Junior School, and 34 junior boarders in the Boarding House. For years now the Junior School and the boarding house have been our main feed for the main school and senior boarding house, and they have also proved a very paying proposition.

The school that greeted the end of hostilities retained only nine of its 1939 staff, though a further six eventually returned from the Forces. Inevitably, the staff body had been drastically affected by the war, and stability was desperately needed. In fact, for many, especially the younger men, the post-war period offered great opportuni-ties, and it became increasingly the case that teachers did not stay a long time in their posts before moving on, either to promotions elsewhere or to other professions. There were, in short, to be fewer "Mr Chips". One temporary member of staff during the war, Dr FM Friedmann, Head of a Berlin grammar school before fleeing from the Nazis, returned to Germany to take charge of a school for survivors of the concentration camps. He was a red-head, and his stock phrase was, apparently, "You prowoke me, but I am not prowoked"! Dr Friedmann's work is justly celebrated in Martin Gilbert's book *The Boys*.

In the first five years after the war, long-serving staff CT Freeman (who taught science and mathematics from 1920 to 1946) and the Glaswegian T Nichol (1922-48) retired, as did MM Clark (1899-1949). The latter, who came with HS Pyne in 1906, served as Second Master, Bursar, Tuck Shop Manager and Stores Manager and offered his entire professional life to the school, continuing beyond his planned retirement in 1936 in order to help the new Headmaster, AHB Bishop, settle in, and

New Buildings, the temporary range of classrooms which lasted from
1919 to 1974, pictured in 1961.
(RF Wilmut)

then staying throughout the war. In "retirement", he continued to work for the school
and to devote himself to the OW Club. He died in 1955 and is remembered as truly
one of the major figures of the school's 20th-century history. It took two men to
replace him: RN Mitchell, who became Second Master (until 1954, when he left for a
headship) and AL Hues, who became Bursar. In 1954, Rev HE Cullis retired from
classroom and tutoring duties, though he remained as Chaplain until 1960. As a
King's Middle School pupil under Pyne, teacher of chemistry, Junior Housemaster,
Chaplain and OW Secretary, he provided continuity and an example of true
Christianity throughout some 60 years. Major DG Pearman, who, prior to coming to
the school in 1923 to teach physical education, had fought alongside Lawrence of
Arabia, retired in 1957, followed two years later by AS Wolstencroft, who, apart from
his gifts as a Modern Linguist, edited *The Portcullis* magazine and played the organ in
chapel. Mention should also be made of the long-serving Head of Geography, EL
Gates Warren, who retired in 1962. As House Master of School House, he had
married the Matron, Miss Southorne, when they were both well into middle age. The
psalm *Lift up your Heads, O ye Gates* was always sung with extra gusto in chapel when
they were present!

Roger Wilmut (Warwick School 1953-1961) has supplied some notes as to the
origins of nicknames of the staff at this time:

ELG Warren's nickname was "Caz" – we were never sure why, but the theory was that it was derived from "Quasimodo" because he was rather round-shouldered. Wolstencroft was "Wol" – he was rather owl-like. Simmonds didn't have a nick-name as such but boys would exaggerate the S at the beginning – he would get very annoyed if he thought he heard anyone hissing at him. Boys do waste their energy on some stupid things!

"Wol", of course, was the way in which Owl in AA Milne's *Winnie-the-Pooh* spelled his own name!

Dick Mann recalls that ELG Warren (who during the war was referred to as "Cassey") was fond of making statements that he probably immediately regretted, such as "Half way up the Alps, the sheep turn to goats" and "This morning, we will just run through Asia." ELG Warren also taught chemistry during the war, and Dick Mann recalls that his skill at demonstrating rather violent chemical reactions created rather more entertainment than was intended.

Although the headmaster regularly bemoaned the difficulty he had in recruiting suitably qualified teachers, Warwick School did, in fact, cope well with the shortage. In 1954, Bishop considered that it was of great credit to the calibre of the post-war staff that five of them had been appointed to headmasterships in the previous three years. Equally, many of his appointments lasted for generations of schoolboys: Messrs LJ Charman, HCG Sawyer, JMA Marshall, HJ Sheppard, HE Owen, RH Thornton, J Swindlehurst, KG Brocklehurst, BW Young, RW Long, PA Adcock, RN Heaton, E Blackshaw, IJ Beeching, DW Keighley, KW Freeborn, RP Usherwood, HB Robinson, GF Eve and Miss M Lanspeary all gave sterling service, many serving well in excess of twenty years.

The post-war period was beset with change and challenge: the winter of 1946 to 1947 was one of the coldest on record, and there were significant effects on attendance and school sport for many weeks, whilst lessons were concentrated in those areas of the premises that could be kept tolerably warm! The acquisition of the school's first "radiogram" must have helped keep spirits up. Pupil numbers remained healthy despite the school's independent status (though, where physical health was concerned, reports from the Boarding Houses suggest that 'flu' epidemics, amongst others, were much more common than today), but academic standards were slow to pick up, and only in 1948 were they approaching pre-war levels. Bishop did not approve of the introduction of the General Certificate of Education, known to us as 'O' and 'A' levels, which were to replace the old School Certificate. He extended the main school course from four to five years (though one form would soon be doing 'O' level in four years) and reintroduced Classical Greek (at the pupils' request!). He thought that fewer subjects should be taught to the 14–16 age group so that the abler boys could join the sixth form as soon as they were ready: he believed that depth rather than extent of knowledge was preferable. Despite concerns that the school was

The effects of the harsh winter of 1946-7, as photographed by the Bishop family
from their front door

no longer as accessible to its local clientèle as before, the move to independence was
seen as successful. Only one in three of those who took the entrance exam could be
accepted in 1950, but the headmaster expressed the hope that the school would
remain, via the Endowment Fund, "open to boys of all types". The 1953 public examination results were the best on record, though in some subjects the standards
required for a pass grade were felt to be too high!

There were objections in some quarters to the popularity of "trashy literature"
and to the growth of new subjects at the expense of proper leisure time: the school, it
was felt, should concentrate on the whole man, rather than the academic excellence
of the few. In order to develop pupils' thinking, a course in general studies was first
introduced to the sixth form in 1955, and, in a revised format, it survives to this day.
By 1958, an 'A' level examination course in economics had been introduced. Within
ten years of the war ending, sixth-form numbers had doubled, especially in the
sciences, which were attracting some 60% of the year group – hence the pressing
need for building work. Philosophical questions about the real purpose of education
at Warwick were frequently discussed at this time: Was the school there to produce
leaders in management, administration and technology? Was it doing what it should
for the "less able" boys? This was an era when about half the fifth form used to leave

The view towards the Engineering Shop and the new Science Block, taken by a pupil, Robin Kenward, from PNG Whitlam's room by the tower in 1960. All three of the 1887 lime trees shown have since been destroyed.

at 16. Certainly, the quality of examination results did improve: in 1957, all twenty-three U6 applicants gained university places, and the 'A' level pass rate was 95%. Subsequent years produced strong results, with record 'O' level results achieved in 1960. As will be seen in the following chapters, this is an area where, statistically at least, the school has continued to improve!

In October 1959, twenty-three years after his appointment as Headmaster, Arthur Bishop was able to report to the governors:

The school is in good heart. For the first time there are well over 700 on the roll. The Junior School and Lower School are overflowing, and the Sixth Form is larger than ever. Both boarding houses are more than full.

At Advanced Level we gained 87.5% passes. At Ordinary Level subject passes improved from 54% in 1957 and 60% in 1958 to 69%. Mr Beeching deserves special mention for the outstanding science results.

The music of the school – orchestral and choral – is improving rapidly. The CCF maintains its high standards. Discipline is good, and the reputation of the school is good. The experiment of admitting boys on Common Entrance from preparatory schools at 13 is going well; the list is already full for next year and a reserve list is being built up.

Much of the credit for this flourishing state of affairs must go to the Second Master, Mr Dugdale, and the staff who are most loyal and co-operative. Theirs is a 6 day week as against a 5 day week in the state schools and they willingly give up time to other activities in the dinner hour and after school. I trust the governors will continue their wise policy of recognising this extra work by the staff in their salary allowances.

When the school became independent it had to improve or fall back on state aid. Our scholarship must, at least, compare favourably with neighbouring state schools and in games, society and tone we must excel. That is why we must have a good staff and pay them well to expect so much of them.

The only surviving picture of an assembly in the old Big School, taken (with permission) by Roger Wilmut in 1961. The headmaster on the stage is AHB Bishop.

Sport has always had a central role to play in British boys' independent schools, and during Bishop's time significant progress was made. The war had inevitable and far-reaching effects upon the school's ability to provide what it wished: provision of basic equipment was cut back to the extent that, in 1945, cricket was limited to seven balls for the whole season, and getting playable pitches relied much upon the good nature of the remaining ground-staff. Nonetheless, in 1945, the First XI played 16 matches, despite transport difficulties, and, later on, PH Bromley was selected to play for Warwickshire on his seventeenth birthday: he scored 121 against Essex (for whom OW Dickie Dodds played with distinction for many years) in 1952 and later captained the county's Second XI. Jack Marshall, like Dodds, was a capped county player, and his return to his old school, where he became Head of the Junior Department, ensured that the profile of sport was enhanced. The 1949 cricket XI was regarded as the best since 1939, and in the late 1950s DR and MS Cook performed with distinction. The prime school sport remained rugby, superintended primarily by Jack Marshall and Ralph Thornton, and in 1952-1953 the first three teams remained undefeated. The arrival, in the late 1950s, of Ken Freeborn and Roger Hosen, with his first class playing experience, enabled the burden to be shared. The development of rugby was evident in the fact that the school now played on equal terms at First XV level with every school except Rugby. Provision for sport was assisted by the purchase of 15 acres of playing fields in the early 1950s, and by 1956 the school, which had formerly rented three-quarters of its fields, owned them all. Tennis as a summer sport, initially for the "non-cricketer", developed, thanks to the provision of courts, so that by 1960 there were four grass and five hard courts. Official school tennis fixtures started in 1958, and in 1961 the basketball squads, also playing "officially", achieved six wins out of seven. As a result of the unfailing enthusiasm of Ken Freeborn (staff 1957-92), athletics and water polo became successful sports. The new gymnasium, which opened in 1957, also guaranteed a substantial increase in facilities.

The Junior Training Corps and Air Training Corps (from 1941) had more than justified their existence in the years up to 1945. With the peace came a change in focus, but numbers remained healthy (127 in 1945, and some 200 in 1955 – a record number, with a waiting-list). The JTC took part in the Victory Parade in Warwick in 1945 and was reviewed in 1947 by Field Marshal Montgomery. The cadets had also formed a guard of honour when Monty, as he was popularly known, received the Freedom of the Borough of Warwick late in 1945. On his visit in 1947, he signed the drum of the Band. The drum-skin was cut out and mounted and is still on display in the modern CCF HQ, although the signatures are extremely faded.

Surprisingly, perhaps, Montgomery did not go down too well with the boys, who may have been all too ready to deflate apparently-inflated egos. Roger Wilmut recalls:

A bus waiting to take pupils home at the end of the school day, pictured in 1961.
Clearly visible is the fives court, later to become the Medical Centre.
(RF Wilmut)

Most of the boys thought he was an idiot. We used to "quote" him as saying: "As the Lord said unto Moses – and *I* think he was right..."

An opposing view comes from Ron Jones:

Monty was a very self-assured individual – surprisingly small in stature to what one might have imagined. He had a contrived upper class accent, delivered in short, clipped sentences. Pompous, but certainly not an idiot!

The JTC was renamed the CCF (Combined Cadet Force) in 1948. Camps are the essence of the CCF, and in 1947 some 33 boys took part for the first time since 1938. As many as 70 boys subsequently trained at a variety of destinations, such as Rhyl, Oswestry, Castlemartin, Aldershot and Gandale, Yorkshire. In recognition of his service over the decades, the Curator, Philip Whitlam, described in 1950 by Bishop as "virtually a master", was promoted to the rank of Lieutenant Colonel and awarded the OBE. The announcement of the end of National Service in 1956 brought with it a decline in numbers of recruits, but also a determination to diversify, hence the introduction of Arduous Training and Outward Bound. Thus it was that the Corps

The school orchestra of 1961 rehearsing in Big School.
(RF Wilmut)

celebrated its 75th anniversary in 1959 in good heart. Those who did not fancy the military aspect had had the opportunity since 1945 to join the School Scout Troop, which rapidly reached full strength. Its first camp, on Jersey in 1946, enabled boys to see at first hand an island that had, until some 18 months previously, been in German hands. The 1947 scouts sent part of their sweet ration to a centre for German boys and girls in Berlin, and were represented at the World Jamboree in France.

During the war, the cause of school music had been largely in the hands of temporary staff such as Mrs German, Miss Blenkinsop and Miss Overbury, and the arrival of CPP Burton as the first Director of Music in 1946 was a significant change. Soon the school was winning prizes at the annual Leamington Music Festival, and the Choral Society had 100 members. TN Tunnard replaced CPP Burton in 1950 and stayed until 1958, when EG Holmes arrived. During this time, two distinguished OWs, Denis Matthews and Eric Hope, put on piano recitals in aid of the Memorial Fund. Holmes, in his early years at the school, oversaw an increase in music-making: the orchestra had more than 30 members; the Choral Society had a waiting-list; and the Gramophone Society met weekly, alternating between classical and jazz music. There was a major performance of *Elijah* in 1961. Attitudes to music were fairly conventional: Holmes disapproved of the excessive growth, as he saw it, of interest in woodwind and brass, and supported the cause of the strings. His distaste for pop is on record, too!

Drama was in the hands of Messrs EA Morley and RN Brayshaw during the period between 1943 and 1950. Performances of *The Rivals, Julius Caesar, Henry IV Part 1, Coriolanus, The Critic* and *The Comedy of Errors* were given at this time. From this era comes the celebrated actor Charles Kay, who was known as AC Piff during his time at Warwick School (1944-1948). The arrival of RW Long, known to the staff as Ron but to the boys as Tom, brought a lively and modern perspective to performance: he put on *Twelfth Night, Journey's End, Hamlet, Our Town, A Midsummer Night's Dream, The Devil's Disciple, The Taming of the Shrew* and a modern-dress version of *Macbeth*. In so doing, he brought on the dramatic talents and interests of his pupils, the most celebrated of whom is Michael Billington, drama critic of the *Guardian*. The return of the dramatic musical after some 25 years was welcomed when, in 1959, Roger Usherwood put on the first of his many Gilbert & Sullivan "Savoy operas", *The Pirates of Penzance*, to be followed, two years later, by *Iolanthe*. Throughout this period, the traditional Staff Play continued, examples of which were: *The Ghost Train, The Importance of Being Earnest, When We Are Married* and *The Happiest Days Of Your Life*. Occasional travelling drama groups came to perform French classics in the original, and many boys travelled to Stratford to benefit from such well-remembered performances as Dorothy Tutin's Juliet, and Michael Redgrave's Hamlet.

School societies were at the heart of the community, especially in times when television had yet to become widespread. Some reflected the mood of the times and went into decline as fashions or needs changed – so it was that the Allotment Holders' Society experienced a falling off in interest after the war. The League of Nations Society (LNU) became the United Nations Association (UNA) and enjoyed a membership of over 150 at one stage, holding talks entitled "A Soviet village after liberation from the Nazis" and "Life in post-war Japan". The Cinema Society benefited from the purchase by the headmaster of a ciné projector; the Geographical Society often boasted attendances of over 50; the Modern Languages Society was revived; and new societies, for example the Archaeological and the Art & Architectural, came into being. The oldest society, the Debating, celebrated its 350th meeting in 1955, the motion being that "this house would bring back the birch." It is not recorded whether the society's chairman, JW Wilson, later to become a judge, was in favour. Not long before, the future MP Harry Greenway had been described as debating "in his best Churchillian manner". By 1960, however, contributors to *The Portcullis* are beginning to lament the decline in attendance at societies, wondering whether television, the concept of the "angry young man", or exams were to blame!

The CCF and scouts long provided the main means of enabling boys to escape the confines of Warwickshire, but in the post-war years groups ventured abroad more and more, mostly guided by Harry Sheppard, who took trips to various parts of

A panoramic photograph from 1957, showing the new Memorial Gymnasium and
changing rooms (on the right-hand page) and the Altar, Tuck Shop, original 1890 gymnasium and
the second Coronation Oak of 1902 (on the left-hand page).
(WCRO and Leamington Courier)

France, Belgium, Italy and Austria. Occasionally, other members of staff, such as
Felix Dugdale, would take a cycling trip to the Rhineland, and, by 1960, Jack
Marshall was creating the tradition of the annual ski trip. It is not clear whether the
experiment of taking one class away to Somerset for a week's fieldwork was repeated,
despite its apparent success in 1949.

Warwick School continued zealously to guard its reputation as a combined day and
boarding school. Of its 670 pupils in 1954, 107 were boarders. From 1952, the Senior
House was largely in the care of Messrs Warren, Young and Whitlam. The needs of
the younger boarder were catered for through the family atmosphere created by Rev
HE Cullis (1944-52) and then by Felix Dugdale. The tradition of boarding still ran in
families at this time, with six of the 13 new boarders in 1952 being sons of OWs.
Dugdale describes the typical interests of his young charges as "model boats and
aircraft... they do not seem to change much." Critics of boarding were reminded, one
Speech Day, of its virtues in character-building. The chapel, too, was at the centre of
school life, with 50 boys being confirmed in 1954.

In the 1950s, the school benefited from visits by Viscount Montgomery of Alamein and the local MP, Sir Anthony Eden (who was Foreign Secretary from 1951 onwards, and Prime Minister from 1955 to 1957), both of whom distributed prizes at Speech Day. During Monty's visit on 9th June, 1955, the veteran soldier also laid the foundation stone of the new Memorial Gymnasium. The fact that the gymnasium was not ready for this ceremony (the building contract was not awarded for another month) did not deter the headmaster from arranging this publicity exercise! Whether Monty ever found out that the pile of bricks, hastily assembled in the middle of the school field and intended to resemble a corner of the new gymnasium, was surreptitiously dismantled at the end of his visit is not known! The foundation stone was later built into the side of the entrance vestibule of what is now the Sports Centre.

An interesting view of life at Warwick School comes from Mrs Caroline Sterratt, who was AHB Bishop's younger daughter:

I was born on 18th September 1946, just at the time of the enormous changes which took place in the school, of which I was of course blissfully unaware. Warwick School was my home and my playground. I didn't have much contact with the day-to-day workings of the School, but had more contact with the "infrastructure"; in fact I have some of it tattooed in my knee! I came off my bike rounding a corner on the ash path which went between the bike sheds by the Junior House. My father's study was where the home and school worlds met.

My father had an interest in Church Architecture, and when the Tuck Shop was extended, he named the semi-circular wall round the enclosure "the Apse" – presumably because it was near "the Altar." It was an excellent place for doing a dramatic turn on a bike or roller-skates.

I believe the Monday morning Sixth Form RE slot was also used for gauging the customer satisfaction for the previous day's sermon. If the Sixth Form Boarders had enjoyed the visiting preacher, then he would be invited again. I know Dad really enjoyed these sessions.

One person I remember very well was Roger Usherwood. He came to the house to tutor me in Latin. He had a great sense of humour, notably in making up strange English sentences for me to translate into Latin. While I laboured away he would practise his singing.

On most summer days, whilst the boarders were in tea, staff and their families could use the swimming pool. Those of us living "on site" were the most frequent visitors. Swimming was, as I remember, compulsory when the water temperature was over 60 Fahrenheit (15°C). The temperature was taken every day under the supervision of Col. Whitlam, who dealt with the chlorination plant, which was at the right of "the Altar." The temperature was notified on a blackboard. I used to nag my mother to let me go in briefly when it was 58 or 59. When the summer got really warm she had to nag me to get out before the boys were out from tea. At the end of the summer term the chlorination was turned off and it took only a few days before the pool was a no-go area – used only for the sailing of toy ships. The wildlife took over and we used to fish for gnat larvae.

About 1957 we had acquired a West Highland White terrier, "Smiley", who was technically mine, but in fact more fond of my mother. My parents took to walking round the perimeter of the school field with him at lunchtime (our previous dog had preferred to "go it alone"). This provided a fine opportunity for speaking to the boys he met in an informal way, and Smiley was a great icebreaker.

Each October, the Town Crier came to visit to announce the Mayor's Half-holiday. One year this was broadcast, and I have a 78 rpm record which I think contains the broadcast. The Town Crier was called Henry Thistleton.

The major visit in Bishop's time was unquestionably that of Queen Elizabeth the Queen Mother on 6th November, 1958. The main reason for her visit to the town was to open the new Shire Hall, but in her half-hour visit to Warwick School she dedicated the new school gates, replacements for those melted down in wartime, and made brief visits to the chapel, gym, Big School and the chemistry lecture room, as well as signing a Visitor's Book. Having been lost for perhaps nearly 40 years, the Queen

The Queen Mother, watched by Alderman Guy Nelson, Chairman of Governors, opens the new school gates at the start of her visit in 1958.

The Queen Mother signs the autograph book in 1958, while Jack Marshall looks on and the headmaster holds her flowers!

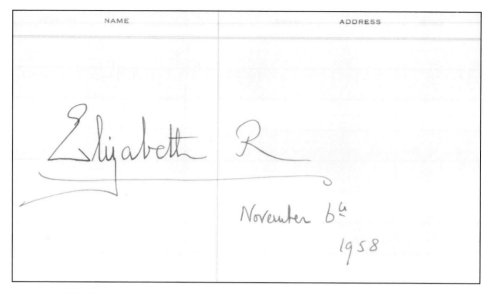

NAME	ADDRESS

Elizabeth R

November 6th

1958

The Queen Mother's autograph - the only one in the book - written in 1958.
(Warwick School Archives)

Mother's signature in an otherwise empty book (in a pile of unpromising junk) turned up to greet EB Halse at the start of his headmastership in 2002. Film of the special day in 1958, which Bishop regarded as the high point of his career, survives to this day, thanks to the diligence of Lt Col Whitlam and the first school archivist, Gervald Frykman, and it featured in a regional BBC TV news programme, *Midlands Today*, in February 2003.

An interesting 'boy's-eye view' of the Queen Mother's visit comes from Roger Wilmut:

> The Queen Mum's visit in 1958 was rather sprung on Bishop. He told us that they rang him up, offering her visit, and asked what she could do. He said "Open the new gates" (this was the first time the idea had entered his head) and then had to set about actually getting some new gates. She visited the new Science Block, where she got a demo of a Tesla coil: I was one of the boys stood in two rows, the second on benches, along the south side of "The Wynd" to hide the mess behind us from building work.

The high-voltage Tesla coil, which was used to power some fluorescent tubes in front of the Queen Mother, has survived, and it now gives the impression of being a singularly lethal piece of apparatus – and is never fired up. Mrs Ros Partridge says that the Queen Mother spotted some boys standing in rows and asked her father, "Why are those boys standing there?" The headmaster replied, "Screening, Your

Majesty." Walking a little further, they came upon another oddly-placed group. "More screening?" she enquired.

Mrs Caroline Sterratt explains:

The Queen Mother arrived late, and left later still, as I remember. The "screening" was partly to hide the numerous unsightly heaps of coal which were all round the school, in the bays at the back by the changing rooms, and partly to make sure that if people could not be introduced, they would at least have a clear uninterrupted view from no more than two back. Staff wives and children, myself included, were in Big School. The route had been so planned that the royal party would enter Big School from the door to the corridor nearest the dining room, and leave by the outside door diagonally opposite, thus allowing the maximum number of people to get a good close look. Before she arrived we were schooled in how to bow or curtsey at the appropriate time. I was on her right as my father ushered her past me. Much further down on my side she stopped, but I could not see why. My father told me later what

The Queen Mother inspects the CCF during her visit in 1958.
(Birmingham Post and Mail)

The Queen Mother talks to some of the pupils during her visit in 1958.
(Mrs Ros Partridge)

The end of the Queen Mother's visit to the school in 1958. She is flanked by Paul Ramage, the
head boy, and AHB Bishop. Behind the headmaster is Guy Nelson, Chairman of Governors.
(BW Young)

had happened. Apparently a very small staff son had been so overawed by the whole thing that he had preferred to look at his mother's skirts. The QM had stopped, put her hand on his head and gently rotated him so that he was facing in the right direction. When asked about this afterwards, he had said, "But I only like my Mummy and my Daddy to touch my head."

The Old Warwickians continued to support their old school faithfully and much appreciated the open lines of communication set up via the headmaster's war-time letters. The post-war era began soberly – a reflection upon the many deaths and injuries in service experienced by former pupils. The return of prisoners-of-war from Germany and Japan was dutifully catalogued – nor was this to be the end of it, as losses were later reported from Korea, Malaya and Egypt. The military has long been close to the heart of the school, and the developing career of Peter Cleaver, later to be an Air Vice-Marshal, was watched with interest. In addition, at one time four OWs were studying Russian under the aegis of the Royal Navy or Air Force. The cricketing achievements of Jack Marshall and TC Dodds have already been mentioned, and it was with great delight that the OW Cricket Week tour resumed in 1946. OWs contributed to the cost of paintings of HS Pyne and of MM Clark; Fred Mulley was elected MP in 1950; Dennis Castle performed in one of the first TV pantomimes, *Dick Whittington*; the school's first Olympian, AGK Brown, was appointed Head of the Royal Grammar School, Worcester; and RW Wilson became the school's first double Blue at Oxford in rugby and cricket. By 1955, the OWA numbered 1,190 members, and in 1957 at least 53 OWs were in residence at universities. As the school grew in size, it was not surprising that numbers of undergraduates reached the 100 mark.

It is fair to say that, of AHB Bishop's 26 years as Headmaster, the early ones were supremely demanding, given wartime conditions. Contemporaries recall that, though not a logical and consistent thinker, Bishop usually got the right answer, and he certainly saw the school through to calmer waters whilst presiding over a huge increase in pupil and staff numbers, numerous building crises and educational changes. It is, indeed, probably fair to say that he saved the school in 1946. He handed over a thriving school to Pat Martin – and whilst it took only twelve further years after his retirement to achieve his desire that the New Buildings be demolished, it was a full fifty years before his hope for a new history of the school (expressed in 1954) should at last be fulfilled. After a brief second marriage to Irene Titcomb in 1965, he died in 1969, at Bladon in Oxfordshire, after a short illness.

CHAPTER 19

Patrick William Martin

When Pat Martin took over the reins in September 1962, he brought with him the benefits of some seven years as Headmaster of Chipping Norton Grammar School and Lincoln School. Born in 1916, he was educated at Windermere Grammar School and Balliol College, Oxford, where he read modern history, but his short teaching career at Abingdon School was interrupted by war service from 1940 to 1946. He then taught at Workington Grammar School, before being appointed Assistant Education Officer for Brighton in 1952. At Warwick he inherited a well-established staff of 44, and a school of some 648 Senior School boys and 117 Juniors. In a period of 15 years, he presided over massive changes in both the fabric of the school and the fabric of society. By 1977, the Senior School numbered 732 boys, whose academic achievements included some of the best the school had ever known, and, in common with schools elsewhere, whose attitude to hair style, musical taste and much else previously held to be conventional would have seemed unthinkable in 1962. It was a major achievement to superintend this sea-change with a sense of proportion, something which his term of office as a magistrate enabled him to do so well. The Junior School developed significantly over these years, too, gaining new buildings and an increase of some 60% in pupil numbers. Pat Martin's reputation spread and, as his retirement approached, he was honoured with the Presidency of the Headmasters' Association. He was a long-serving member, too, of the Headmasters' Conference Committee. Within the school, he developed a number of initiatives: the concept of the Parents' Meeting was extended; the Friends of Warwick School was set up; Community Service was introduced on a much wider scale; and, to the chagrin of few, the school cap was abolished. As headmaster, he had authority. One example is given of a "difficult" lower fifth form who were proving recalcitrant. PWM asked to be given that form to teach for Religious Education – the gesture was appreciated by the teaching staff, if not by the boys! Certainly, he left behind the reputation of a man who would give support to those in need of it.

The staff as a body grew to 62, and the curriculum took note of changes at a national level, such as Nuffield Science; the Schools' Mathematics Project; the Cambridge Classics Project; and audio-lingual methods in Modern Foreign Languages, which led to the installation of Warwick's first language laboratory. In 1967, the first "computer"

Headmaster PW Martin talks to some prefects in his study, photographed in 1969.

was built, though modern-day informaticians might not wish to recognise it as such! Buildings were also a prime concern over this period, and projects great and small were undertaken, with plans for the more distant future also put in place. So it was, in 1965, that an appeal was launched for the School Hall, later to bear the name of Guy Nelson, long-time Alderman, and Chairman of the Governors from 1938 to 1963. Fittingly, the architect was the father of a pupil, Henry Fedeski. The eventual cost, when the building was completed in 1969, was some £95,000, which does not, perhaps, seem a large sum, but it should be borne in mind that schoolmasters earned less than £2,000 per year at this time. In reality, the new hall cost almost exactly one million pounds in 2003 values. Buildings continued to reflect the inflation that affected the national economy, and during the 1974-5 school year *The Portcullis* recorded that the latest classroom block had come in over its budgeted figure of £500,000. The "New Buildings", dating from 1919, were eventually demolished, but new blocks for the Junior School, Modern Languages (at a cost of £35,000), biology and mathematics had to be constructed first. In 1971, the Art Department moved to Bridge House (purchased by the governors in 1957, in poor condition, for £7,800, principally to

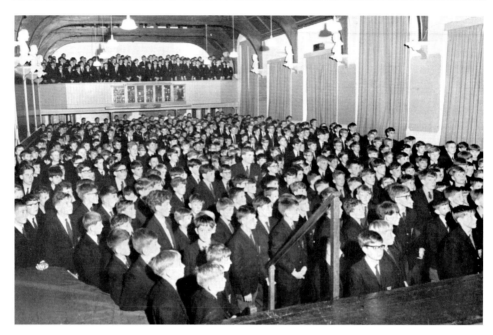

A staged, very crowded assembly in Big School, photographed in 1966 – for the
appeal brochure for a new hall.
(Warwick School Archives)

New Buildings, pictured immediately before their demolition in 1974.
Construction of the ground floor of the Design and Technology Block, with English above, has
already been started. The tree on the extreme left, a Judas Tree, has survived.

31. The demolition of the old Tuck Shop in 1995, in order to create the new Tuck Shop and Sixth Form Centre. The forlorn tree on the right is one of WT Keeling's Coronation Oaks, planted in 1902.

32. The new Tuck Shop and Sixth Form Centre, photographed in 1995.

33. The demolition of the Orlits building in 1996.

34. The new Arts Block, photographed from the Limes in 1996.

35. The new Drama Studio at the back of the Guy Nelson Hall, pictured in 1996.

36. The foyer of the new Bridge House Theatre, photographed in 2002. (GN Frykman)

37. The Masefield Centre, housing the library and ICT department, pictured in 2002. (GN Frykman)

38. The new buildings of the Junior School, with the Sports Centre behind, pictured in 2002.
(PJ O'Grady)

39. The last photo ever taken of the venerable mulberry tree, photographed a few months before being destroyed in a gale in 2002. (GN Frykman)

40. The Junior School and Senior School staff, pictured in May 2002.

Back row: Mrs D Caswell, Mrs A Williams, Mrs A Bungard, Mrs J Perry, DJ Rogers, Mrs C O'Grady, Mrs L James, K Marshall, Miss A Bond.

Second row: Mrs A Wilson, P Wheaton, M Byrne, Mlle, D Papin, Mrs C Morel-Bedford, T Butcher, C Thomas, P Nield, BL Davies, J Hanson, Miss G Beck, J Elston, N Oakden, T Lewis, Miss L Burridge.

Third row: IB Armstrong, JP Morris, R Thirlwell, T Jefferis, Mrs B Rossay-Gilson, M Jackson, RA Chapman, JD Stone, Mrs P Orme, A Debney, WM Newton, C Gibbs, Miss Z Keyte, D Pyrah, Mrs C McNee, Rev AW Gough, D Barr.

Fourth row: Miss A Ecclestone, J Jefferies, Mrs RE Jefferies, Mrs L Bain, GA Tedstone, D Seal, SR Chapman, CG McNee, Mrs EM Halborg, T Hoyle, DC Menashe, JR Daws, IS Dee, DEJI Lloyd, R Appleyard, Mrs SL Sephton, TG Barr.

Fifth row: PJ Duckworth, EJ Hadley, MW Shield, RA Bradley, DJ Shield, CH Watmough, PA Snell, GS Wilson, R Flintoff, G Ward, GN Frykman, RR Cousins, GIR Ogdon, Mrs LM Haines, Mrs K Ellison, Mrs JE Tait, D Snatt, Mrs M Yates.

Front row: JW Clift, PJ O'Grady, R Hudson, PA Johnson, MJ Green, AJ Reilly, P Russell, SHL Williams, PJ Cheshire, S Wheeler, B Emmerson, HE Collis, CG Daniel, IB Moffatt, WG Adams, JA Cooper, RW Fair.

(Gillman and Soame)

41. An aerial view of the school, taken by Peter O'Grady from an RAF helicopter in 2003.

42. The Charity Concert in the Bridge House Theatre, 26th March, 2004. (PJ O'Grady)

43. The first ever Staff Reunion, held in May 2004, attracted former staff from as far back as 1946. Several current senior staff, including the two authors of this book, also attended. (PJ O'Grady)

ensure that no adverse development ensued), as part of a plan, never to be fulfilled, to combine there the needs of art and what was then known as "handicraft". In the late 1960s, plans were unveiled for the building of a school for 5- to 7-year-old boys and girls on the site of the Bridge House orchard. Thus came into existence what we now know as the Squirrels, officially Warwick Preparatory School, on the Warwick School site. Previously, they had enjoyed accommodation in The Butts in the centre of town, until a fire destroyed their premises in 1970. Later on, of course, the site of Bridge House itself, deemed, even in 1957, to be "unsuitable for any school purpose", was used to construct a brand new theatre for the new millennium. The last tenants of Bridge House were the stalwart men of the Maintenance Department, and they had to wait until 2004 to get a purpose-built new facility.

Pressure on space, caused by increasing numbers of pupils, is revealed in governors' minutes of the 1950s. An example is the thorny problem of the Scout Hut, which belonged to the Boy Scout Association. It had been built on the edge of the playing fields in 1948, but scouting had ceased in 1955-6, and the cub pack dissolved in 1957. In desperation, the school had used the hut for teaching purposes, finally buying it for £100 in 1959. There were alterations to the administrative facilities of the school, to the benefit of the school office, the Bursary and the teaching staff, whilst a cafeteria-style dining room was created out of the space between the old Big School and the original, oak-panelled dining room. Big School itself was converted in the early 1970s into the school library, unfortunately largely destroying the painted "Honours Board" panels dating from the First World War. The panels were professionally photographed before being covered over, but it wasn't until thirty years later that the extremely large, and presumably very expensive, colour photographs were found. Not knowing that these photographs were ever supplied to the school, KG Brocklehurst also recorded the panels for posterity, using a single hand-held bulb and a step-ladder! The library survived in this format until 1999.

During the headmastership of Pat Martin, academic standards continued to rise: the 1965 results were praised as the best ever, with an 86.4% pass rate at 'A' level (whereas in the very different days of the early 21st century, a figure of at least 99% is expected!), and the greatest number of boys yet proceeding to higher education. In 1967, it was noted that the school's best-ever 'O' level cohort had produced disappointing 'A' level results, but records continued to be broken as the 1970s arrived: in 1972, 42% of 'A' level grades were A or B; the 1973 'A' and 'O' level results were again the best ever; and in 1975 the 'A' level pass rate exceeded 90%. That year, the school's Oxbridge results were among the best in the country. An average number of 7 'O' level passes per boy was now achievable. The entire curriculum was reviewed: the abolition, in 1967, of the "early" taking of some 'O' levels in the fourth form (middle fifth, or Year 10) was regretted by some, but it was followed shortly after by the introduction of a more open choice of 'A' level subjects, something which has reached its maximum extent today. It was a cause for regret in 1968 that boys doing a second

The new school library, created out of the old Big School, photographed in 1971.
(Warwick School Archives)

The gallery of the new school library, photographed in 1971.
(Warwick School Archives)

modern language or Greek could not do a "full" science course at 'O' level. Then, as now, there were strains upon the option system, even though there were far fewer options.

Warwick School has always taken the performing arts seriously, and during Pat Martin's 15 years many boys were given the opportunity to set out on a cultural journey which wasn't just reflected in the participation of OWs in *University Challenge* and *Songs of Praise*, nor in boys performing live on the radio in 1965, in a series called *Bright as a Button*. Within weeks of his arrival, PW Martin attended the official opening of the new Music School (now part of the Staff Common Room) by Eric Hope (OW), concert pianist of international repute. It is interesting to note the forceful view of the then Director of Music, EG Holmes, regarding the pernicious influence of pop music on pupils' appreciation of orchestral music, in various issues of *The Portcullis* in the early 1960s. Certainly, it was in the more traditional modes of music that Warwick boys made their names at this time. In 1967, Paull Boucher went to Canada to perform with Benjamin Britten in *Burning Fiery Furnace*. A year later, the school was treated to an organ recital by Kevin Passmore (OW), and the talents of flautist William Sleath were developing so fast that the first Summer Concert to be directed by David Nichols (Director of Music 1969-95) was truly memorable. During DN's reign, much musical development was evident: with the support of Paul Russell (who gave his first lesson as teacher of brass at Warwick back in 1959 as a teenager, and who remained on the staff until 2003), the May 1970 Sounding Brass

The school's first language laboratory, opened in 1972.

Boys outside the Tuck Shop at break, photographed in 1963.
(Photo-Reportage Ltd)

Concert set the standard that was still filling halls in the early 21ˢᵗ century. Folk music was given its due, with performances by Dorita y Pepe and Cy Grant, names familiar to those born in the 1940s; and major musical forces such as Anthony Hopkins and Leon Goossens came to the school. Thanks to a Music Marathon in 1974, the then significant sum of £700 was raised to buy instruments. Support staff in the Music Department increased over this period: the appointment of Hugh Large as Assistant Director of Music in 1968 reflected the new opportunities the school was now offering its musicians – and, indeed, those who did not realise that they had musical potential – and there was great sadness at his early death some five years later. His replacement by Miss Mary Eels, who was later to be replaced by Mrs Ruth Johnson, ensured that the cause of womankind in the Senior School would develop.

The tradition of the major school play, for example, one by Shakespeare, being interspersed, perhaps, with a Gilbert & Sullivan "Savoy opera", such as *Ruddigore, Trial by Jury, Yeomen of the Guard* or *Patience* (directed by Roger Usherwood), has lasted for many years: performances of *Much Ado About Nothing* and *Julius Caesar* (the first play to be performed in the Guy Nelson Hall in 1970) made an impression, as did *A Penny for a Song* (reprised in 1994 by Warwick's first Head of Drama, John Daws), *The Caucasian Chalk Circle, Sweeney Todd* (with all proceeds going to fund a camp for underprivileged children), *The Crucible* (the first of David Stooke's very

Mr PW Martin, in the foreground, having just received the keys of the first minibus owned by the school, photographed in 1969. Mr KG Brocklehurst is getting out of the driver's seat.

special contributions to Warwick's drama), *The Importance of Being Earnest*, and *Oliver!*, to name but a few. Junior School drama was given a special boost by the appointment of Allan Wilkins in 1972. His direction of *Oliver!* in 1976 was deemed the best thing since the opening of the Guy Nelson Hall, and *Emil and the Detectives* gained plaudits from all who saw it. During this time, George Brightman partici-pated in the National Youth Theatre, and some years later the talents of Louis Hilyer began to develop. Meanwhile, the tradition of the Staff Play (or pantomime) continued, uninterrupted by examination pressures, and *Queen Elizabeth Slept Here* was followed a few years later by *Cinderella in Transit* (the purpose of the show being to raise money for a minibus), *The Thwarting of Baron Bolligrew* and *The Happiest Days of your Life*. Stalwarts of these shows included Ken Freeborn (who frequently wrote the scripts, which were sometimes followed...), Brian Emmerson and David Stooke. From this time also dates the regular involvement of girls from King's High School and The Kingsley School, Leamington, in school productions. As he himself said in May 2004, David Stooke "was wont to boast of his initiative in this area".

The importance of sport in a boys' school can never be underestimated. Rugby remained the school's prime sport, but success in a number of areas was recorded. In 1963, Roger Hosen toured Australia and New Zealand with the England Rugby XV, before leaving the staff for a Head of Department post. In 1969, Tim Dalton became

A games session on the school field, taken in 1963.
(Photo-Reportage Ltd)

the first OW to be capped by England at rugby football and simultaneously the first substitute to play in an international rugby match for England. A year later, John Reardon won an England U19 cap, and in the early 1970s RC (Tim) Barnwell (U19) and Martin Clifford (U15) gained England honours. In 1970, the school entered the Rosslyn Park Sevens for the first time – and so began another episode in the history of the school's rugby football. The 1974–75 season was notable for the six players who were selected for Warwickshire. The following season saw Ralph Thornton hand on responsibility for the XV to Ken Freeborn after many years of building up Warwick's rugby. His dedication had extended to long journeys, supporting youngsters playing representative sport. Although the Victorians at Warwick School had no problem, it is now, perhaps, sacrilegious to mention soccer in the same breath as rugger; it should be noted, however, that, in addition to being the one sport that boys can be guaranteed to play spontaneously on any sports field, soccer was the game played during a tour of Holland, led by Ken Freeborn, in 1964, though there is no record of this being repeated.

At various times in Warwick's modern, or even Victorian, history there have been outbreaks of interest in hockey, but there were also lengthy fallow periods when, at best, the sport survived as a club activity. By the late 1960s, however, thanks to the persistence of Phil Heelis, the status and popularity of hockey rose rapidly. Competitive matches against other schools were increasingly successful, and the 1973–74 season was a milestone, as the U16 team won the county knock-out championship. In 1974, Roger Thurman was selected to play for England, and Neil Thomas was selected to play for Wales – hockey was well and truly on the map!

During this period, cricket continued to be the major summer sport without generating any "big names". However, the XI remained a strong competitive force on the local "circuit", guided by Jack Marshall until 1976, when he retired from his sporting responsibilities. The cricket photographs of the early 1970s are good indicators of changing hair-styles! The swimming pool benefited from heating at this time, and water polo produced heroes in Bob Jelfs, who captained the Great Britain U18 team in 1964, and, at the end of the decade, Keith Tallett, who played for the U20s against Spain. Water on a wider scale attracted other pupils: Jason Holtom and Tim Fillmore took part in *The Observer* Single-Handed Transatlantic Yacht Race in 1971. Just over 30 years later, the latter's son Guy looks set to repeat his father's achievements. Tennis, too, had its moments, with MA Walter representing Great Britain at U14 level against Germany and Italy in 1976. Badminton enjoyed a revival as an acknowledged school sport in 1967 (having had its first mention in 1935) under Messrs Jackson and Underwood. Within five years, the brothers R and J Wallace were making a name for themselves, one in the all-England Junior Final and an Under-18 European tournament, and the other in the finals of the all-England Doubles championship. Pip Elson played golf for England at U18 level and went on to a successful professional career, as did his son Jamie later. Cross-country experienced particular success in its early days as an official school sport: in 1964, the first "proper" competitive fixtures took place, and 1969 was described as the busiest and best season to date.

The Combined Cadet Force remained an important aspect of the school's extra-curricular provision. New Ministry of Defence regulations did have an effect, however, in that only 20% of the contingent was allowed to serve more than nine terms, that proportion being used as NCOs. This led to the creation of a pre-CCF for younger cadets. From 1963 till 1966, in addition to his many other duties, Roger Usherwood took charge of the CCF. In 1964, an RAF section was created, commanded by Phil Heelis. Within a short while, it had nearly 50 cadets, not far short of the number in the Army section. Camps and Arduous Training in places as far afield as Snowdonia, Germany and Norway were popular, and individuals gained flying scholarships and took part in the international Air Cadet Exchange. Closer to home, Colonel Whitlam was delighted to be able to open an indoor rifle range on the school site. Additionally, the Duke of Edinburgh Award Scheme, which had been instituted in 1962, was available from 1965 onwards, initially only within the CCF. It was fitting that Warwick's first Gold Award winner, David Summers, should receive his prize from the Duke himself in 1967.

The school holidays were regularly used for a variety of trips. In the early 1960s, walking holidays to destinations such as Lyme Regis and the Lake District were followed by more distant travels to places such as Greece, Czechoslovakia, Sicily, Hungary and Brussels, often organised by the senior chemist, Harry Sheppard – a man with an international reputation, as it happens, as a scholar of alchemy! The geographers explored Iceland, as well as their more traditional haunts: North Wales,

Mr GT Simmonds teaching geography to M.V.1 in 1963.
(Photo-Reportage Ltd)

A woodwork class in the old Engineering Shop, photographed in 1963.
(Photo-Reportage Ltd)

A Lower Fourth science lesson in C2 (before it was made smaller), taken in 1963.
(Photo-Reportage Ltd)

A Middle Fifth chemistry lesson in C1, pictured in 1963 in what would now be regarded as
severely over-crowded conditions.
(Photo-Reportage Ltd)

Break in the Masters' Common Room, photographed in 1969.
Mr RH Thornton stands in the centre.

Arran and Skye. The biologists continued their field-trips, too. Another regular feature of the school's extra-curricular activities was the educational cruise. It should be remembered that in the '60s and '70s foreign travel was altogether more exotic than it is now. Cruises around various parts of the Mediterranean enabled groups of up to 200 boys at a time to see parts of the world that they would not otherwise have got to know. Trips and exchanges (for example, with the Grammar School in Ahlen, Germany) continued to be organised by members of the Modern Languages Department. Ski trips to Switzerland and Austria retained their attraction.

School societies reflect the times very effectively: in 1963, a Fine Arts Club was set up, followed shortly afterwards by the Angling Club, the Motor Film Club, the Aeromodelling Club and the Folk Music Club. These 'went the way of all flesh', although at least the Ringing Society and the Film Society came back at a later date. The Outdoor Pursuits and Personal Survival groups experienced a period of strength, linked as they were with the ongoing CCF activities. A different form of society was the Community Service Unit. Initially known as the Voluntary Service Unit, this organisation rapidly enabled the school to strengthen its links with the community by running concerts for the elderly, a Day Club for OAPs (Old Age Pensioners, as they were then called), a Grand (Fundraising) Walk and summer camps for "deprived children", as well as supporting the elderly in their own homes and helping out at Hatton Central Hospital – the county's major psychiatric hospital,

Mr BW Young teaching Latin to Lower Remove A in 1963.
(Photo-Reportage Ltd)

now the site of what might be called an urban village. Income was generated by sponsored events and the collection (and subsequent sale) of waste-paper. In the early 1970s, as many as 80 boys a week were involved in Community Service, thanks, in the main, to men like Peter Johnson and Colin Byfleet.

Speech Day enabled the school to invite learned speakers to distribute prizes in the traditional way. During Pat Martin's time, the school was privileged to receive some eminent politicians – local MPs Mr (later Sir) Dudley Smith and Sir John Hobson: Warwick's only Cabinet Minister, Fred Mulley; RHS Crossman (future member of the Wilson cabinets); Sir Edward Boyle (a Conservative Minister of Education); and Sir Henry Plumb (then of the Farmers' Union, later a Conservative MEP). OWs Air Vice-Marshal Peter Cleaver and Denis Matthews complete a memorable list.

The teaching staff changed radically between 1962 and 1977. The pre-war generation approached or reached retirement age; many new and younger members of staff moved on to major promotions elsewhere; and the staff as a body grew as a consequence of greater pupil numbers and curricular change. Boarding remained a popular option, with over a hundred boys in the two houses, and Junior House regularly having its maximum complement of 40 boys. As he came up to retirement in 1969, Felix Dugdale handed Junior House on to Roger Usherwood. Given that he had been Second Master and a senior Modern Linguist, Mr Dugdale had shouldered a heavy burden over the years. In 1971, Barry Young handed the Senior House on to

A biology practical with M.V.2,
pictured in 1963.
(Photo-Reportage Ltd)

A 1963 biology lesson in what is now
the Music Block.
(Photo-Reportage Ltd)

David Nichols after 15 years; he was to continue full-time teaching of Classics for a further 14 and to sing with the choir for at least a further 30!

The departure of long-standing members of staff merits some attention: in 1964, CCC Lewis retired after 34 years teaching Modern Languages; the deaths of Messrs AD Hainworth (1907-38) and AS Wolstencraft (1922-59) were reported; Lt Col PNG Whitlam had completed 44 years as Curator – his films survive as a memorable example of life at Warwick; HC Deykin retired as Head of Art after 30 years' service; LJ Charman retired after nearly 20 years as Head of Mathematics; and the Headmaster's secretary for 30 years, Miss Mann, passed on her baton. RW Long left the English Department in 1966, and in 1968 Rev BS Maitland moved to a headship, having spent the better part of 15 years at the school. Miss Margaret Lanspeary completed 22 years' service in the Junior School the same year. In 1969, the Director of Music, EG Holmes, moved to RGS, High Wycombe, and the school's Bursar since 1946, AL Hues, retired. GL Bousfield moved to a Deputy Headship after 13 years, during which time he had helped to introduce economics to the sixth-form curriculum. The retirement of Geoffrey Simmonds (OW), after 30 years of teaching geography, and the death of Rev HE Cullis (staff 1921-54) marked the end of a line of OW teachers stretching back to the First World War. In the final six years of Pat Martin's headship, three "major" retirements took place: in 1975, Henry Sawyer, who had taught mathematics since 1946; in 1977, Harry Sheppard (Head of Chemistry) after 30 years; and Edgar Blackshaw (Head of Modern Languages) after

21 years. By this time, however, there were increasing numbers of young members of staff – some of whom remain at Warwick in the early years of the 21st century and have worked under four headmasters. Even in these days of professional mobility, the school has succeeded in retaining the affection of members of staff who are prepared to spend virtually their whole career there.

The Old Warwickians continued to play an important part in the life of the school, and their section in the *Portcullis* magazine (which appeared as many as three times a year until 1970) shows what a variety of professional activities pupils went on to after school. Some families, such as the Hiorns and the Hains, have supported the school through the generations. Some have had lengthy uninterrupted periods when their sons were in the school: few could outstrip the Wilsons of Kenilworth, who had a boy in the school every year from 1942 until 1974, or the Wardles, whose line goes from K Wardle, Head of Mathematics from 1933 to 1946, to great-grandson James, who left the U6 in 2004 – and who went out in style by holding every single school swimming record. Some families, such as the Thorpes, have habitually taken the "boarding route", though such traditions are virtually extinct now. The musical career of Denis Matthews was followed keenly at this time, as were the successes of Michael Billington, who celebrated 30 years as Drama Critic of the *Guardian* in 2001 – he was Drama Critic of the Year in 1976. Another feature of OW life has been the Portcullis Club, which opened in 1964, and where many contacts are maintained.

As mentioned earlier, Pat Martin shepherded the school through times of change. He extended the Warwick School Code (established in 1942) to include:

> Members of the Sixth Form may drive a car, motorcycle or scooter to School as long as their parents have sought general permission in advance from the Headmaster. They may not park the vehicle at School and must undertake to do so either at a public car park, or in the private garage or grounds of friends.

The days of the "permissive society" were just around the corner, and the automatic authority of adults was about to be questioned. Some staff, just as some parents, found this hard to take. Yet the school did adapt, as it has throughout the decades, and one senses that Pat Martin was doing more than just 'keeping the lid on things'. Standards were still expected, despite the period of student unrest which he commented on in 1969, and it was still appropriate to remind the school of the need to take pride in their appearance in his 1971 Speech Day report. Schools were a political 'hot potato' for much of his headship, since, of his 15 years, nine were under a Labour Government, which was ideologically opposed to Public Schools, but the pressures were seen off. The school continued to retain the support and affection of the community, reflected not least in the 1966 fête, which attracted some 1,500 visitors. Described as a headmaster with "flair and street-cred among the boys" by Eric Ives, Chairman of Governors from 1985 to 2003, Pat Martin lived in retirement in Kenilworth, and died in November 2000, aged 84.

CHAPTER 20

John Anthony Strover

❧

In 1977, the governors appointed John Strover to replace Pat Martin as Headmaster. Born in India, he was aged 46 when he took up the headmastership, as were to be his two successors. An Oxford mathematician and Hockey Blue (he had captained the university team and represented England at the 1956 Olympics), he had ample teaching experience at Canford, Harrow and, as Headmaster, at Kingston Grammar School. So it was that he 'hit the ground running' and rapidly gained the appreciation of his staff and pupils, thanks to his friendly and approachable manner. His style – and domestic arrangements – were different from those of his predecessor and his successor in that he had four sons, one of pre-school age, and they did not really appreciate having to grow up in so public a place as the headmaster's house. However, the Strovers' eventual decision to move out from the headmaster's house to a property that they bought in Leamington did not go down well in some quarters and did eventually have an impact upon his tenure of the post of headmaster. Others quite liked the idea of the headmaster arriving at school on his bicycle!

John Strover's time as head coincided with significant changes in education and politics: the arrangement by which the Local Education Authority funded 45 free places per year was phased out, which was potentially a very serious loss for the school. The boys nominated by the LEA were, by definition, local boys, many of them very bright, and it was Strover's achievement to navigate his way successfully through the consequences of this loss: numbers held up, and the quality of intake was more or less maintained. The Assisted Places Scheme was introduced thereafter, lasting until the early years of the 21st century. It was the introduction of this scheme, with its insistence on the complete absence of corporal punishment for those benefiting from it, which finally led Strover to abolish corporal punishment completely throughout the school. During this period, the school had to market itself more vigorously than before: Open Days and a new prospectus were just two of the approaches adopted, and communications with parents, via more regular meetings and reports, were sharpened up. Not everyone was in favour of this, since, in the past, parents had been 'kept at arm's length', but it proved to be beneficial. Appraisal of senior staff, now seen as a normal aspect of management, was introduced. A major step forward in terms of modernisation, and harmonisation with other schools, was the abolition of Saturday morning school, as from September 1982. This radical step was brought about after two consultations with parents and staff – after the first there was no clear wish to change.

Examination results, too, came under scrutiny. A pass rate of 83% at 'A' level in 1978 (when an average of 6.7 passes at 'O' level was achieved) would no longer be seen as sufficient, and by the end of John Strover's time a pass-rate in excess of 90% was seen as a minimum requirement for the school. Academic excellence was unquestionably achieved, however, and the school's success in obtaining ten Oxbridge awards in 1980 is but one example of this. 'O' level and CSE examinations were replaced by GCSE (the General Certificate of Secondary Education) in 1988.

The curriculum changed in relatively small, but highly significant, ways – for example, when Technical Studies became Craft, Design and Technology, raising its profile and improving its workshop facilities to take in metals and plastics; at the time, these were seen as state of the art, and much visited by other schools. Even more significant was the growth of computing, and in 1981 plans were put forward for the

Mr JW Clift (centre), with maintenance staff Peter Yurkwich and Fred Burden, on the completion of the school's first full-sized computer room in 1986, complete with 17 BBC computers.

school's first dedicated computing room. John Clift, the school's first Director of Computing, has supplied the following note about the early development of the subject at Warwick School:

> Warwick School was amongst the pioneers in the introduction of computers in the classroom. Our first desktop computers, then called microcomputers, were purchased in 1980. The maximum memory capacity of these computers, Commodore PETs, was 32 kilobytes. Programs and data had to be stored on unreliable cassette tape. There was no applications software, apart from the BASIC programming language. Even so large numbers of boys volunteered for after school courses in the new technology.
>
> The pace of change in this field was such that each generation of computers had to be replaced after about six years. In 1986 the former Science Library was converted to become the Upper Computer Room, holding 17 BBC micros. This enabled computing lessons to make their first appearance in the timetable. One consequence was that computing was established as a separate academic department in the following year. Previously all computers had been the responsibility of the mathematics department.
>
> Something that did not change was the enthusiasm of Warwick School pupils. Many seemed to spend all their lunch breaks at computer club and school teams regularly reached the national stage in competitions, such as those run by the British Computer Society.

Building work went on apace: assisted by a successful appeal in the late 1970s, the school now had its first English Block, and this was followed by the creation of a Sixth Form Centre in the main building (formed from three of the original 1879 ground-floor classrooms), improved facilities for music, a dedicated Economics Block in 1982, and a Design Centre in 1986, which provided two art studios, and extensions for mathematics and biology. Facilities for hockey and cricket were enhanced by the laying of new pitches on the Banbury Road side. The Junior School, too, benefited from the building plan, gaining a science laboratory and new facilities for art and music, whilst the Staff Common Room was substantially extended.

Throughout this period, the school continued to offer a developing range of extra-curricular opportunity. One aspect of this was its commitment to broadening its pupils' minds through the means of expeditions and travel, including field-trips for geography and biology; annual trips and exchanges to France and Germany; regular trips to Spain (at a time when curricular Spanish was yet to develop); ski trips to Austria; and educational cruises – for example, to the Baltic and the former Soviet Union. The Hovercraft Club even took part in a competition in the former Czechoslovakia. Annual CCF camps and Adventurous Training ensured that boys could develop other skills, and it is perhaps significant that at this time a number of Army and Flying Scholarships and University Bursaries were awarded. Members of

The new English Block on its opening in 1979.

the school had the opportunity to participate in the Tall Ships Race, thanks to the ingenuity of Paul Stainsby, who had developed a highly successful Sailing Club, with numerous sailing weekends and longer cross-channel trips. Clubs and societies retained their popularity, even if the most popular ones of the time are no longer favoured these days! The Archaeological, Industrial Archaeology, Poetry, Stamp & Coin, Transport and Ornithological were but a few of the successful clubs of the time, whilst new ones sprang up, including Fencing and Archery. A major sporting expedition was the 1985 Rugby tour of Zimbabwe, followed up by a tour of Canada in 1987.

Sport prospered throughout this period. In cricket, the school had two players who went on to represent their counties, and another who gained one-day international honours. As Young England cricketers, Gordon Lord and Geoff Tedstone toured in Australia and the West Indies, later representing Warwickshire at first-class level. Lord, an opening batsman who finished his career playing for Worcestershire and is currently employed by the England and Wales Cricket Board, scored 199 (run out) against Yorkshire in 1985. Tedstone, now Director of Sport at Warwick School, kept wicket for Gloucestershire after leaving Edgbaston. Neil Smith, son of MJK Smith, former England cricket captain, made his début for Warwickshire in 1987, going on to captain the county in 1999 and 2000. An off-spinner and aggressive batsman, who was good enough to be used as a "pinch hitter" in the 1998 World Cup, held in India and Pakistan, he played seven times for England. He is well remembered for his exploits in winning the 1989 NatWest Trophy Final for his county. In his "off season", he regularly helped with sports coaching, joining the staff of his old school on a more formal basis in September 2004. In the mid-1980s, the Oxford and Warwickshire off-spinner, Simon Sutcliffe, taught history at the school. Squash was especially successful in the early 1980s, thanks to the exploits of the Robinson brothers, one of whom, Gary, became the 1985 British U19 Champion.

Hockey also distinguished itself at this time, 1982 being described as the school's most successful season to date. The 1st XI, captained by Denys Shortt, won 22 of its 30 matches. It was rugby, however, that made much of the running in the 1980s. In 1984, rugby at Warwick celebrated its centenary, and this was commemorated in a special publication, prepared by Martin Green. Rugby football continued to expand during John Strover's headmastership, with more "B" team matches at the younger levels and more games played by the 3rd and 4th XVs. In 1982, the 1st, 2nd and 3rd XVs beat Rugby School, and the 1983-4 centenary season was especially successful, with only two matches lost to school opposition. The devoted coaching of men like Ken Freeborn, Ian Moffatt, Martin Green, Alex Hughes, Brian Emmerson, Geoff Lane, Tony Sparks and Robin Flintoff undoubtedly played its part. Brian Emmerson took over from Martin Green as 1st XV coach in 1984 and set about organising the school's first major tour, to Zimbabwe. Twenty-one boys took part, not losing a game and experiencing at first hand the reality of Robert Mugabe's post-colonial republic. Amongst the most successful Warwickians at this time were Mark Calverley, who played at scrum half for the England U18 team in 1985, and James Freeman, who went on to obtain a Cambridge Blue in 1987. Martin Green coached the England rugby team on its New Zealand tour in 1985 and in the first World Cup in Australia in 1987. The success of the 1985-86 team was noteworthy: 17 out of 19 games were won, as were all six 7s competitions. Victories in the North of England, Oxford and Rosslyn Park tournaments (in which not one game out of 36 was lost or drawn) were high points indeed. Although the following season was something of an anticlimax, it did lead to another tour, this time of Canada. An itinerary leading from Edmonton to Vancouver provided an all-round experience for 24 boys and their coaches, leading to a season in 1987-8 which was one of the best three in recent memory.

The school's commitment to the wider community was very much in evidence in the 1980s. The Community Service Unit, formerly called Voluntary Service, and run until 1981 by Colin Byfleet (thereafter by Andrew Parkes and, from 1987 to 2002, by Gervald Frykman), made much money from its newspaper collection and from activities such as a 48-hour table football marathon (which got into the Guinness Book of Records) and sponsored walks. The school was the headquarters for the Warwickshire Talking Newspaper for the Blind, and the CSU's work once featured on regional television. The 1984 appeal for Ethiopia raised the sum of £2,200, and when, in 1985, Andrew Hughes, son of a master at the school, was diagnosed with a life-threatening illness (from which he mercifully recovered in due course) and had to go into Great Ormond Street Children's Hospital, it sparked off some imaginative

A robot butler, with its designers and constructors,
Simon Tweed, Peter Wilson and Henry Rivera,
which won first prize in a national competition in 1985.

and dedicated fundraising in support of the hospital's Wishing Well Appeal. Two members of staff, Martin Green and Rob Howard, ran marathons, and over sixty separate projects helped to raise £13,000. This sum was handed over in assembly to Graeme Hick and Phil Neale of Worcestershire Cricket Club. The annual visit of the Town Crier of Warwick raised sums for the Mayor's chosen charity, too. Raising money was not the sole objective of Community Service, however: the drama group took its wares out to local primary schools and homes, and individual pupils spent Thursday afternoons doing domestic and gardening chores for elderly folk.

Substantial sums were raised for the school by the Friends of Warwick School (FOWS), as a result of which such items as video recorders, cellos, a scrummaging machine, stage-lighting for the Guy Nelson Hall, sailing dinghies, seven PET computers and a minibus were bought in a period of six years. The 1977 Appeal for bursaries and buildings succeeded in its aim of raising a sum in excess of £200,000. An approach to industry and trusts bore fruit, and the 1979 Warwick School Fiesta also made a useful contribution.

Drama remained a strength. The regular pattern continued – a Gilbert & Sullivan opera, directed by Roger Usherwood, interspersed with plays such as those mentioned below. The role of David Stooke in fostering and producing plays cannot be overstated. Major Senior School productions included: *Incident at Vichy*, *Joseph and His Amazing Technicolor Dreamcoat* (narrated by Louis Hilyer, who went on to success in the theatre), *Henry IV Part 1*, *HMS Pinafore*, *Noye's Fludde*, *A Man For All Seasons*, *Bartholomew Fair*, *Iolanthe*, *Journey's End*, *Waiting for Godot*, *The Tempest*, *Oliver!* and *She Stoops To Conquer*, the latter three being directed by Graham Ogdon. Staff plays and pantomimes continued to cater for a wide audience in those days when the pressure of work was a little less acute than it became in the last decade of the century. *Snow White*, *Arsenic and Old Lace*, *Babes in the Wood*, *Forty Years On* and *Sweeney Todd* were but a few of the offerings. The Junior School put on memorable shows, such as *Toad of Toad Hall* (directed by Allan Wilkins) and *Murder in the Cathedral*, and Stephen Woodward continued to stage his own translations of Molière comedies. Opportunities continued to arise for boys to work with the Royal Shakespeare Company at Stratford, as, for instance, in the 1984 production of *Measure for Measure*.

Accommodation for music improved over the period, though the aim of a single, large departmental building would have to wait until the mid-1990s. David Nichols continued to direct the school's music, assisted from 1979 by Richard Springate on strings and from 1983 by Charles Watmough. Numbers of peripatetic music teachers increased as the school strove to cater for developing interests among its boys.

Art moved from Bridge House to a purpose-built Design Centre, which opened in 1986. Following Bryan Hornsby's retirement in 1979, his assistant, Robin Flintoff, was appointed Head of Art, a position he still occupies, and Grahame Ward, with his complementary skills and interests, became the latter's assistant.

The generation of staff who had known war service was now reaching retirement age (generally 65, rather than the 60 which is now the contractual norm at Warwick), and many characters who had defined the school over previous decades came to the end of their careers. In 1977, the Senior School had 62 staff for 732 pupils; this grew to 74 staff for 802 pupils by 1988. During this period, the size of the Junior School remained constant at around 180. The management of the school was, essentially, in the hands of the Headmaster and the Second Master – John Beeching until 1980, and thereafter Ralph Thornton until the latter's retirement in 1989, after more than forty years of service. Both of John Strover's Second Masters had held lengthy departmental responsibilities, as Heads of Science and Mathematics respectively; indeed, Ralph Thornton continued as Head of Mathematics until 1982. Both men embodied the virtues, which are no longer so common, of very long service in one institution, to which they gave continuity and unfailing dedication. These men "knew their stuff", knew their staff and understood the needs of their charges. Continuity was also the keyword regarding the 17 years that Jim Palmer spent as Chairman of the governing body between 1963 and 1980, when he was succeeded by Air Vice-Marshal Peter Cleaver. Thereafter, the governing body became much more influential.

The Junior School, too, had benefited from the long service of two men with distinguished war records. Jack Marshall, its Headmaster since 1946, had been the very essence of the school, a county cricketer of repute, a man who was known and respected in the community to the extent that his personal example was enough to persuade parents that this was the school for their sons. On his retirement in December 1979, he was replaced by Keith Winterbottom. Harold Robinson, like JMAM an OW, served as Deputy Head and was on the staff from 1961 till 1982, when he was succeeded by David Rogers, who, unfortunately, had to resign, owing to ill-health, at the end of 2003.

Amongst the staff who retired during the Strover years were a number whose service began shortly after the war: Ellis Owen (1947-84) taught French and German; Jack Swindlehurst (1948-81) oversaw major developments in design and technology; Keith Brocklehurst (1948-83) completed his years at Warwick as Head of Science; Barry Young (1949-85) taught Classics and also ran the Senior Boarding House for a significant period; and Peter Adcock (1950-85) became Head of English. Such brief, bald facts give no flavour of each man's unique contribution and service. Arriving in the 1950s were David Keighley (1957-86), a keen cricketer, who taught French and took responsibility for careers; Roger Usherwood (1957-86), a Classicist, who also took responsibility for the Junior Boarding House – his wife, June, was Matron to both boarding houses – and within the CCF (where he inaugurated the RAF section in 1963); and Robert Heaton, whose death "in office" in 1980 was a tremendous shock. As Head of History, he had also introduced economics to the curriculum. The 12-year service (1968-80) of Rev Michael Robinson, the first of two economist-Chaplains, seems momentary in comparison, but, by the 1970s, a greater mobility was the route to promotion within the teaching profession. Nineteen eighty-seven was, therefore, a rare year – no member of the teaching staff came or left!

Warwick's reputation as a forcing-ground for young talent continued throughout John Strover's time as many left for Head of Department posts: Colin Byfleet, Peter Smythe, Peter Wales, Chris Aldred, Carol Gray (the first full-time female teacher in the Senior School for some time – she had two spells on the staff) and Simon Sutcliffe, to name but a few. Peter Johnson both went and returned, having worked in the interim for the Scouts' Association. His wife, Ruth, also has a claim to fame, having been one of the rare women (at the time) to be appointed to a regular post in the Senior School. For many years after Mrs Johnson's departure, Elisabeth Freeman, a Modern Linguist, was the sole female member of staff, although she only worked part-time. By 1987, she was one of four.

(*Top left*) Cubicles in the boarding house immediately before the complete refurbishment of 1985. (Warwick School Archives)

(*Left*) A boarding house cubicle, for two boys, pictured just before its demolition in 1985. (Warwick School Archives)

(*Above*)The main boarding house dormitory just before refurbishment in 1985. This photograph should be compared with that of the Elstow dormitory of 1930. (Warwick School Archives)

Study bedrooms built in the boarding house in the summer of 1985. (Warwick School Archives)

The teaching staff gained from an increase in ancillary support over the years up to 1988: more technicians (for example, Steve Rowlandson in the audio-visual department and Tish Pipitone in computing) and reprographics assistants were employed, and a full-time librarian, Teresa Smith, was appointed, enabling Robert Hudson to return to full-time teaching. Steve Rowlandson's appointment to the post of audio-visual technician seemed to bear little relationship to one of his first major tasks – that of modernising the telephone system. Little did he realise what he was to set in motion when a PABX system was installed in 1986. This lasted until 1992, by which time there were 42 extensions around the school, and each individual telephone could be used internally or externally. Gone – finally – were the days when Jenny Langley (the Headmaster's secretary) or, indeed, frustrated members of the teaching staff, had to hold two handsets, one to each ear, in order to relay messages between an incoming caller and his target! The idea of having a telephone receptionist finally bore fruit in 1989.

The maintenance and ground-staff grew, too. Norman Horner, the head groundsman, was formerly Warwickshire's distinguished opening batsman, and he undertook the mammoth task of re-laying the entire cricket square. When carpenter Bill Hughes retired in 1980, after 50 years' service, he represented the end of an era, in that, these days, a fifty-year career in anything is hard to achieve! The duties of the Bursar developed as the school grew. In 1983, Major Peter Waterworth retired after 14 years' service. Air Vice-Marshal David Bates (an OW), whose father had been the music master from 1929 to 1940, replaced him for a while. In 1986, Lt Col Francis Daniell took up office. He was to stay until 2001.

The traditions of the school remained in place. Speech Day guests frequently had a high profile: Lord Carver, Anthony Quinton (the Oxford academic), Sir Adrian Cadbury, Tim Devlin (later to become a Conservative MP), John Egan (then Chairman of Jaguar) and Enoch Powell all addressed the school, the latter giving a powerful defence of the Classics in October 1984, whilst a small group of demonstrators protested on the Myton Road – not against the Classics, of course, but against what they perceived to be his racist views.

A stronger tradition, indeed the historic basis of the school, was to be found in boarding. In the early 1980s, this became a point of conflict between those who felt, largely for financial reasons, that the boarding houses should be closed rather than refurbished, and those who believed in their continuance. The former believed that boarding had had its day, and that the cost of upgrading the facilities to the standard parents and boys would require in the modern age could not be justified. Somewhat to their surprise, a counter-attack was launched, with a strong OW involvement, spearheaded by the President, Bill Billington, and the governors reversed their decision to close the boarding houses. Thus the summer of 1985 saw the start of a complete refurbishment of the boarding facilities – and a change in the chair of governors. By 1986, the necessary improvements had taken place, and the future of boarding seemed secure once more. Numbers of boarders tended to be around 55-60

Headmaster John Strover, MP Enoch Powell and Chairman of Governors Peter Cleaver on
their way to Speech Day, October 1984.
(Warwick School Archives)

each year, and no significant decline was noted. For the greater part of John Strover's
headmastership, Stephen Woodward was Senior Housemaster; his immediate predecessor, David Nichols, stayed on in Junior House, latterly with Grahame Ward as
Junior Housemaster. Certainly, no talk of closure was heard for a while, although in
the early 1990s rationalisation led to the combining of the two houses, and the issue
of boarding was considered again in 2003. Demand for the existing places remained
high. Traditions of another kind lived on, in that departing sixth-formers had for
some time marked their final day as schoolboys with antics of one kind or another,
and a somewhat dangerous tradition of jumping from the bridge into the Avon
needed eventually to be discouraged!

Old Warwickians continued to make their way in the world, some more publicly
than others. In the 1979 General Election, Harry Greenway and Fred Mulley were
returned as MPs for their constituencies in Ealing and Sheffield respectively. In the

same year, Sir George Catlin, father of Shirley Williams (Liberal Democrat leader in the House of Lords), died. OWs of a younger generation are frequently represented amongst the armed forces. In the Falklands conflict of 1982, Squadron Leader RD Iveson was shot down behind enemy lines, and JK Brocklehurst was mentioned in despatches for his action as chief officer of the "Atlantic Conveyor", which was sunk. Happily, both men survived. OWs also often go on to great academic success, typified by Paul Dupree, who left in 1987, and who served for a time as Admissions Tutor (Sciences) at Magdalene College, Cambridge. During this period, the Chaplain, David Houghton, was a boarding house tutor, and his benign influence may well have led to Justin Forsyth and Tim Cole achieving prominence in later years as senior functionaries in Oxfam and Christian Aid respectively.

An appraisal of John Strover's headship is given by Eric Ives:

> With reference to the boarding row in 1983-4, everything started with the governors asking about the economics of boarding and its likely future. An enquiry established that, with the decline in numbers (largely following Britain's retreat from Empire), Warwick could no longer claim to offer a genuine boarding experience. Boarding at Warwick had become marginal. There were doubts about costs and space. We had, for example, two sanatoria.
>
> On those criteria, the decision to close (though opposed by the HM and staff) was right, but it caused a furore. The OWs were particularly militant. The governors felt that they were not wrong, but that their conclusion had not taken into account the social utility of boarding for particular boys, nor the way it supported the out-of-class activities of the school which every boy benefited from. But there was a downside to retaining boarding. First, it could never be more than a convenience to boys and parents. Secondly, a great deal of money had to be spent. The governors discovered that existing conditions were Dickensian, for both boys and resident staff, and that if boarding had to be retained, it must be modernised.
>
> Under Strover the big challenge was to weather the withdrawal of county places. He was also a strong advocate of Warwick's separate identity (reciprocating the feelings of staff and governors at King's and the Squirrels) and (with the whole-hearted backing of the staff) was determined to see the school in control of its own facilities. For example, he felt that the needs of Warwick justified having its own un-shared swimming pool and sports hall and locating them where they eventually were. He also had an educational vision, and, in particular, foresaw the need for CDT provision. He had to persuade a sceptical governing body, and some staff who had other priorities, but events have more than justified his assessment. We should have built even larger facilities. The modernising of boarding also made possible better staff provision.

CHAPTER 21

Philip James Cheshire PhD

୶

Philip Cheshire came to Warwick following a period in cancer research and some years as Head of Science at Rugby School, where he had taught since 1972. A doctor's son from Lincoln, he was a pupil at Oakham School and went on to read physics at King's College, London, proceeding to a doctorate. He brought with him a determination to prepare the school for the twenty-first century by developing the curriculum, the range of extra-curricular activities on offer and the fabric of the school. His style of headmastership gained the praise of the *Daily Telegraph Good Schools Guide*, which stated that he "ran a tight ship". His diligence was formidable, and he expected high standards of everyone. Tall, lean and possessed of a quick intelligence that resulted in a speedy delivery, he was a man who got things done. Results in public examinations, reflecting parents' desire for high-quality achievement, pupils' talent and the determination of the teaching staff, became increasingly distinguished, even though some cynics mentioned the words "dumbing down" with regard to the standards required in public examinations in the late 1990s. Others spoke darkly of the pressures created by League Tables!

The fabric of the school developed dramatically throughout Dr Cheshire's 14 years at the helm, thanks to the support of a strong governing body, chaired by Professor Eric Ives. Barely one academic department was unaffected by these changes, and, at the time of his departure, radical plans were put forward for science and mathematics. The temporary Orlits buildings (built in 1949) gave way to a purpose-built History and Geography Department, opened by Lady Antonia Fraser in 1996. Music transferred to the old Arts Block (the original Science Block of 1905) and gained massively in space for practice and performance as a result. The chapel benefited from the building of a new organ in 1992, something that would have been unlikely without the generosity of Ralph Thornton. Facilities for sport were transformed. The 1911 outdoor swimming pool was replaced by a 25-metre indoor pool, and a brand new Sports Centre was opened by former England Cricket Captain, MJK Smith (a former parent), in 1993. An astroturf pitch was laid at the far end of the school field, offering improved facilities for hockey and tennis. The old gymnasium was imaginatively turned into a Sixth Form Centre, accommodating a revamped Tuck Shop and modern facilities for Careers. Classics moved into new premises above economics,

The filling in of the old outdoor swimming pool in 1991...

... and the opening of the new indoor swimming pool in 1992.

Dr PJ Cheshire helps Viscount Daventry and Christopher Campbell, the youngest boy in the school, to plant a tree on the site of the outdoor pool in 1992.

Dr PJ Cheshire and MJK Smith at the official opening of the new Sports Centre in 1994.

having endured the discomforts of the rooms behind the Guy Nelson Hall for some years. It should also be placed on record that biology teacher Paul Snell and his group of conservation volunteers were responsible for the planting of an avenue of horse-chestnut trees from the centre of the school field in a southerly direction, in the early 1990s, to replace elms lost to disease.

In the neighbouring building, Modern Languages gained an updated satellite system and a state-of-the-art language laboratory. English said farewell to its flat roof, and various parts of the school were re-roofed. The dining hall underwent significant refurbishment. The library moved from the old Big School to the newly-built Masefield Centre and instantly became hugely popular with pupils. The downstairs floor of the Masefield Centre, stretched to its limits within two years, holds the Information and Communications Technology Department. Here is an area where even experts struggle to keep pace with the growing possibilities of ICT! A drama studio was attached to the back of the Guy Nelson Hall, and in 2000 the Bridge House Theatre, based on the style of the Swan Theatre in Stratford, was opened by Dame Judi Dench. An attractive piazza was constructed between the theatre and the hall, marked by the beginnings of a sculpture trail. Improvements were made to the administration end of the old Victorian building and within the boarding house; increased space was found for design and technology and for art; and, finally, the entire Junior School was rebuilt and extended during 2001-2002. It represented a major triumph of vision and good housekeeping that the School was able to do this in just over ten years!

Evidence of the pace of change can be seen in the further development of the school telephone system during this period. Not only did it have to be enlarged to cope with more and more buildings, but it also had to encompass two new aspects – growing computer usage and security applications, that is, the use of public and hidden cameras. In the 1992 ISDX Mercury network there were 43 extensions, but within five years this had grown to 64 extensions, and in 1998 work started on a complete change to a full digital service from a local cable company, Telecential. Full implementation had to wait until repairs to the Avon bridge allowed the company to complete the school's own private circuit. Telecential became Comtel, and then NTL, and by April 2004 there were 122 extensions covering data, security and voice. Steve Rowlandson's "ultimate goal" was to achieve total telecommunications integration across all Foundation schools before he retired – time will tell!

Dr Cheshire's arrival coincided with major educational and political issues. In 1988, the General Certificate of Secondary Education (GCSE) replaced the previous exams at 16+ ('O' level and CSE). Top GCSE grades at Warwick increased from 33% in 1988 to 59% in 2002. Changes in the nature of 'A' level examinations, followed by the introduction of the first 'AS' (Advanced Supplementary) and its eventual replacement by a different kind of 'AS' (Advanced Subsidiary) in 2001, all added to the pressures felt by sixth-formers and staff alike. Results at A and B grade, which were 47% in 1987 and 52% in 1988, had reached 71% by 2001. The Government's desire to raise national standards was reflected in the introduction of tests at 7, 11 and 14 (Key Stages 1, 2 and 3). GCSE was Key Stage 4. The Junior School was happy to adopt Key Stage 2 testing, but after trying out Key Stage 3 tests, the Senior School decided not to use them again, feeling that they offered less information about the real standards achieved at Warwick than existing internal examinations. Independent schools were not required by statute to carry out these tests, and fears that the government would specify all major detail of the 11-18 curriculum were not realised. Clearly, had that happened, certain valued elements of the Warwick School curriculum would have been lost or threatened. An area where government decisions have affected the school since 1997 has been the loss of the Assisted Places scheme. This scheme enabled children of parents whose income could not sustain school fees of some £6000 per annum (after tax) to receive support and ensured that the able pupils from the locality obtained an education otherwise closed to them. The governors were able to plug some of the gaps created by the ending of the Assisted Places Scheme by introducing Foundation Places. They also supported the HMC East European Scholar initiative, whereby highly talented teenagers from countries like Croatia, Bulgaria or Estonia spend a year as lower sixth-formers in the boarding house free of charge. At least three of these scholars have been offered places at Oxford University.

The school curriculum continued to evolve over this period. The status of design and technology, always a popular subject within the school community, rose consid-

Computers old and new, pictured in 1991, celebrating the retirement
of the school's first commercially-purchased micro-computer.

erably, and it became a respected examination subject at GCSE, AS and A2 level.
Information technology became more than just a hobby for teenagers during the 14
years of Dr Cheshire's headship: "IT" and "DT" were usually taken by over 50% of
GCSE pupils. The use of the Internet and e-mail developed rapidly, and the school
created its own website and intranet.

The development of computing in the 1990s carried on under the guidance of John
Clift, who says:

> Between 1992 and 1993, the two computer rooms were expanded and re-equipped
> with Acorn A series computers. The Internet became a major focus of attention in
> 1995. At first its use was restricted to an Internet club, which met from 8.00 to 8.40
> each morning. A further development was to allow all pupils access to e-mail across
> the school's network. The change in name from Computing to Information and
> Communications Technology reflected the increasing importance of the World
> Wide Web.
>
> The governors realised that the ever-increasing demands for access to computers
> could not be met within the existing facilities. A new, much-expanded ICT depart-
> ment opened in 1999 on the ground floor of the Masefield Centre. At the same time,
> another new generation of computers was installed, running the (by now) ubiqui-
> tous Microsoft Windows operating system, and the school's network infrastructure
> was completely replaced. The original Upper Computer Room, focus of so much
> activity, has been converted back into a mathematics classroom while the Lower
> Computer Room has been divided between physics and chemistry.

Classical Greek remained a "protected" subject, with a small but dedicated clientèle, and new languages – Russian and Japanese – were introduced at sixth-form level. The school rejoined the Foreign Language Assistant scheme, having had no French assistant since 1968, and in 2004 gave careful consideration to the compulsory nature of French, given the rise in popularity of Spanish. Drama and theatre studies received curricular acknowledgement. Meanwhile, from the outset, the headmaster gave passionate support to the idea of the three sciences being compulsory for all boys to GCSE level, dual award science only being introduced in 2000 for the slower-moving science pupils. All three sciences remained very popular sixth-form choices, with a majority of leavers going on to science-based university courses. Not every pupil found the going easy, and some were not well organised: in order to counteract this, there were a number of different approaches, two of them based in the Sixth Form Centre, where "Springboard" and MULT (Making Up Lost Time) sessions were designed to guide boys to better understanding and results. The appointment of a teacher for Learning Support in 2000 was a valued step, especially for the many boys whose learning difficulties masked their real talents. Provision for those whose first language was not English was also stepped up.

The school was not just an academic institution, of course. It welcomed many eminent visitors over this period, in a variety of contexts. These included Sir Ben Kingsley (parent of two Warwickians); Dame Judi Dench and her late husband, Mr Michael Williams; the late Sir Nigel Hawthorne (who came as a guest of the Politics Society to talk about his experience of being Sir Humphrey Appleby in the memorable BBC series *Yes Minister!*); the Lords Howe, Tebbit, Hurd and Parkinson; Viscount Cranborne; Miss Ann Widdecombe; and local MPs Messrs Plaskitt, Maples, Robinson and Howarth. It was a rare coup to entice the Chinese Ambassador and, a year later, the German Ambassador and the Russian Deputy Ambassador to visit. The Politics Society built up a formidable reputation for attracting notable speakers, and the rise in popularity of political studies at AS and A2 level was no coincidence. The History Society also attracted major figures, including Lord Skidelsky and, memorably, Paul Oppenheimer, a survivor of Belsen, who delivered his first talk on the sixtieth anniversary of *Kristallnacht* (when many outrages were committed by Nazi Germany against German Jews and their property). Not every guest was a celebrity in the accepted sense of the word, but visits by Georgian and Chinese teachers, and by Counsellor Oku at the opening of the Japanese Garden, remain in the memory.

The popularity of school societies frequently waxes and wanes according to national taste or the initiative of individual members of staff. By and large, their success depends upon boys being able to get 'hands-on' experience, as is the case with the Astronomical Society, Circus Skills, Young Engineers, Young Enterprise, the Walking Society and the Scholars' Society, all of which entered the 21st century in rude health. Societies like Transport, Coin & Stamp Collecting and Gramophone, popular until the 1980s, have, on the other hand, disappeared. The Amateur Radio Society, with popular camps in the Isle of Man and the Channel Islands as highlights, finally bowed to modern technology in 2000 and was killed off by the Internet! Large numbers of boys regularly attended meetings of BAYS (The British Association of Young Scientists), held either at Warwick or King's High School, where topics had much contemporary application. Smaller, but dedicated, numbers of boys were involved in Debating and Public Speaking; the school was highly successful in a number of competitions, including those run by the English Speaking Union, in the late 1990s and at the beginning of the 21st century.

Cultural opportunities galore were provided by the Directors of Music, the Head of Art and Design and the Head of Drama over this period. Building on the foundations of David Nichols' work, Trevor Barr guided the Music Department through its move from the Orlits to the former Arts Block (WT Keeling's 1905 Science Block) and superintended a huge increase in the number of peripatetic teachers (and, therefore, of instruments offered) as ever more boys studied an instrument. Indeed, the policy for every lower-fourth boy to learn an instrument was continued, as those teaching near the Orlits in the late 1980s will remember well! Teachers of jazz guitar, the double bass and singing are among recent appointments. The selection of James Fox as Radio 2 Choirboy of the Year in 1999 gained much local publicity, but the performances of other talented musicians were equally memorable. The Swing Band, conducted by Paul Russell, achieved the highest professional standards. Robin Flintoff strove to find every possible way of bringing the distinguished work of his artists to a wider audience, exhibiting at local venues and using the foyer of the Bridge House Theatre. Former 'A' level artists have passed on to prestigious courses at university and art school. Members of the school also achieved notable success in local photographic competitions.

The appointment of a Head of Drama, John Daws, in 1993 took some of the pressure off others who had had responsibility for school drama, and ensured that talented thespians, and also those who might otherwise never have discovered an interest in the theatre, were catered for. The appointment, in 1999, of Wallace McDowell as Manager of the Performing Arts Centre was a further landmark, and he and biology teacher John Cooper, who was responsible for so much excellent technical support in Guy Nelson Hall dramatic productions, soon started afresh in a brand new theatre. In the 14 years of Philip Cheshire's headship, there was usually one major school, one Lower School and one Junior School production per year, though that increased after the opening of the Bridge House Theatre. Major productions explored not just the classical, but also the modern European, tradition (Dürrenmatt's *The Visit* and Brecht's *The Good Person of Sichuan*). Plays on a grand scale, such as *Oh, What a Lovely War!* and *The Royal Hunt of the Sun*, were followed by Thornton Wilder's *Our Town* and Woody Allen's *Don't Drink the Water!* Shakespeare was not ignored: performances were given of *Macbeth* and *King Henry*

Bridge House, pictured immediately prior to its demolition in 1999 to make way for
the new Bridge House Theatre.
(Peter Yurkwich)

IV, Part 2, and, to inaugurate the Bridge House Theatre, *Romeo and Juliet*. Other
major Senior School performances were John Daws' début *A Penny for a Song*,
Sweeney Todd, *Becket*, *Our Country's Good*, *Cat on a Hot Tin Roof* and a return to the
big-cast musical with *Oliver!*, the Guy Nelson Hall's dramatic swansong.

In the period up to 1997, there was a long-standing tradition of "the Staff Play".
Usually comic, these productions involved many staff at a busy time of year, and the
increasing demands on teachers' time eventually spelt death for this form of entertainment. Plays such as *Daisy Pulls It Off*, *The Happiest Days of Your Life*, *Charley's
Aunt* and *Cold Comfort Farm* live in the memory, not least because of the outrageous
costumes worn by certain male "actors". Visiting companies, such as The Actors of
Dionysus and the European Theatre Company, made regular appearances, and, until
his retirement in 2001, Stephen Woodward continued to produce many a Molière
play, demonstrating the humour that is to be found in the classics. Young actors occasionally found unforgettable opportunities by performing for the Royal Shakespeare
Company, for example, in *The Lord of the Flies* and on tour as far away as the USA
and Japan. From a single year-group, three pupils went on to drama courses or acting
school (Tom McKay, Marc Elliott and Karl Ude-Martinez). Interest in modern
drama was further stimulated by a visit from Michael Billington (OW), drama critic
of the *Guardian*, who talked about Harold Pinter, to the accompaniment of extracts

from the great man's *oeuvre*. An outline of the cultural possibilities at Warwick School around the time of the millennium should also mention the themed evenings devoted to such topics as John Masefield's verse and Gothic literature, as well as the outstanding achievement of Matthew Finch in having his own work published at the tender age of thirteen.

Culture can be seen in a variety of guises; not everyone would recognise sport among them, perhaps, but Warwick continued to achieve high sporting standards over this period and to encourage the less obviously sporty as well. Rugby remained the school's major sport, managing, at the turn of the century, to put out successful teams involving over half an entire year-group. The tradition of the Rugby Tour, developed by Brian Emmerson in the mid-1980s, continued with a four-week marathon trip to Australia and Fiji, involving 26 boys. At this time, major players such as Steve Thompson, Charlie Mulraine and Steve McCluskey gained Midlands and even England honours. Not all seasons were as successful as others, and in the 1991-2 season the only major record was for injuries – 32 boys represented the 1st XV that year! The following year was, however, one of the best, with a XV reaching the national semi-final of the *Daily Mail* Knockout Competition. That summer, the fourth major rugby tour took place, this time to Australia and New Zealand, followed by tours of South Africa and Argentina. The fact that at least 15 teams played some twenty opponents in 1999-2000 is an indication of the commitment of coaches and pupils. Ken Freeborn had retired in 1992, after 35 years of service to the school (without a single day off sick, as he told his younger colleagues in his farewell Common Room speech), being replaced as Head of PE by Tim Hoyle, who looked after the 1st XV until 2002, when he handed it on to Richard Chapman. By this time, Geoff Tedstone (OW), former wicketkeeper for Warwickshire and Gloucestershire, had become Director of Sport. One feature of Geoff's appointment to the staff in 1994 was the further development of hockey as a major sport in the school: by 2002, upper fourth-formers could opt for it, and successful teams were put out at all levels. Many boys achieved county and regional standard in both sports.

Former pupils achieved fame in a number of fields: David Neal and Andrew Grimes obtained Blues for Hockey at Oxford; Michael Ramsey, for Association Football (a first and last?); and Edward Green, son of Senior Master Martin Green, for Cross-Country at Cambridge. The school cross-country team was particularly successful at the turn of the century. Cricketers of distinction, such as Charlie Mulraine, Huw Jones and David Young (who scored an undefeated 200 against Solihull School in 1996), found the step up to first-class level just that bit too far, but gave plenty of entertainment to those who could otherwise have claimed that cricket was boring. OW Neil Smith made his England one-day international début and took part in the 1996 World Cup, thereafter becoming captain of Warwickshire.

Inspiration for sport comes from various sources; the tour to distant parts is but one of these, but through sport many generations of Warwickians have travelled the world. In a ten-year period, the rugby senior squads visited Australia, Fiji, New Zealand, Argentina, and South Africa. Hockey teams travelled to Ireland, Holland, and Australia; basketball teams to France and Holland; and the cricket team to Singapore and Malaysia. For a five-year period from 1997, the school's swimming teams remained undefeated in fixtures against other schools. In 2000, the Sports Centre Manager, Mark Rickhuss, swam the Channel for charity, achieving the remarkable time of 9 hours 18 minutes. Whilst sailing enjoyed a brief renaissance in the mid-1990s – and remains popular with individual pupils – rowing came back into vogue at the turn of the century, when the school took part in a number of regattas. Tim Wurr's success as a shot-putter, the achievements of the school's fencers over this period, and Christian Horner's motor-racing exploits are also worthy of mention.

The CCF retained its significant role in the extra-curricular life of the school. In 1990, Major Morris Rodham handed control over to Lt Col Humphrey Collis, who remained Officer Commanding until his retirement in 2000, when he was succeeded by Major Peter Johnson. Throughout this time, numbers of cadets joining at 13 remained healthy, with many boys taking part in the annual camps and competitions. Flying Scholarships were obtained, and the Canada Cadet Exchange scheme enabled individuals to spend a challenging, but unforgettable, month in the wilds. Those who pursued their interest in the forces after leaving school and university found plenty of opportunity: one example is Julian Buczacki, who served in Bosnia in the late 1990s, and who memorably returned to the school, in full dress-uniform, to participate in the Remembrance Day service in the school chapel in 2003.

It was not just sport and the CCF that provided the opportunity for travel between 1988 and 2002. The school continued to take its pupils to various parts of the world. Although the cruises that had been popular for generations ceased after 1989, the biennial trip to Greece and regular trips to Italy were organised by the Classics Department, in particular by Jeremy Rider, who retired in 2000, and James Morris, his successor. Despite the unfavourable political situation, the History Department ran trips to Turkey and Egypt until, in the aftermath of the outrage in New York on 11th September, 2001, a planned trip had to be cancelled, though their trip to Washington and the Civil War battlefields did go ahead. Annual trips to the First World War battlefields of the Somme and to the site of the Normandy landings remained popular with successive generations of younger pupils. A number of expeditions to Russia were undertaken – the biggest, to Moscow and St Petersburg in December 2002, being truly memorable. Modern Linguists organised the usual "homestays" and exchanges, frequently in conjunction with King's High School, to France, Germany and Spain. Various destinations were visited, though Paris remained the most popular. From 1989 until 2000, the Junior School organised a long weekend in Northern France for all the Upper Twos (9-year-olds). Long-standing relationships were established with the Gymnasium St Mauritz in Münster. In the early 1990s, Messrs Wheeler and Woodward bravely took a minibus load of senior boys on camping expeditions to Prague, and the Geography Department went further afield, benefiting from its fundraising initiatives to go to New Zealand. Annual ski trips were organised, the Junior School once striking out for Canada. The regular retreats to Caldey Island attracted a small, but faithful, clientèle. Perhaps the most challenging trips of all, however, were those undertaken by John Cooper to Baffin Island, and those taken to Iceland were unforgettable, too.

Travel in a more mundane sense also reflects the changes in our society. The Geography Department intermittently surveys how Warwick boys come to school. In 1984, we learn that 61% travelled by car, 14% by bus, 12% by bike, 7% on foot and 6% by train. By 1994, the figures were 50% car, 35% bus, 1% bike, 4% on foot and 2% train. We may conclude that congestion on the Myton Road and a better provision of bus services to outlying parts are, in part, the reason for these changes. By 1994, too, the school had learnt from bitter experience that teenage driving needs the highest standards. Following a number of 'scrapes', which should have been warning enough, there was a fatal crash in which a front-seat passenger was killed during out-of-school time. The shock to the school community was very real, and measures were undertaken, with the help of the AA and the father of the victim, Mr Kerr, to ensure that Warwick boys acquired the best driving habits. In the subsequent ten years, no pupil has been involved in a serious teenage driving incident.

The school has committed itself in recent years to various fundraising tactics for its own development: the Towards 2000 Appeal, co-ordinated by Ralph Thornton, was notably successful as a means of kick-starting the building programme mentioned at the beginning of this chapter. Subsequently, great efforts went into raising money for charity. Such sporting activities as the Triathlon for the Acorns Children's Hospice and the sponsoring of a given Saturday's matches by the number of points scored, organised by Tim Hoyle, raised substantial sums. The Walking Society, led by John Jefferies, Robert Hudson and John Clift, undertook a number of sponsored walks (across the Black Mountains, along Hadrian's Wall and the Pilgrims Way, and across Dartmoor and Exmoor) in order to assist a Ghanaian village to develop its facilities and a Tanzanian school in Kiganamo to obtain better premises. In 2001, Gill Beck from the Junior School went to see for herself what was needed, and she was followed a year later by the Head of Classics, James Morris. Each year, under the guidance of the Chaplain (Huw Mordecai from 1990 to 1996 and, subsequently, Andrew Gough), staff and boys strove, with considerable success, to raise useful sums for a variety of local and national charities. Young Enterprise companies, organised largely by sixth-formers, also made a measurable contribution to charity, as did one of the most unusual exploits, the building of a rocking-horse in 1995. Whilst Community Service did not raise money, it continued to offer a valuable link between the School and the local community. Contacts were forged with local primary schools, charity shops and individual, often elderly, people.

The school retained close contact with its Old Boys, whose Association celebrated

AGK Brown and Fred Mulley – portraits that accompanied their obituaries in 1995.

its hundredth birthday in 1998, and a number of reunions were held towards the end of the twentieth century. As indicated above, OWs made their mark in numerous fields, and, amongst those not mentioned in any category so far, we should note the achievement of the following: Dan Byles, who rowed across the Atlantic with his mother; William Sleath, who played the flute in productions such as *The Lion King* on the London stage; and Denys Shortt, whose company, DCS Europe, has gone from strength to strength. OWs and retired colleagues of distinction did, sadly, die during this period: Warwick's only cabinet minister, Fred Mulley; the pianist Denis Matthews and the actor Dennis Castle; former Headmaster Pat Martin; and teachers Geoffrey Simmonds, Harry Sheppard, Felix Dugdale, Edgar Blackshaw and Ellis Owen, to name but a few. Contemporary readers may never have heard of them, but in their day they made their mark. Memories are preserved in the school's annual official publication, *The Portcullis*. Numerous shorter and shorter-lived publications have existed, too, of which *The Warwickian* is the slickest and most regular, being sent to parents each term.

The staffing of the school increased during Philip Cheshire's time at Warwick. One of the first challenges he faced was the first ever claim by a member of the teaching staff for maternity leave – the birth of Mrs Louise Haines' daughter Charlotte only temporarily interrupted her teaching career, however. In 2002, there were 95 members of staff teaching in the two schools. Many stayed a relatively short time before moving on to promotion elsewhere. It was said that Warwick provided almost too good a training-ground for other schools! After "bedding in" the new head, Ralph Thornton retired in 1989, having served 41 years, latterly as Second Master. He took the title with him, for his eventual successor, William Duggan, became Deputy Headmaster and stayed until 1995. The subtle difference between the two titles is that the position of Deputy Headmaster is a governors' appointment, rather than a headmaster's choice with governors' agreement. William Duggan rapidly gained a reputation for forensic efficiency, which gained him much respect among staff and boys. His successor, Alistair Hector (1995-97), also moved on – even more rapidly – to a headship, and in January 1998 the school welcomed its next Deputy, Simon Williams, who held the post for nearly seven years before being appointed to a headship in Hampshire in September 2004.

Retiring in the early stages of Dr Cheshire's reign were Geoff Eve, Trevor Pritchard, Keith Winterbottom, Eric Kennett, Pat Bannerman, Ken Freeborn, David Dews and Phil Heelis, whilst Tony Sparks moved to a senior position at Arnold Lodge School, and Andrew Parkes went into the world of books. Sadly, Don James died after 20 years on the staff. It was hard to believe that colleagues such as these could be easily replaced, but, however much teachers may think themselves indispensable, they seldom are! Even though a new generation is making its mark, the school did have in 2002 fifteen members of staff who had each served over 25 years. In what might be termed the middle period of Dr Cheshire's time, the following retired: Geoff Lane, Pauline Fawcett, Judith Fogg, Llew Grimes and Elisabeth Freeman. They were followed by Alex Hughes, David Nichols and Charles I'Anson. Carol Gray and Barry Meatyard moved on to university positions; David Elston and Simon Morris, to promotions leading to Deputy Headships. The later phase of Dr Cheshire's tenure was marked by the retirement of David Stooke, Jeff Marshall, Jeremy Rider, Humphrey Collis, Stephen Woodward, Francis Daniell (Bursar 1986-2001), Josette Tait, Ian Moffatt, Angela Bungard (whose service in the Junior School had started in 1970) and George Adams. Memories of some of these figures can currently be found on the Internet site *Friends Reunited*, most of them affectionate.

Over the many years outlined in this chapter, the school's infrastructure was strengthened by the appointment of many more ancillary staff, be it in reprographics, the library, the bursary, the school office or on the ground, technician and maintenance staff. The retirement of Pearl Lock, Bursar's secretary, in 1990, and the sad death of Jenny Langley, Headmaster's secretary, in 1992, marked the end of an era. The retirement after so many years as technicians in the Science Departments of Peter Westerman (1965-2000) and of Marjorie Bland (1968-1999) left a big gap, too.

The school, long regarded as predominantly a boarding school, has, in fact, for some years had in the region of only 50 boarders out of an overall pupil population of over 800 Senior School boys, so the combining of Junior and Senior House was a logical step. After his retirement from the Senior House in 1988, Stephen Woodward handed the housemastership on to Simon Letman, and since the latter's departure in 1992 Junior Housemaster Grahame Ward has had responsibility for all boarders. For all the talk of the decline, and even death, of boarding, numbers at Warwick have remained robust.

Relations over this period with the sister school, King's High School, did develop, albeit patchily. Girls from KHS would regularly take part in dramatic productions, and there was the annual joint concert. On Thursday afternoons, many girls would take part in activities, such as Young Enterprise, with sixth-form boys, and numerous boys learnt a variety of skills, including cooking, at KHS. Joint discos for the younger pupils were a regular feature, too. There were for many years Warwick School boys on the KHS exchanges to France and Spain and on other trips as well. What developed more slowly, largely for practical reasons, was joint teaching at sixth-form level, but in minority subjects it looked to be the only way forward.

Right at the end of Dr Cheshire's headmastership, an unseemly row broke out in the local press concerning the distribution of income from the Charity of King Henry VIII. This ancient charity, which had been reconstituted in 1978 (and re-named The King Henry VIII Endowed Trust, Warwick, in 2003), had amassed total funds exceeding £20m and was required by its constitution "to benefit the Church (50%), King's School at Warwick (30%) and Warwick residents (20%)". The income that Warwick School, King's High School and Warwick Preparatory School thus received was seen in some quarters as not benefiting all of the schoolchildren in the old Borough of Warwick, which roughly corresponds to the CV34 postcode area, but the position of the charity was very ably defended by Professor Eric Ives, deputy chairman of the trustees at the time:

> Like the trustees of any charity, we are bound by act of Parliament to follow rules laid down by the Charity Commission. We cannot decide to change or try to change them, just because we or other people might not like them or think them unfair. The Charity Commission decides who is to benefit, not trustees. This has been explained to the headteachers in discussion and in correspondence. We simply do not have the remit to do what they are asking us to do. Nor do we have any control or influence on what the other beneficiaries of the charity, including the Warwick School Foundation, does with the money we pay over to them.
>
> We have kept the Charity Commission fully informed of the media coverage of recent months. On January 24th, 2002, the Commissioners wrote to confirm the Warwick School Foundation is legally entitled to the income it receives from the charity in perpetuity. We know this will disappoint the headteachers of the state schools, but the law is clear and we have to obey it
>
> The trustees recognise the financial problems faced by the headteachers of the state schools. We already do what we can to help them and to contribute to the general progress of Warwick children; last year we provided over £125,000. We could have done more if suitable applications had come to us, but the Charity Commission specifically forbids paying for anything which ought to be provided out of taxes. The charity cannot make up for inadequate public funding.

One other extraordinary incident during this period deserves to be mentioned, and that is the marriage in 2001 of a pupil, Robert Walters, at the end of his lower sixth year, to a Swiss girl whom he met using the Internet. Eventually, the presence of a married upper sixth-former was almost regarded as normal, but his status was probably unique in the history of the school.

The school marked Philip Cheshire's retirement with an Evening of Celebration, in which performances of music, drama and dance preceded the official unveiling of his portrait. Professor Ives, shortly to stand down as Chairman of Governors after 17 years, spoke warmly of the Cheshire years and reminded his audience of the tremendous contribution to school life made by Philip's wife, Pam. They retired to Stratford-upon-Avon.

Eric Ives assesses this period of the school's history:

Philip Cheshire arrived at the start of agitation about educational tests and standards and his brief was to respond by raising Warwick's academic performance from the perfectly satisfactory (and sometimes brilliant) to excellent overall. One of his first jobs was to improve staff/governor relations, which had been damaged by the boarding and sports issues. The result was the annual Governors' Soirée, which convinced each side that they shared the same aim. Academic improvements also necessitated better facilities and these were provided to different areas in turn. The first was sport, with the swimming pool and sports hall. The former nearly came to disaster, as the company constructing it went bankrupt mid-way. Fortunately, the pool shell had just been completed, so that Francis Daniell, the Bursar, was able to complete the work. A week or so earlier and we would have been left with an expensive hole. A rolling programme gave most departments dedicated rooms. Special attention was paid to the arts, with music coming first. All boys had to study a musical instrument for at least a year. The Orlits were abandoned and the move of history and geography to a new block allowed music to occupy the block opposite the chapel. PJC was repaid by an increasingly good programme of music making and a brass group (of which he was especially fond) which appeared on many special occasions. Drama came next, with a new studio behind the Guy Nelson and eventually the Bridge House Theatre. The arrival in a big way of computing in education eventually led to the Masefield block, which allowed the library to move and so achieve PJC's wish to improve behaviour by adding to the dining space and putting down a carpet.

The governors, meanwhile, were becoming increasingly concerned about modernising the Junior School – which, it is fair to say, both John Strover and Philip Cheshire saw more as a longer term requirement. For once the governors became insistent, found more money and the head then enthusiastically seized the offer. The result was a triumph and the end to a Junior School 'tacked on'. Its new cohesion was not only emphasised by its new plan (and the colonnade) but by another of the sculptures which PJC saw as valuable additions to the cultural impact of the school. After some debate about having giraffes, the boys decided (thankfully) to have bears.

All this leads to the issue of funding to pay for new facilities and the increased sophistication in teaching method. Most of this came from brilliant financial management at which PJC was a wizard. The financial difference which efficiency makes is enormous. The pool and sports hall were largely paid for by the appeal. We began with a professional company which cost the school a good deal in fees and did nothing. Ralph Thornton came in, took it over and achieved a triumph. An important factor in better financial management was a major modernisation of the machinery of the Foundation under Philip Gomme, and later David Russell and Adrian Blyth. Without that the school would certainly have gone into serious decline.

CHAPTER 22

Edward Barrington Halse – Into the Future

Edward Halse, only the fifth headmaster that the school has had since 1936, was 46 years old when he arrived in August 2002. He had spent the previous seven years as Headmaster of Kent College, Canterbury. A graduate of the University of Wales, his teaching career had taken him from Bridgend Boys' Grammar School to King's College, Madrid, and thereafter to Kelly College, Tavistock, before he was appointed Deputy Headmaster at Dauntsey's, a leading co-educational school in Wiltshire, where he spent four years before his move to Canterbury. His wife, Jean, was also a teacher, and they had two teenage children. An economics graduate, Edward Halse brought with him a commitment to develop the place of the computer in teaching and administration. The decision to equip all staff with laptops had already been taken when he arrived, but the regular use of e-mail for communication, particularly with the new headmaster, rapidly became taken for granted. Interactive whiteboards sprang up around the school, and all staff were encouraged to take the European Computer Driving Licence, possibly in an attempt to ensure that their ICT aware-ness kept up with that of the younger generation! Mr Halse also aimed to maintain and improve upon the academic standards for which the school had become known and without which its future could not be guaranteed. Distinguished results at A2 level in 2003 (over 71% A and B grades) offered encouragement in this direction, but there were no grounds for complacency in a generation where schools in general were struggling to maintain boys' motivation. The second major inspection took place in December 2002, at the end of Mr Halse's first term, and, to no-one's great surprise, much praiseworthy evidence emerged. The need for some fine-tuning was identified, and a variety of committees sat in order to make recommendations for improvement.

The arrival of the new headmaster did not bring with it immediate radical changes – much of what had worked well over the years continued to be respected. However, a radical review of the school was undertaken through the construction of a school development plan which sought to make major changes – eventually – to 50 areas of school life. Naturally enough, the "usual" trips and sporting and cultural activities took place. Between 2002 and 2004, when this book was published, in addition to the annual exchanges and homestay trips run by Modern Linguists, there were large-

Local author Celia Rees, sculptor Matthew Lane-Sanderson, Thomas Ashworth and
Thomas Gayle of the Junior School, and headmaster EB Halse at the unveiling of the new
bears sculpture at the Junior School on 5th February, 2004.
(PJ O'Grady)

scale expeditions to Russia, Eastern Europe, Greece and the United States. The
sportsmen weren't to be left out, either. Some 30 boys went on the Rugby Tour to
Venice in October 2003, and even more went on the by now regular Australia Rugby
and Hockey Tour in Summer 2004. The U14 XV celebrated its third undefeated year.
The profile of rugby was further enhanced by the appointment of the school's first
Director of Rugby. Meanwhile, the 2002-3 Hockey XI was the strongest in the
school's history, becoming Midlands U18 champions and also national finalists,
finishing in third position; the rowers won their first regatta; the fencers got better
and better, thanks to the performances of Graham Heydon; the school had its first
Judo international success, when Arran Lawson, then aged 13, represented Great
Britain in Holland; and 27 swimmers took part in a fundraising marathon 100-mile

swim, which generated substantial sums for the school's Tanzania Schools Project – and created an official world record.

In music, the departure of three of the school's best pupil musicians for many years, Paul O'Grady and Richard Norris in 2003, and Leo Steeds in 2004, left a hole to be filled, but, as is the way of these things, filled it was. The retirement of Paul Russell, who taught his first lesson in 1959, was marked by the issue of a very successful Swing Band CD, entitled *Ain't Misbehaving*. Much good work was produced in the Art & Design Department, where Alex Ball achieved one of the top five 'A' level results in the country, and in design and technology, where Robert Rigby and Da Feng were awarded prestigious Arkwright Scholarships. In drama, the school's connection with the Royal Shakespeare Company offered opportunities to Tom Spackman and David Jowett to perform in *Richard III*. In public speaking, the team of Matthew Collins, Charlie Samuda and James Langman, guided by Mrs Louise Haines, won the English Speaking Union National Championship and were awarded their prize by the Duke of Edinburgh at Buckingham Palace – a memorable experience for all. A new initiative was the series of lectures sponsored by Sir Ben Kingsley. The inaugural talk was given by Professor Ian Stewart FRS, and some months later the renowned actress Jane Lapotaire gave a masterclass under the same aegis. The Politics Society continued to attract speakers of great repute and interest, such as Lords Hattersley and Alton, Peter Lilley, John Redwood, the Labour MPs Tony Wright and Bruce George, and the Syrian Ambassador. The speeches of the latter two were particularly relevant in the light of the 2003 Iraq War. Perhaps the most successful of recent meetings was the visit of former MP and current political commentator Matthew Parris, uncle of one of the school's younger pupils. As a reward, perhaps, for all of this activity, pupils and staff enjoyed the first ever two-week half-term holiday in October 2003.

There were other "firsts" in 2003: the entire lower fourth had an induction day of activities, and later in September they enjoyed a 3-day "bonding exercise" in and around Paris. Also, the first girls joined the CCF as part of a vigorous attempt by both Warwick School and King's High School to increase collaboration. The drama production, *The Silver Sword*, also reflected greater co-operation between the two schools, something which parents evidently welcomed, given their responses to a survey conducted by an external organisation.

In a dynamic institution, staff come and staff go. In 2003, there were few "major" retirements: indeed, apart from Paul Russell, already mentioned above, only Simon Wheeler (formerly Head of History and latterly Master of the Scholars) and David Rogers, Head of the Junior School since 1990 and Deputy Head before that, retired. In 2004, however, a number of retirements promised to change the shape of the staff list! Alan Reilly, on the staff since 1968, and Head of Science at the time of his retirement; Martin Green, formerly Head of Economics and of the Sixth Form, and latterly Senior Master, who stepped down from an active teaching role to take on advisory work; Bob Fair, Head of Chemistry since his arrival in 1977; and Randal Cousins, Head of Mathematics from 1983 to 2003, all announced their retirements. This left Brian Emmerson, who started teaching PE and games in 1968, and Cliff Daniel, who joined the Mathematics Department two years later, as the longest-serving members of staff. Robert Hudson (Classics and English) and Peter O'Grady (mathematics) have also completed some 30 uninterrupted years, whilst physicist Peter Johnson started his career in 1970, left and came back. The staff, as a body, now contains more women than ever before – 19 in the Senior School, where in 1987 there were but three. The year 2002-3 was a record one, in that three children were born to serving female members of staff!

After a brief lull on the building front, following the completion of the new Junior School building, the only major construction was on the site of the old Bridge House, where a proper Maintenance Department was completed early in 2004. A particularly interesting development was the digging up, while a soak-away was being constructed in February 2004, of an empty Warren's Blacking pot, in almost perfect condition. Bridge House was already in existence by 1886 (and can be seen on the Ordnance Survey map of that year), and the blacking factory went out of business in the 1870s. The pot was found close to where the front door used to be, and to the west of the venerable monkey puzzle tree, which is presumably contemporary with the original house, but about 60cm underground, and may have been used in the porch (blacking was a very messy process), before being thrown into a pit when empty. A famous former employee of Warren's Blacking Factory (at the age of 12 years, in 1824) was Charles Dickens; he was put to work in the factory at Hungerford Market, London, in order to clear some of his father's debts. At first, he lodged in Camden and walked four miles to the factory every day, visiting his family at the weekend, until they found lodgings for him close to their location, and while it is fanciful to suggest that Dickens was involved with the Bridge House pot, it is nevertheless a fascinating and rare archaeological find on the school's own land.

It seemed that the mechanical diggers would be mustering again as this book went to press. The long-spoken-of development in science would come to fruition with, perhaps, the demolition of the caretakers' cottages (the school's original sanatorium of 1879) to the west of the Masefield Centre, and the construction of a state-of-the-art building for the sciences at the cost of some six and a half million pounds – and new homes for the caretakers! Despite being equivalent to half of the capital spending incurred at the school over the last 20 years, this would free up space to bring all the mathematics teaching in the school under one roof, to the delight of the school's most peripatetic teachers, and also provide extra space for art, design and technology. Even then, there would be times in the school week when there was a shortage of rooms, and thought was given to adding a third storey onto the Modern Languages building, the only one still having a flat roof. At present, that idea remains on the table.

In May 2004, a new scheme was being formulated to increase the level of co-operation between local independent and state schools, and this was being led by Warwick School. The headmaster writes:

> Following a meeting with Mr Eric Wood, the County Education Officer, I arranged to meet Mr John Botten from the Warwickshire Education Business Partnership to form an Independent State School Partnership between nine of Warwick's primary and secondary schools. This partnership offers an exciting collaborative programme which seeks to develop genuine partnership between state and independent schools, and was supported by the DfES (Department for Education and Skills) to the order of £50,000. Its aim is to improve standards in English, ICT and staff development.

As the school marched further into the 21st century, it was as full as it had ever been – in September 2003, there were 848 pupils in the Senior School and 230 in the Junior – and it seemed likely to withstand all the changes that governments and examination boards could throw at it, as GCSE, AS and A2 examinations came under increased scrutiny, and the question was asked, "Do we examine our pupils too much in England?" "Indeed we do," might be our answer, but whilst the systems exist, it is good to know that the parents of the school's pupils trust us to provide the best way round them and to ensure that we strive to educate the whole man by offering, in addition, the widest range possible of sporting and cultural opportunity. Particularly relevant in view of the fees charged by the school – currently £7,782 per annum for tuition, with an extra £8,826 for full boarding or £7,740 for weekly boarding – the future of the school would also be safeguarded by further developing local and community contacts, and by examining every possible avenue to ensure that no pupil capable of benefiting from a Warwick School education would be barred from doing so by a shortage of funds.

Index

ᗥ

Note: References to illustrations are in *italic*.

Names of Subscribers up to July 2004 and their years at Warwick School

Rev Wm E K Allander 1926–1932
Richard K Guy 1926–1935
A J Hassall 1928–1932
F R Salkeld 1928–1934
George Pantry 1928–1936
W J Grimes 1930–1938
Desmond Scarr 1931–1937
Keith N Powell 1935–1939
Harold Sampson 1935–1940
M G Sawyer 1935–1943
Dick Mann 1935–1944
P F Payne 1936–1940
A E Currall 1936–1942
R Derrick Hughes 1936–1943
Roger Smith 1937–1944
Tom Flynn 1937–1945
A E Fretwell 1938–1943
Mark Thomas 1939–1943
G W Malins 1939–1944
W H Jackson 1939–1944
Anthony Randle 1939–1946
G T Horn 1940–1944
R G Binks 1940–1945
E Colman 1940–1945
W H Waldron 1940–1947
John Winterburn 1940–1947
J E Blakstad 1940–1951
P J Hall 1941–1945
Ron Jones 1941–1946
R A Hoggett 1941–1947
Ian Painton 1941–1947
P G Butler 1941–1947
Tom Bellamy 1941–1947
John B Lucas 1941–1951
H J Hooper 1942–1946
J G Binks 1942–1948
John Porter 1942–1949
P H E Bailey 1942–1949
Neil F J Thurley 1942–1951
J A P Blakeman 1942–1952
C D Davis 1943–1947
A Saul 1943–1948
Cecil Hinton 1943–1949
A E Sturley 1943–1959
John L Randall 1944–1952

John Hinton 1945–1950
Peter J Price 1945–1950
Christopher M West 1945–1955
A P Wright 1945–1956
John Grew 1946–1947
Malcolm Shrimpton 1946–1949
R T J Allen 1946–1953
Timothy J Fowler 1946–1956
J T Gridley 1947–1954
M J F Stephens 1947–1956
John E Price 1948–1955
Peter Johnson 1948–1955
Ralph H Thornton (Staff) 1948–1989
D A Parsons 1949–1955
C S and S E Bellerby 1949–1958 and 1973–1983
Keith G Brocklehurst (Staff) 1949–1983
B W Young (Staff) 1949–1985
David J Gardner 1950–1954
David Westlake 1950–1957
Michael Foster 1950–1960
R V Capps 1951–1958
Ralph Hulme 1952–1959
K C K Scott 1952–1961
N A Robinson 1953–1961
Roger Wilmut 1953–1961
M W Hewitt 1953–1963
F J S Dight (Staff) 1953–1968
Derek W Usherwood (Staff) 1954–1960
William H Clarke 1954–1961
John Bolton 1954–1962
Ian M Baker 1954–1963
M W G Scott 1954–1964
N J Robinson 1955–1966
S S Davis 1956–1961
Norman Hyde 1956–1963
D J Payne 1956–1965
Roger P Usherwood (Staff) 1957–1986
John Hawkesford 1958–1966
E G Holmes (Staff) 1958–1968
Ian Macdonald 1959–1970
A R M King 1960–1966
P M and R C Tacon 1961–1969 and 1991–1998
G F Eve (Staff) 1961–1989
Michael E Barnwell 1962–1968
T R Harry 1962–1973

John Abbotts   1963–1968
W Stuart Peacock   1963–1975
N A W Davis   1964–1975
Philip Heelis (Staff)   1964–1991
M A Garrett   1965–1972
M H Patterson   1965–1972
Peter Dalrymple   1966–1977
Alan Pugsley   1966–1977
Martin and Simon Richards   1966–1977 and
   1967–1975
Peter Crafter   1967–1971
G A Thompson   1967–1974
Jeremy Grew   1967–1978
Mark Bellamy   1967–1978
David Stevens   1968–1974
Gerrard Tyrrell   1968–1975
Martin Hewitt (Pupil and staff)   1968–1975 and
   2003–
Michael John Barrett Turner   1968–1977
John Cavanagh   1968–1979
Alex (Staff) and Andrew N H Hughes   1968–1995
   and 1981–1989
A J Reilly (Staff)   1968–2004
B Emmerson (Staff)   1968–2005
John and Josh Clegg   1969–1975 and 1998–
N G G Binks   1969–1976
Ken Vivian   1969–1976
Bill Adridge   1969–1979
David Charles Turner   1969–1980
Mrs Penny Birt (Staff)   1969–1986
T A Pritchard (Staff)   1969–1989
David Nichols (Staff)   1969–1995
C G Daniel (Staff)   1970–
Ross Cheshire   1970–1977
Pete Johnson (Staff)   1970–1979 & 1986–
Andrew Holley   1970–1980
D W Stooke (Staff)   1970–1998
M J Green (Staff)   1970–2005
M J Calderbank   1971–1976
Geraint Lewis   1971–1978
Martin Hill   1971–1981
Mark Aldridge   1971–1981
T J Priest   1971–1982
Stephen Woodward (Staff)   1971–2001
David Pirie (Staff)   1973–1977
Ian Pilling   1973–1980
Roy Dixon   1973–1981
Andrew Parkes (Staff)   1973–1990
Charles I'Anson (Staff)   1973–1995
George Adams (Staff)   1973–2002
Stephen Haywood   1974–1981
Alan Haywood   1974–1984
Elisabeth Freeman   1974–1994
James Dickson   1975–1980
D A Scott   1975–1983
Simon Bellamy   1976–1987

John Cooper (Staff)   1977–
J W Clift (Staff)   1977–
Jonathan C Rayner   1977–1981 and 1982–1989
J A Strover (Headmaster)   1977–1988
Judith Fogg (Staff)   1977–1993
R W Fair (Staff)   1977–2004
Matthew Boulter   1978–1985
R Flintoff (Staff)   1979–
C J Marshall (Staff)   1979–1998
Charles Scott   1980–1991
Llewellyn G Grimes (Staff)   1980–1994
Simon Wheeler (Staff)   1980–2004
Reg Skelton   1981–1986
Stuart D A Walker   1981–1988
Charles Watmough (Staff)   1983–
Randal Cousins (Staff)   1983–2004
C J Skilbeck   1984–1995
Graham I R Ogdon (Staff)   1985–
P G Yurkwich (Maintenance)   1985–
Derek J Shield (Staff)   1985–
Steve Rowlandson (Audio-visual)   1985–
Morris Rodham (Staff)   1985–1990
Anthony Coulls   1985–1992
James A Hanson (Pupil and staff)   1985–1995 and
   2001–2003
R Higgs (Caretaker)   1986–
James A Heatley   1986–1991
Edward Higgs   1986–1993
M J Huitson   1986–1994
Francis A F Daniell (Bursar)   1986–2001
Mark Johnson   1987–1994
James H Lawless   1987–1997
Charles Rashleigh   1987–1998
Gregory C D Musson   1987–1998
O P Bowden   1988–1995
S D Wurr   1988–1995
Simon Morris (Staff)   1988–1995
R A Kennedy   1988–1995
Christian Culley   1988–1998
Simon L S Bond   1988–1999
Ross A Bradley (Staff)   1989–
Janet Turner (Office)   1989–
Iain A Bell   1989–1996
Tom Bullock   1989–1998
Alyson Pettifer (Bursary)   1990–
David Snatt (Staff)   1990–
Andrew and Christopher Cathcart   1990–1997 and
   1996–
N, A and M Stanojevic   1990–1998
Alun Vaughan (Staff)   1990–1998
George Darby   1990–2000
Murray Forsyth   1990–2001
Matthew T Shield   1991–1998
Alexander Grieve   1991–1999
Iain Grieve   1991–2000
Jonathan Wilkinson   1991–2002

Ravi Lal-Sarin   1991–2002
Mark C and Josh C Noble   1991–2002 and
   1994–2005
C G McNee (Staff)   1992–
K Marshall (Staff)   1992–
A J R Berrow (Staff)   1992–1997
Eileen M Halborg (Staff)   1992–2002
Jonathan Hitchman Stone   1992–2003
Edward Beningfield   1992–2003
Paramdeep and Manveer Dosanjh   1992–2004
D Seal (Staff)   1993–
Jonathan Begg   1993–2001
Owen G James   1993–2003
Henry Begg   1993–2004
Hugh Rashleigh   1993–2004
M J K Hickman   1993–2004
Ashley J Belcher   1993–2004
Anant Patel   1993–2004
Angus Grieve   1993–2004
Benjamin O'Sullivan   1993–2004
Jordan J Lake   1993–2005
Guy Fillmore   1993–2005
Tom Pavel   1993–2005
Steven Norton   1994–1999
Timothy J and Richard J Ward   1994–2001 and
   1994–2005
Paul James and Phillip John Rothwell   1994–2001
   and 1996–
Alex Smout   1994–2004
Amar Lal-Sarin   1994–2005
Philip Antrobus   1994–2005
Richard Michael Bennett   1994–2005
J Harry Stephenson   1994–2005
Charles E G Dickson   1994–2005
Hayden W Belcher   1995–
L S McDonald (Staff)   1995–1999
B E Cahill   1995–1999
Benjamin Twynam   1995–2002
R J Caine   1995–2002
Robert Taylor   1995–2002
Neil and David Cauldwell   1995–2002 and
   1997–2004
Stephen and David Marshall   1995–2002 and
   1997–2004
Philip Rashleigh   1995–2006
James Shipton   1995–2006
Freddie Dixon   1996–
Huw Richards   1996–
B J Illingworth   1996–
Adam D Cross   1996–
Rev Andrew Gough (Staff)   1996–
Sarah (Staff), Josh and George Sephton   1996–,
   1997– and 2000–2004
Adam Griffiths   1996–2001
Simon Beaumont   1996–2003
Tim Jacques   1996–2003

Simon Williams (Staff)   1996–2004
Robert Balmer   1996–2005
James Hambleton   1996–2005
RA and RC Lawson   1996–2006
Richard Guest Wilson   1996–2006
Michael O'Sullivan   1996–2007
J D Stone (Staff)   1997–
W A Homer   1997–
J J M Dargan   1997–
T A Lewis   1997–
Rob Howard   1997–
Adam Preston   1997–
C Harry Benfield   1997–
Peter McKenna   1997–
Callum A W Stein   1997–
James Twynam   1997–2004
Joseph S Warren   1997–2004
William David Roskelly   1997–2004
Rupert Millard   1997–2004
M P McDermott   1997–2004
Jonathan Ewles   1997–2004
Tom Newton   1997–2004
Philip J Hodges   1997–2005
Peter Hall   1997–2005
Craiglyn Wallace   1998–
Jonathan Kiefert   1998–
Calum C A Swain   1998–
Richard A Chapman (Staff)   1998–
Edward J Lawless   1998–
D R Caine   1998–
Matthew E C Clark   1998–
Benjamin Riddle   1998–2005
Kyran Spalding   1998–
Stephen D Donnachie   1998–2003
T W B Hughes   1998–2004
Matthew D Collins   1998–2005
Lewis Scott   1998–2005
Matthew Woof   1998–2005
Jack Navein   1998–2005
Justin Houghton   1998–2005
Roddy Green   1998–2005
James Lee   1998–2005
Ravteg Singh Dhesi   1998–2005
W O Chaundy   1998–2006
Edward J S Tainsh   1999–
Alex Lakin   1999–
T D Robbins   1999–
Jamie R A Glanvill   1999–
Thomas R R Wilson   1999–
Khyle Raja   1999–
Charles A G Fox   1999–
Richard Calcutt   1999–
Leopold W R Hughes   1999–
Daniel H Wood   1999–
Joe and Max Jennings   1999–
C W Burrows   1999–

Joshua McGuire   1999–
R A McDermott   1999–
Richard Sykes   1999–
Tom and Elliott Callard   1999– and 2000–
T J Jefferis (Staff)   1999–2002
James D Langman   1999–2004
R J Thirlwell (Staff)   1999–2004
George F B Rose   1999–2005
Nicholas Edwards   1999–2005
Anthony Baxter   1999–2006
Edward Scandrett   1999–2006
Chris Leadbetter   2000–
Robert S W Day   2000–
Daniel G Kitchen   2000–
Adam Revill   2000–
Paul Revill   2000–
Jonathan Cook   2000–
James A D Morgan   2000–
Nathaniel D O Adeyemi   2000–
Harry Gillespie   2000–
E A W Gillespie   2000–
Jonathan Gill   2000–
Adam Simmons   2000–
James Hargreaves   2000–
Joshua Greig   2000–
Michael Stevens   2000–
Henry Dodd   2000–
Peter Harrison   2000–
Luke and Oliver Richmond   2000–
Benjamin Francis Grazebrook   2000–
M L and DL Simpson   2001–
Adam M Moss   2001–
James A Taylor   2001–
Richard Wilson   2001–
Luke Harry Yates   2001–
James G J Cumberland   2001–
Daniel F Drummond   2001–
Daniel H Marcus   2001–
James and Charles Brooke-Taylor   2001–
T W Bloomfield   2001–
William J W Hopkins   2001–
Hugo C D Dyas-Catton   2001–
N J F Couzens   2001–
Samuel T Hooker   2001–
Josh Collier   2001–
Thomas D Spackman   2001–
J A Wiltsher (Staff)   2001–
Julian Darby   2002–
Boris Davis   2002–
T P Jee   2002–
Callum T Keightley   2002–
Jack Peter Leggatt   2002–
Richard T Jones   2002–
David Stone   2002–
Michael J F Heap   2002–
Jonathan Brown   2002–

T J F le Druillenec   2002–
S U McCarthy   2002–
Matthew Partridge   2002–
James Taylor-Hoff   2002–
Ferdinand L von Holstein   2002–
J S Dryden   2002–
J W Dryden   2002–
C R Chapman   2002–
Nicholas Hero   2002–
James Mower   2002–
Samuel Miller   2002–
Thomas R Cooper-Cocks   2002–
Shawn Hughes   2002–
James H W Lam   2002–
Dominic P C Hayes   2002–
Michael Moreton-Smith   2002–
C T F Streeten   2002–
E B Halse (Headmaster)   2002–
Bruce Fitzpatrick   2002–
Matthew Hull   2002–
Christopher Hull   2002–
Myles E Furness   2002–
C L Tyner (Staff)   2002–
Edward Hambleton   2002–
BP and TD McElholm   2002– and 2003–
Laurel Glockner (Staff)   2003–
J C M Worlidge   2003–
T A Worlidge   2003–
Alexander Beese   2003–
Andrew J F Heap   2003–
Alessandrio Luciano   2003–
Derek Jouppi   2003–
Patrick J C Forrester   2003–
Jonathan Wylie   2003–
William McGovern   2003–
Gus Gillespie   2003–
Harry D Drummond   2003–
A J Murrell   2003–
Alex Carvell   2003–
Piers J Furness   2003–
M A Williams   2003–
William D Spackman   2003–
Simon Hogg (Staff)   2003–
Thomas A V Karnik   2005–

Peter Taylor
Mrs Rosalind Partridge, née Bishop
Harry Fitzpatrick
Warwick School Library
Mrs Caroline Sterratt, née Bishop
R J Grieve
Mrs Margaret Esther Jones, née Clark
Dr Sarah Richardson
Dr Jonathan Davies
Norma Jones
Angela Robinson

Floreat Domus.

Written by
Rev. W. T. Keeling M. A.

Composed by
J. Haworth Esqr.